Dark Age Liguria

Studies in Early Medieval History
Series Editor: Ian Wood

Dark Age Liguria: Regional Identity and Local Power, c. 400–1020
Ross Balzaretti

Inventing Byzantine Iconoclasm
Leslie Brubaker

Pagan Goddesses in the Early Germanic World: Eostre,
Hreda and the Cult of Matrons
Philip A. Shaw

Dark Age Liguria

Regional Identity and Local Power, c. 400–1020

Ross Balzaretti

B L O O M S B U R Y

LONDON · NEW DELHI · NEW YORK · SYDNEY

Bloomsbury Academic
An imprint of Bloomsbury Publishing Plc

50 Bedford Square	175 Fifth Avenue
London	New York
WC1B 3DP	NY 10010
UK	USA

www.bloomsbury.com

First published in 2013

British Library Cataloguing-in-Publication Data
A catalogue record for this book is available from the British Library.

ISBN: PB: 9781780930305

Library of Congress Cataloging-in-Publication Data
Balzaretti, Ross.
Dark Age Liguria : regional identity and local power, c. 400–1050 / Ross Balzaretti.
pages cm. – (Studies in early medieval history)
Includes bibliographical references and index.
ISBN 978-1-78093-030-5 (paperback : alk. paper) – ISBN 978-1-4725-1710-4 (ePub) –
ISBN 978-1-4725-1711-1 (ePDF) 1. Liguria (Italy)–History. 2. Regionalism–Italy–Liguria–
History–To 1500. 3. Liguria (Italy)–Politics and government. 4. Liguria (Italy)–Antiquities.
5. Liguria (Italy)–History, Local. 6. Genoa (Italy)–History–To 1339. 7. Vara River Valley
(Italy)–History. 8. Italy–History–476-1268. I. Title.
DG55.L5B35 2013
945'.18–dc23
2013000825

Typeset by Newgen Imaging Systems Pvt Ltd, Chennai, India
Printed and bound in Great Britain

Contents

Figures

Acknowledgements

First, I would like to thank Ian Wood without whom there would be no book as he suggested that I write it: he has been supportive and encouraging at every stage. I am equally grateful to the following friends and colleagues for help and advice of many kinds: Karen Adler, Isabel Alfonso, Frances Andrews, Pantellis Arvanaitis, Julia Barrow, Rob Bartlett, Anthony Blane, Louise Bourdua, Tom Brown, Raffaella Bruzzone, Helena Carr, Roberta Cevasco, Roberta Cimino, Harry Cocks, Katy Cubitt, Wendy Davies, Gwilym Dodd, Georgina Endfield, Nick Everett, Gabriella Figone, Raffaele Figone, Carlo Gemignani, Richard Goddard, Dennis Gowans, Jenny Gowans, Edoardo Grendi (who died in 1999), David Groves, Robert Hearn, Liz Harvey, Rob Houghton, don Sandro Lagomarsini, Fulvio Landi, Steve Legg, Rob Lutton, Simon MacLean, Bryony McDonagh, Roberto Maggi, Alessandra Marcone, Marco Marcone, Michela Marcone, Eleana Marullo, Giampaolo Massa, Bruna Ilde Menozzi, Linda Merciari, Diego Moreno, Chiara Molinari, Carlo Montanari, Jinty Nelson, James Palmer, Claudia Parola, Mark Pearce, Pietro Piana, Osvaldo Raggio, Susan Reynolds, Mark Riley, Eirini Saratsi, Sara Scipioni, Elina Screen, Susanne Seymour, Trish Skinner, Anna Maria Stagno, Naomi Sykes, Setsu Tachibana, Claire Taylor, Faye Taylor, Claudia Vaccarezza, Charles Watkins, Mark Whittow, Chris Wickham and Alex Woolf. I was lucky enough to be elected to the Donald Bullough Visiting Fellowship at the University of St Andrews in 2010–11, which enabled me to draft the book. I am also grateful to librarians in Genoa, Leeds, London, Nottingham and St Andrews. The anonymous reader for Bloomsbury made very useful suggestions, as did Julia Barrow who read and commented on the whole draft saving me from many slips. I'd like to thank Sally Phillips for compiling the index. Finally, at Bloomsbury Deborah Blake, Michael Greenwood, Dhara Patel and Chloë Shuttlewood all helped the production process go smoothly, as did the staff at Newgen.

Sources and Debates

Liguria in the early Middle Ages (c. 400–1020 CE) is the subject of this short book. This north-west Italian region is known to outsiders mostly from holidays on its stunning coast at places such as Portofino, San Remo, Santa Margherita and the villages of the Cinqueterre. Its many fascinating inland settlements of considerable charm and historic significance are usually bypassed in the rush south and with the exception of Genoa its larger cities – Savona, La Spezia and Imperia – remain unknown and largely unstudied by non-Italian scholarship. A long coastline has played a major part in its history, but some historians have over-emphasized the sea at the expense of the land forgetful of Liguria's role as a region 'of transit' linking northern Europe to the Mediterranean and France to the rest of Italy. Several valleys were vital arteries for northerners, notably the Polcevera which connected Genoa and the sea with the Po plain, and the Magra in the east which was an important pilgrim route throughout the medieval period (Figure 1.1). Oddly, given Liguria's distinctive geographical situation, it is barely mentioned in the mammoth surveys of the early medieval period fashionable of late (McCormick 2001; Wood 2006; Wickham 2009). *Dark Age Liguria* therefore seeks to fill this specific gap explaining why Liguria in this period should be studied more than it has been.

Most early medievalists would shy away from 'dark age' in a book title as it is regarded as an old-fashioned and culturally loaded term: the positive qualities of this much-maligned historical era are now generally preferred. As I have taken the same view in earlier work, I am fully aware that 'Dark Age Liguria' is a rather provocative title which needs defence. My view is that the inadequacies of the surviving sources especially the written ones historians rely on, mean that the 'dark age' label is more appropriate to Liguria than either 'early medieval' or 'post-Roman'. Other European regions are different as more is known about their immediately post-Roman history and connections

Figure 1.1 Map of Liguria in 1908.
Source: Gordon Home, *Along the Rivieras of France and Italy* (London, 1908).

can be more plausibly made with medieval societies (Delogu 1994). Most problematic is the near-total absence of narrative sources from which local political frameworks might be re-constructed, and even for Genoa – by far the best documented site – there are long periods of time for which we have little idea of what happened (see Chapters 4–6, for what is known). Such serious gaps in evidence necessitate a brief introductory chapter about the surviving sources and the key debates which have emerged from them.

More positively, it has been a pleasure to synthesize much fascinating and important recent local archaeological research, most of it carried out under the auspices of the *Soprintendenza per i Beni Archeologici della Liguria*.[1] Liguria is one of the smallest Italian regions bordered by France, Piemonte, Emilia-Romagna and Tuscany. The region has many archaeological sites including those underwater and in caves as well as the more conventional ones of villa, farm, village and city. Research has been largely confined to Genoa and the western coastal strip (the Riviera di Ponente), although thought-provoking discoveries have surfaced in the east and at a few inland sites, which promise more complex future histories, which at the moment remain hard to envisage. This recent surge in archaeological work, which reflects trends across Italy (Brogiolo and Casteletti 1992; Brogiolo and Gelichi 1996a, b; Brogiolo 1996a, b, 2001, 2005, 2006; Brogiolo and Cantino Wataghin 1998), has made it possible to connect Dark Age Liguria with wider and newly energized debates between historians and archaeologists about the historical meaning of the early medieval period (see Wickham 1999, 2005, 2009; McCormick 2001; Ward-Perkins 2005; Collins 2009; Moreland 2010). Was this region 'normal' or 'exceptional'? As we shall see, Edoardo Grendi's clever formulation of 'exceptional normal' may be the most appropriate way to see Ligurian history in this period (Wickham 2002; Raggio 2004; Raggio and Torre 2004; Grendi 2006). Was early medieval Liguria really as 'dark' as the gaps in evidence imply? Is its history typical of the 'transformation of the Roman world' in general,[2] or was Liguria in this period simply a precursor of a more interesting later history as a medieval 'crusading republic'? Liguria is a fascinating site for historians to debate these and other questions because archaeology must be taken seriously by anyone who writes its Dark Age history. Curiously, many historians have not done this because they see this period of history as a warm-up act for what followed: the glories of the Genoese Middle Ages (e.g. Pavoni 1992; Epstein 1996; and even Airaldi 2010). My disagreement with this teleology is the main reason why I have omitted the phrase 'early medieval' from my title: this book concentrates on how Dark Age Liguria can be related to what came *before* rather than what came after.

In terms of political geography 'Liguria' only designated the current region from the late 1960s when the Italian regional governments came into being. Modern Liguria is divided into four provinces based on the largest towns: Imperia (IM), Savona (SV), Genoa (GE) and La Spezia (SP). These divisions have determined how the history of Liguria has been written because of where archives are housed and organized, and how archaeological research is currently funded and who carries it out. For reasons of convenience I have adopted the late twentieth-century regional boundaries of Liguria as the main study area, but there were many earlier territorial divisions including those discussed in the rest of this book (see Guglielmotti 2005). 'Roman Liguria' was part of 'Region 9' (*Regio IX*), a larger unit which encompassed Turin, Asti and Tortona as well as Nice and parts of the French Alps. It was succeeded – perhaps, the sources are far from definitive – by a Byzantine Province, a Lombard Duchy of Liguria, a Carolingian County of Genoa, an Ottonian County of Lavagna and many smaller divisions besides. From the early eleventh century until 1797 Genoa was an independent republic (the 'Genoese Republic'), whose internal boundaries extended a little further north than they do now (taking in the northern town of Novi Ligure for example), but whose colonies could be found across the eastern Mediterranean. Even so it was not until the 1550s that the eastern Ligurian valleys finally became part of this republic when a rebellion by the powerful Fieschi clan, counts of Lavagna whose fief this area was, was crushed by Andrea Doria. Therefore a 'greater Ligurian' identity comes into the picture at times, especially in the east for much of the time part of the Lunigiana, a distinctive borderland with a strong cultural identity which linked the far east of Liguria with the far north of Tuscany, as far as the town of Pontremoli.

Knowledge of Liguria outside Italy is not great and in Britain the region was probably better known in the past than now because of tourism. I have argued elsewhere that nineteenth-century tourists only partially appropriated Liguria as they took the coast to their hearts but not the inland valleys (Balzaretti 2011). Since the 1960s differential development of the coast and interior has continued, although the depopulation of the interior valleys which began in the mid-nineteenth century and continued until recently has made it easier to study 'traditional' landscapes and cultures here than on the much-changed coast and in the larger conurbations. Of the latter, the region's capital is – and arguably has always been – Genoa, one of the most fascinating of Italy's historic centres, politically powerful throughout the medieval period and as the Genoese Republic one of the more successful states in Ancien Régime Europe until conquered by the French in the late 1790s. The city never recovered its political independence and although significant phases of industrialization in the wake of Italian unification dramatically transformed its cityscape with modern apartment blocks and commercial buildings, for much of the twentieth century it experienced significant economic decline to the point where it is now in a post-industrial phase.

Genoa is nevertheless Italy's sixth largest city, with a population around 600,000 within the city limits and a sprawling hinterland. Its history is quite well-covered in English, with the exception of the period dealt with in this book. Interest in Genoese history has pushed the rest of Liguria to the historiographical margins and only recently has a popular 'History of Liguria' appeared in Italian (Assereto and Doria 2007). Other places featured in this book include the sizable towns of Imperia, Savona and La Spezia, and the smaller coastal centres of Ventimiglia, San Remo, Albenga, Finale, Rapallo, Portofino, Chiavari, Sestri Levante and the Cinqueterre. This litany of names is quite well-known to outsiders, but their histories are little studied outside of the region. Inland, the picture is utterly different: who outside of the region could locate Pieve di Teco, Cairo Montenotte, Torriglia or Varese Ligure on a map, let alone discuss their history? I have tried to unearth some of this buried past in what follows.

The chapters of this book deal with historical ecology, settlement patterns, political and religious change, the city of Genoa and the Vara valley, the eastern border of the region. Each draws on many types of source, but Chapters 2, 3 and 5 deliberately focus more intensively on particular sources so that readers can get a good sense of what sorts of history can be written from what sorts of evidence, as well as find a way through the shadowy records to uncover what actually happened, or at least what may have done. My own route into Ligurian history has been via the Vara valley where with Charles Watkins I have co-led an annual fieldtrip for undergraduates since 1995. These field visits to Varese Ligure – and the large amount of information recorded then – have involved multi-period landscape history research, and resulted in *Ligurian Landscapes* (Balzaretti et al. 2004; Torre 2008).

Varese Ligure provides an instructive example of the problems posed for historians by the documentation of this period. The earliest written text dealing with the town and surrounding villages is a *libellus* – a type of charter – copied into the Genoese archiepiscopal register (Belgrano 1862: 290–4) in 1147, but dated there to 1031 CE.[3] The register lists episcopal properties, how they were held, who rented them, who the church's vassals were, as well as tithes owed. It is organized by parishes beginning in Genoa itself, and most of the records date to the mid- to late-twelfth century. The latter sections of the document deal with properties in eastern Liguria, in the parishes of Lavagna, Sestri (Levante) and *Varia* (Varese Ligure). The document of 1031 has been transmitted in a somewhat garbled text like many others in this complex collection (discussed below 121–5). Even the reference to Varese itself is not straightforward, as the town is not mentioned as such but merely the 'Vara parish' (*plebs de Varia*) which had jurisdiction over *costa de castro*, Marchesano (*in casa martinasca*), Scioverana (*Sivelana*), Cassego (*Caxano*), Chinela (*Quellena*), Trensenasca (*casa terezanasca*), Zanega (*Zanica*) and *Kastro*. This most likely means that in the eleventh century Varese did not exist as a nucleated settlement where it is now – on the floor of the Vara valley – but that a group of nucleated sites, some fortified, did exist and these were part of a large, rambling parish. Although the details of the text are problematic its wider meaning is not: by the early eleventh century Genoese bishops were interested in this part of the upper Vara valley as a source of income, and the 'central' place of Genoa had finally caught up with developments in this remote 'marginal' mountainous interior.

In contrast, Genoa is much better documented but still poorly recorded by comparison with other urban sites of this period in other Italian regions and elsewhere in Europe, especially France and Spain. As it is impossible to produce a continuous narrative of Genoese history across the early middle Ages I have resisted the temptation to try, instead explaining what different types of surviving written sources reveal by paying attention to the forms and conventions which shaped them (Tyler and Balzaretti 2006: 1–9). These sources are entirely the work of people who in all probability did not know the town first hand, at least until the first local charters dated to the early tenth century (Epstein 1996: 15–18; Calleri 1999). Outsiders mostly dealt with administrative and business matters in isolated royal and papal letters, records of the proceedings of synods, royal grants and monastic inventories. Historical writers such as Procopius, Fredegar, Bede, Paul the Deacon, Carolingian annalists and Liudprand of Cremona always presented Genoa as incidental to their narratives, a sideshow to the main actors and stage. To flesh things out, a few funerary monuments have survived to document the dead and one or two go beyond the conventional pieties to say specific things about local society. The small amount of local hagiographical writing is obviously helpful in understanding the formation and development of Christian communities within the town, but has to be treated cautiously as a historical record of the period it describes, given its preservation in late manuscripts only. Lastly, the small corpus of charters permits social history of a limited sort to be attempted. The earliest charter dates from 916 during the episcopate of Ratpertus (Belgrano 1862: 159–60), and deals with property in Bargagli in the upper Bisagno valley 20 km northeast of Genoa. According to one recent count there are 56 tenth-century texts and 132 of the eleventh century (Calleri 1999: 57–85) but not evenly distributed, as there were only 8 before 960. These documents all revolve around Genoese concerns to some degree even when they deal with land in other parts of Liguria as most texts have survived in the Genoese episcopal registers rather than as original single sheets (see Belgrano 1862). Trying to find patterns across such a long time period from within this disparate material can be very interesting traditional historical detective work, and I've tried to explain why it is interesting for any non-historian readers as I have gone along. But nothing really startling can emerge from it in the end, as many people have worked over this material before even if with rather different aims and agendas, and the best that can perhaps be hoped is to bring it to the attention of a new audience.

One relatively little-studied aspect of these charters is what they record about land management, for which they are in some respects very useful sources. Some give quite detailed lists of how land was exploited, and others record detailed property bounds which can help when thinking about how farming worked in a given area. Other charters refer in intriguing ways to forms of land use. The first few charters can serve by way of example. The earliest charter of 916 states that rights to the revenues raised from pannage (*scatico*) and the pasturing of flocks on high mountain sites (*alpiatico*) were to be reserved for the Genoese church, revealing that pigs, sheep and goats would have been especially important (Belgrano 1862: 160).[4] In a charter dated 946, tenants were growing wheat, rye, barley and spelt, and raising sheep and goats, as well as chickens (Belgrano 1862: 387–8). In 952, the presence of 'chestnut wood' (*castaneto*) in the generic formulae of a text relating to Bavali tells us that we are in inland Liguria, but it is more interesting that the wood in question is named as the *castaneto de Colloreto* which suggests that a specific site was in mind (Belgrano 1862: 161–2). In the property bounds the reference to chestnuts takes a different form: *castanea baronciasca*. The use of two different words for a chestnut wood – *castaneto* and *castanea* – might well reflect different forms of management, perhaps for fruit and for timber (Figure 1.2). Similar material is discussed below (57–8).

Figure 1.2 Managed Chestnut Wood, Colli di Valetti, Spring 1999.
Source: Photograph by Ross Balzaretti.

Much more exciting are the results of modern archaeological science which
is at last yielding dateable concrete evidence (C14, thermo-luminescence,
dendro-chronology), which gives a much better idea of what it was actually
like physically to live in Liguria at this time and how life may or may not have
changed over the years. This evidence – pollen records, charcoal fragments,
ice cores, fossilized trees and the like – is site-specific, and I have stressed
throughout the crucial importance of place (see Torre 2002, 2008). All sites
are unique, but have to be understood comparatively for their uniqueness
to be fully grasped. Sites can be compared with others of the same period –
perhaps the most common method – but also they can be compared over
long time periods, sometimes very long periods of thousands of years. The
latter is something I have attempted in Chapter 2, and it was that comparative
process which encouraged me to believe that 'Dark Age' is an appropriate
way to describe much of Liguria in the post-Roman period. It transpires that
many Dark Age sites are more like prehistoric sites in their cultural profiles
than like Roman or later medieval ones, especially those in inland valleys.
Alongside the archaeology, I have discussed types of ecological study almost
completely neglected by early medieval historians, at least those who rely on

the written word for evidence. This is, in one respect, perfectly understandable as the discipline of historical ecology has not often examined early medieval societies. But my field work has suggested that the general approach may be useful, particularly because it stresses the dynamic nature of human relationships with land, something clearly relevant in a period as fluid as the early middle ages was. For example, in the last few years important work has emerged from several sites high in the Apennines in the Aveto valley which suggests that climatic changes in the fifth to seventh centuries may have had a significant impact on the settlement history of Liguria as a whole: a wetter and colder climate seems to have persuaded many people to move from water-logged flatter land – itself in short supply in hilly Liguria – to hilltop settlements, around 500–700 m asl. It is possible that these ecological changes in combination with other things, helped to hasten the departure of the eastern Roman state from Liguria in the mid-seventh century, undoubtedly the major political event of the entire era.

This returns us to the distinctive nature of Ligurian political history. The date when Liguria ceased to be part of a much larger state is very late when compared with most other western parts of the old Roman Empire meaning that it provides a distinctive example of the wider developments now termed the 'transformation of the Roman world'. Quite what happened to 'Byzantine Liguria' after the Easterners left is therefore a sufficiently important question to necessitate detailed consideration in the chapter about Genoa.[5] Without wishing to pre-empt the arguments, my conclusion is that throughout the early medieval period the Genoese were as much part of political and social networks which looked inland as those that responded to the call of the sea which puts me at odds with other historians – notably Steven Epstein of those writing in English – who continue to see Genoa as exemplary of a 'Mediterranean-wide' cultural system which persisted down the centuries, almost as an unquestioned trope, with early medieval Genoa as the first stage in a process which led to the later medieval Crusades. I prefer to see these later colonial developments as choices rather than inevitabilities. Genoese history is certainly a story of expansion, but in the first few centuries after the Romans left it was all about the town's connections with its immediate Ligurian hinterland and more distant inland sites, notably the old Roman capital of Milan – whose bishop had been exiled in Genoa as a consequence of the initial Lombard conquest of much of northern Italy in 568 – and the increasingly powerful monastic community at Bobbio, founded in the early seventh century (c. 612–13) and the beneficiary of early Carolingian patronage which included the gift of land and a church in Genoa itself. The political and social networks which developed around the Genoese bishops as the result of these and other transactions can be compared with similar networks at other urban or proto-urban coastal sites, such as Albenga, now sufficiently well-studied archaeologically for recent excavations to have revealed a place of some social complexity, even though its political history remains resolutely hidden by the lack of a written record.

Another distinctive feature of Liguria is its physical geography which certainly helped to shape its political history. Liguria is a small region with a long, mostly rugged, coastal strip which does not extend far inland. As there is little flat land anywhere apart from the valley floors, large urban settlements are few and coastal with Genoa the most significant. The Apennine interior is hilly and often mountainous, the highest peak being Monte Maggiorasca (1,780 m) in the Aveto valley. Its numerous valleys are narrow, steep-sided and extensively terraced, and only a few are even now extensively settled, notably the Polcevera and Scrivia immediately north of Genoa. Routes along these valleys can be very ancient, and the high passes – such as the Bocco, the Bocchetta and Cento Croci – were always important sites to control. At many valley sites aspect has been crucial for successful cultivation; the north-facing side will generally be densely wooded while the south-facing is sometimes agricultural but more often pastoral in character. Currently the climate is wet all year round, among the wettest in Italy (Cruise et al. 2009: 988), and although the coasts are usually very mild in winter it can be very cold for quite long periods inland. Geologically Liguria is varied, but soil quality is often low and unable to support much cereal cultivation: wheat in particular was historically uncommon with rye, barley and other 'lesser grains' often preferred. On the coast there is classic 'Mediterranean' vegetation as olives, vines and figs flourish at lower altitudes but the interior is very different dominated by oak, beech and especially chestnuts which still cover the hills in an increasing state of neglect. The current situation is characterized by natural regeneration, reforestation and the disappearance of traditional woodland management (Watkins 2004: 145–51). Past landscapes, however, could be very different from current ones even though the basic facts of geography are mostly similar.

My main aim has been modest therefore: to map out a clear path through the fragmentary and complex evidence without constructing an artificial and misleading master narrative based on knowledge of what happened after the period in question. Inevitably in a short book finding space for all this evidence has proved impossible, and I regret that some important material has been largely ignored, most notably place name evidence.[6] Nevertheless I hope that readers will be inclined to fill these gaps by following up the references and notes I have provided to investigate and discover in the process a region which ought to be much better known than it is.

Notes

1 www.archeoge.liguria.beniculturali.it/ (accessed 10 May 2012).

2 The 'Transformation of the Roman World' was a multi-disciplinary research project funded by the European Science Foundation to reassess the history of Europe in the post-Roman period. It reflected the tendency of modern scholarship to see the 'end of the Roman Empire' as a slow transition and not a cataclysmic break (see Wood 1997).

3 Luigi Tommaso Belgrano's edition (Belgrano 1862, 1887) is not perfect and should be read alongside recent scholarship (e.g. Calleri 1999). Where better editions exist I have used them: Calleri 1997 and 2009.

4 Other references to this form of land-use are found in charters of 972 (Belgrano 1862: 223–4) and 981 (Belgrano 1862: 257–8) but being few the formula probably refers to something which really existed at these sites in the Val Bisagno: Bargagli, 'Monte Butonio' and Molassana.

5 The Byzantine Empire is the name from the eastern Roman Empire which continued as a state after the 'fall' of the western Empire in the fifth century. Liguria was part of it until conquered by the invading Lombards, a northern European 'barbarian people' in the mid-sixth century.

6 Readers should therefore consult the excellent works of Giulia Petracco Sicardi (1962: 30–5, 46–8, 2003; and Petracco Sicardi and Carpini 1981, which is divided into sections on Pre-Roman ('celtic') and Roman place names at 7–82 and names of 'Germanic' origin, 83–125).

2

Historical Ecology in the Apennines

For historians, getting out and walking the land should be as important as reading about the land in documents. In Liguria, intensive fieldwork by multi-disciplinary teams at the University of Genoa has completely transformed understanding of the post-medieval histories of many upland valleys, especially in the east of the region. Even so an interesting starting point for this book is a written text, set down by the Greek author Strabo in the first years of the first century CE (Dueck 2000). Strabo made some pertinent observations about Liguria even though these were not meant as a literal description of the place at that time (Meiggs 1982: 30–2; Grove and Rackham 2001: 173–4). In his monumental 'Geography', a description of the known world, this is what he wrote:

> This country is occupied by the *Ligures*, who live on sheep, for the most part, and milk, and a drink made of barley; they pasture their flocks in the districts next to the sea, but mainly in the mountains. They have there in very great quantities timber that is suitable for ship-building, with trees so large that the diameter of their thickness is sometimes found to be eight feet. And many of these trees, even in the variegation of the grain, are not inferior to the thyine wood (i.e. citrus wood) for the purposes of table-making. These, accordingly, the people bring down to the emporium of Genoa, as well as flocks, hides and honey, and receive therefore a return-cargo of olive oil and Italian wine (the little wine they have in their country is mixed with pitch and harsh).[1]

His account mixes the pastoral (flocks of sheep, their milk and hides, presumably meaning fleeces) with woodland (timber and honey), in a context of exchange (for olive oil and wine from elsewhere in Italy at Roman Genoa). The Ligurians' timber, possibly maple wood (*Acer campestris*), may have been destined for the city of Rome (Meiggs 1982: 274, 292). The linkage of mountains with the sea strongly implies transhumance, and plausibly suggests a functioning ecological system adapted to this landscape (Delano Smith 1979: 224–5). His reference to barley is also notable, as this hardy and adaptable grain is suited to the cool climate of much of upland Liguria, and was certainly grown in earlier periods (see Arobba et al. 2003 for an early Iron Age silo full of barley at Monte Traboccheto, near Pietra Ligure).

Earlier in the first-century BCE, Diodorus Siculus had painted a rather gloomier picture of a harsh mountain land, worked only with great physical effort:

> The Ligurians inhabit a land which is stony and altogether wretched, and the life they live is, by reason of the toils and the continuous hardships they endure in their labour, a grievous one and unfortunate. For the land being thickly wooded, some of them fell the wood the whole day long, equipped with efficient and heavy axes, and others, whose task it is to prepare the ground, do in fact for the larger part quarry out rocks by reason of the exceeding stoniness of the land; for their tools never dig up a clod without a stone. Since their labour entails such hardship as this, it is only by perseverance that they surmount Nature and that after many distresses they gather scanty harvests, and no more.[2]

This also gives a plausible impression of possible lives in upland Liguria in this period, even though clearly intended to play up the 'primitive' nature of these Ligurian 'barbarians' when compared to their Roman conquerors (Bertinelli 2007: 5–9). The *topos* of the stones had earlier been relayed by Aristotle, Theophrastus and Posidonius, whose work Diodorus had plundered without scruple.

These two texts are a reminder that the 'Romanization' of Liguria came about in part by conquest, although of course experts now present much more nuanced accounts of these complex cultural processes (Häussler 2007). The *Ligures* had submitted to Roman rule around 155 BCE and the Roman presence lasted with differing intensities from the third-century BCE (Giannattasio 2007: 124–60) until the mid-seventh-century CE, when the final Byzantines left in the face of Lombard armies (Christie 1990). This roughly thousand-year period can meaningfully be seen as an interruption in a more continuous Ligurian history stretching back at least to the Neolithic, as in other parts of Italy and across Europe more widely. Many parts of inland Liguria indeed never appear to have been thoroughly Romanized as Roman settlement was largely focused on the coast (Gambaro 1999; Airaldi 2010) with the exception of a few valleys, notably the Polcevera/Scrivia north of Genoa (Bianchi 1996; Häussler 2007: 62–4). Given the nature of the terrain it is likely that very long-term continuities were normal in the upland valleys: in these places Dark Age Liguria might have been more like Prehistoric Liguria than Roman Liguria, especially as Roman political and economic power began to weaken substantially during the course of the fifth-century CE.

It seems reasonable therefore to challenge the notion that Liguria really underwent the 'dark' age as presented by the stark absence of written documentation between the fourth and tenth centuries CE by making comparisons with both earlier and later periods.[3] When considered in the long term the period studied in this book was like the Roman occupation a relatively short one in the history of human settlement in Liguria: parts of the region have been inhabited, managed and exploited for over ten thousand years. It is therefore appropriate to begin the analysis of Dark Age Liguria with a brief consideration of what came before, taking inspiration from disciplines which deal with long time periods: historical geography, historical ecology, environmental history and archaeology (Quaini 1973; Delano Smith 1979; Horden and Purcell 2000; Grove and Rackham 2001; Balzaretti et al. 2004; Cevasco 2007; Moreno and Montanari 2008; Torre 2008). These disciplines have revealed a complex pre-literate past and a deep relationship of humans with environment in this area. The only caveat is that in this region environmental archaeology (and cognate research in palynology and anthracology,[4] pollen and charcoal studies) has concentrated more on prehistory than on what came after: Iron Age (Bertinelli 2007: 5–10; Giannattasio 2007; Häussler 2007), Roman (Bertinelli 2007: 10–19) and especially early medieval Liguria (Christie 1990) have been less intensively studied even though many of the same concerns apply because of the basic facts of the physical environment with which people had to contend. This means that chronological comparisons are inevitably one-sided.

It can be proposed that although texts such as Diodorus and Strabo provide some insights about past landscapes and their human management, the existing landscape itself is potentially a better guide to past ecologies (Grove and Rackham 2001; Moreno and Montanari 2008; Stagno 2009).

Early modern land management practices can help understand what was and was not possible in traditional agricultural systems such as those known as *ronco/alnocultura* (types of specialized clearance management),[5] *alpeggio* (short-term transhumance), *scalvatura* (tree shredding, Moreno and Raggio 1990: 208),[6] the production of charcoal or what is often termed 'trees without forest' (Moreno 1990; Cevasco et al. 1997–9, 2010; Howard et al. 2002; Scipioni 2002; Lagomarsini 2004; Cevasco 2007, 2010). Probably the most widely studied of such systems globally is transhumance or pastoralism, the economic and social complexity of which is now widely recognized (Cleary and Delano Smith 1990: 34; Maggi et al. 1990). Liguria with its short valleys is ideal country for this practice as flocks can be moved quite quickly from winter pastures near the coast to high, lush mountain summer sites (Cleary and Delano Smith 1990: 28; Maggi and Nisbet 1990: 267; Moreno and Raggio 1990: 195, 199). The routes used have remained broadly similar for thousands of years although the purposes of such practices have obviously fluctuated a great deal as rural economies changed under the pressure of modernity (Delano Smith 1979: 239–56; Moreno 1990; Maggi and Nisbet 1990). Written documents from elsewhere in Europe demonstrate the importance of pastoralism in the early middle ages (Wickham 1988: 167–70; Wickham 1994: 121–54), and the early modern evidence for Liguria (Moreno and Raggio 1990; Raggio 1991) strongly implies that it may well have happened there much earlier too (see Giannichedda and Mannoni 1990).

Prehistoric and post-medieval ecology

Sophisticated methods of post-medieval historical ecology cannot be applied directly to the early medieval past as it is so distant that it has not left many impressions which can be seen with certainty in the current landscape. Nevertheless, post-medieval research can provide both inspiration and occasional nuggets of hard fact for early medievalists. For example, Cevasco's book about 'Green memory' (2007; Balzaretti 2009) makes an excellent case for both existing and past plant cover as meaningful historical evidence. A good example is her reconstruction of a now lost system of *alnocultura* (alder cultivation) in the Aveto valley in which *Alnus incana* trees were managed by peasant farmers as a way to fix nitrogen in the soil and improve its fertility, without understanding the science of it (Bertolotto and Cevasco 2000; Cevasco 2004: 159–62, 2007: 183–7, 2010). This early modern practice could be more ancient, as recent evidence has shown (see below 26). A comparable example is the use at Monte Prò (Rapallo) of the supposedly poisonous leaves of hop-hornbeam (*Ostrya carpinifolia*) as forage which revealed a sophisticated understanding by peasant farmers about the uses of this common plant (Moreno 2004a: 131–9). Both studies emphasize the dynamic nature of 'traditional' peasant cultures and their land-management practices (Moreno 2004b) in ways that should make early medievalists think about largely static images presented by the few surviving written sources (see the much-studied Carolingian polyptychs or those of Bobbio, see below 29–30). Dark Age peasants could have agency in their own environment which can now only be guessed at.

Determinism is not a convincing approach to a physical environment that has been far from unchanging in the last 10,000 years (see Grove and Rackham 2001: 151–66). The current vegetation cover of the region is (crudely): evergreen oaks, tree heather, olives on land up to 200 m; deciduous oaks, birch, chestnut, hop-hornbeam between 200 and 1,000 m; beech, hazel, fir on land above 1,000 m (Cruise et al. 2009: 988). Past tree cover varied a great deal as a series of crucial pollen studies has demonstrated (Cruise 1992; Lowe, Branch et al. 1994; Lowe, Davite et al. 1994; Watson et al. 1994; Watson 1996; Branch 2004; De Pascale et al. 2006; 'Zone Umide 2009'; Menozzi et al. 2010). Silver fir trees (*Abies alba*) which had been widespread before 5000 BP, came to be replaced by beech in the centuries after that, while the management of chestnuts, walnuts and olives is evidenced back to 2000 BP, but hardly before (Branch 2004: 7). Nick Branch's seminal study of the last 7,000 years in Liguria was based on the evidence of four key upland wet sites near the Aveto/Trebbia watershed: Rovegno (812 m asl, upper Trebbia valley), Lago Riane (1,279 m asl, upper Aveto valley, near Santo Stefano d'Aveto), Lago Rotondo (1,331 m asl, upper Aveto valley, near Rezzoaglio) and Lago Lagastro (1,326 m asl, also near Rezzoaglio) (Figure 2.1). He showed that in the Iron Age and after deforestation which might possibly be implied by Strabo and Diodorus had a catastrophic impact, increasing erosion and flood events (Branch 2004: 65); in consequence more shallow mire basins developed, creating our 'wetland' evidence. Around 1700 BP (i.e.

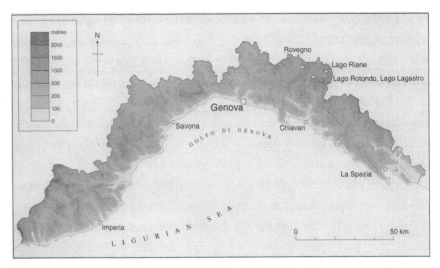

Figure 2.1 Lago Riane, Lago Rotondo and Lago Lagastro.
Source: Ross Balzaretti et al., *Ligurian Landscapes* (London, 2004).

c. 300–400 CE) it appears that as lake levels increased a 'significant reduction of woodland cover occurred'; fir and beech declined, chestnut, walnut and olive appeared although probably not in upland areas until later, and the cultivation of cereals and pulses increased. Crucially, these results were confirmed by those from sites elsewhere in the northern Apennines and in southern Europe (Arroba et al. 2003; Cruise et al. 2009; Menozzi et al. 2010); together they suggest that at the start of the period covered by this book, much of Liguria was both differently and less wooded than it had been for centuries past and probably on balance more like it is now than 7,000 years ago (see Wickham 1994: 155–99 for early medieval woodlands). Seemingly remote upland areas as well as the coastal ones later preferred by Roman settlers have been carefully managed for millennia for food, wood and timber production, but between 5000 and 2000 BP, the domestication of plants now characteristic of the region (particularly sweet chestnut), hunting, pastoralism and transhumance, all indicate a shift from coastal exploitation to encompass the interior uplands as well (Branch 2004: 7–8).

These studies have adopted a site-specific approach which is something replicated throughout this book. Although each site is obviously unique and in some ways evidence only of itself, yet comparisons with other sites do reveal wider patterns. Key sites for the pre-Roman period, in addition to those studied by Branch, include Bargone/Pian del Lago (Maggi 2004: 75; Cruise et al. 2009),

Mogge di Casanova (Cevasco 2007: 76–9, 152–9), Mogge di Ertola (Mariotti Lippi et al. 2007; Cevasco 2007: 40–4; Menozzi et al. 2007),[7] Pian delle Gròppere (Campana and Cevasco 2001; Cevasco 2007: 76–80, 188–90); Prato Mollo, a site where fire was used to create both pastures for *alpeggio* and cultivation spaces (Maggi 2004: 74, 79); the coastal Arene Candide (Maggi 2004: 71–4; Mussi et al. 2008) and Vado Ligure (Carobene et al. 2009); the extraction sites of Rocca di Lagorara (near Maissana, Lagorara valley, Maggi et al. 1995) and Libiola (near Sestri Levante, McCullagh and Pearce 2004; Maggi and Pearce 2005); and the settlement sites (*castellari*) of Camogli, Uscio (728 m asl, inland from Recco, Giannattasio 2007: 91–2, 131–4), Zignago (Maggi 2004; Giannattasio 2007: 62–4, 80–2), nearby Monte Dragnone (Milanese and Giardi 1987) and Pianaccia di Suvero, and Genoa itself (Milanese 1987). Some of these evidence terracing (Uscio), shredding (Arene Candide, Uscio) and the use of fire to clear land for both grazing and arable cultivation (Bargone) all activities which have been well-documented in this region in post-medieval contexts, and which the post-medieval evidence has helped to understand.[8] It has also been suggested that Zignago at the eastern edge of the Vara valley was part of a local network of sites of similar size which demonstrate that human impact on the landscape could be considerable even when population density was low (Maggi 2004: 72). This is a crucial point which has obvious resonances in early medieval contexts when the population appears to have been very low.

Each of these sites shows that Ligurians before the Roman conquest had a very deep history of exploiting 'natural' resources, but more importantly some also evidence early medieval conditions, allowing assessment of relative levels of cultural development over long time periods. The site with the deepest stratigraphic sequence is Bargone (831 m asl) near Sestri Levante, which extends from something like 11000 BCE to 1400 CE, some 12,500 years. The pollen sequence studied in 1989 suggested that 'major deforestation and the development of heath and grassland communities' occurred here during the Iron Age and Roman periods (Cruise et al. 2009: 995, 999), with evidence of the increasing presence of olives, walnut and chestnut (i.e. possibly cultivated trees), although more recent sediment micromorphology studies of deposits from the basin edge (Cruise et al. 2009: 988), have implied that these vegetation changes took place in the later medieval period (1210–1400 CE). The presence of olive pollen at this altitude does not suggest that olives were being grown here in Roman times, but rather that they were grown on the nearby coast which is itself an important observation (Cruise et al. 2009: 1000). Unlike some other higher sites, there was relatively little evidence of deliberate use of fire for clearance in the prehistoric periods (Maggi 2004: 75; Cruise et al. 2009: 998–9), but by the Iron Age/Roman periods, fire was used for light clearance – keeping down unwanted plants for example – but not for full-scale clearance of forest. This evidence matches early modern documentation of similar practices (i.e. that known as *ronco*). The archaeologists have concluded that Bargone was probably part of a regional system of seasonal grazing and transhumance, associated with *compascuo*, common grazing rights; although positive written evidence is lacking, this conclusion is perfectly reasonable.

Liguria has many wetland sites because of its particular terrain, geology and climate ('Zone Umide 2009'). It is this which has facilitated the development of pollen and related studies in the region. As vegetation cover is relatively easy for people to modify given appropriate tools, scientific studies of its historical dynamism can say a great deal about the 'activation practices' employed by people at specific sites at different times (Moreno 2004b). Other environmental factors in pre-modern times have proved much harder to change or even to cope with. Catherine Delano Smith has suggested that Liguria is 'an archetypal "high risk" environment' prone to erosion and flood events because of its extremely mountainous terrain (Delano Smith 2004: viii). Topography, soil fertility and the vicissitudes of climate are all crucial considerations for early medieval historians, as these probably had a more direct sometimes catastrophic impact on past human cultures, less able to control them than our own. But appreciating the ways in which environmental facts have been crucial to the region's historical development is only meaningful when understood in terms of human relationships with the land. The hills of much of the upper Vara valley, for example, in the sixteenth century, were grazed by thousands of sheep which produced vast tracts of pastureland interspersed with intensively managed tree-land (Moreno and Raggio 1990). Since then, population pressure led to the development of a widespread subsistence sweet chestnut culture (Cevasco et al. 2010), a much more wooded landscape characterized by the production of leaf fodder for animals and occupational burning to keep the land under trees free for grazing (Moreno 1990; Cevasco et al. 1997–9; Gentili et al. 2009) which probably reached its peak in the latter decades of the nineteenth century. But now in the face of population collapse the land looks utterly different, covered with dense, largely unmanaged woodland.

It would be wrong to see physical factors as unchanging, and a key theme in this book is the dynamic relationship between people and the land (Grove and Rackham 2001: 13–14). In Liguria, terraces have been one of the most characteristic topographical features of the landscape crucial in combating erosion while at the same time providing flat land for small-scale agriculture (Grove and Rackham 2001: 107–18; Watkins 2004). Some areas, notably the Cinqueterre in the eastern Riviera and the far western province of Imperia are very substantially terraced, but the average for Liguria as a whole is around 28 per cent of surface area.[9] The dating of terraces has proved difficult and is subject to on-going controversy (Grove and Rackham 2001: 112). Although sophisticated Bronze Age dry-stone terraces have been found in excavations at Uscio, Zignago, Pianaccia di Suvero, Camogli and Pigone (Maggi 2004: 76) and some possibly medieval ones near Casanova (Guido et al. 2002b: 121, radiocarbon-dated 890–1270/1040–1380 CE) such archaeologically datable terraces are in fact rare. The creation of a still extant set of terraces in Varese Ligure was recorded in the 1550s by the local historian Antonio Cesena, whose land it was (Lagomarsini 1993: 86–7; Grove and Rackham 2001: 113–14; Balzaretti 2004: 122–3; Watkins 2004: 143–4). This too is a rare case. Indeed, if, as has been plausibly argued, terraces were not much written about in the past because they were a ubiquitous feature of many Mediterranean lands (Delano Smith 1979: 183–5), we ought not to expect early medieval writers to refer to them, and indeed they do not. This does not necessarily mean that terraces are an exclusively post-medieval development as the archaeological evidence just cited makes clear: we just need to 'find' – both literally and metaphorically – early medieval terraces archaeologically.

In the past, as now, climate was unpredictable and impossible to control. Climate alternates between hotter and cooler periods and the Roman Empire coincided with a relatively warm period, followed by a cold period between c. 400 and c. 800 CE, with another warm period from then until c. 1000 CE. Liguria fits these wider European patterns (McCormick et al. 2007; Cheyette 2008; Behringer 2010: 60–84; Squatriti 2010). In cold periods, agriculture tends to be abandoned in marginal areas, whereas increases in cultivation can be linked to warm periods (Tinner et al. 2003). Climate changes therefore are likely to have had significant impact on early medieval farmers, and prolonged periods of rain and water-logging in the absence of the sufficiently large workforce required to undertake the necessary drainage works (see

Squatriti 2002) may help to explain why hilltop sites were settled and those
on valley floors were abandoned at various times (Cheyette 2008: 163). Local
palynological studies can highlight significant changes in recorded plant
cover and provide proxy data about climate, as well as about human activities.
Apennine sites including Prato Spilla, Bargone, Pian delle Gròppere and
Mogge di Ertola have all suggested significant climate change in Late Antiquity
to a colder period. This is especially marked in comparison with a warmer
Roman period, as evidenced by coastal flood data records (e.g. those for the
Rivers Arno and Tiber, Benvenuti et al. 2006: 873), where pollen studies have
been harder to carry out (Bellini et al. 2009). Cores from Lake Massaciuccoli
(N. Tuscany) have shown that evergreen vegetation only became established
in this coastal area during the Roman period, suggestive of land drainage and
reclamation at this time (Mariotti Lippi et al. 2007: 274). Bargone has further
suggested that there was some deforestation in the Roman period followed
by the development of heath land and grassland with transhumant practices.
Deforestation in the upper parts of valleys could certainly have led to the sorts
of catastrophic flooding events seen in this period (see Squatriti 2010).

Dark Age ecologies

This brief foray into the ecologies of prehistoric and post-medieval Liguria has
clear implications for the early medieval period as such comparisons allow
us to grasp what may have been *possible* at a given site with all its specific
characteristics even in the absence of tangible evidence of early medieval
date. Diego Moreno's concept of the 'realistic decoding' (Italian *decifrazione
realistica*) of written documents can be applied to this period as to the early
modern periods he has studied (Moreno 1997a: 313–14). Such speculations
are worthwhile precisely because it is difficult to know what early medieval
landscapes were really like in Liguria. The surviving written sources are hardly
helpful in whatever way they are read, as narrative descriptions of the land even
of the generic sort made by Strabo and Diodorus have not survived for Dark
Age Liguria. While it would be interesting to know what Dark Age Ligurians
thought about the place they lived in and how they may have described and
interacted with it, this will always be unknowable in the absence of meaningful

written evidence. Greek and Roman writers, representatives of an alien culture, had pondered this and for them the word Liguria curiously conjured up the herb lovage (*Levisticum officinale* Koch), a common ingredient in Roman cuisine. For Dioscorides and Pliny, the plant *ligusticum* took its name from Liguria because it was common in the area both wild and cultivated (Andrews 1941): '*Ligusticum* grows most plentifully in Liguria on the Apennine, a hill bordering on the Alps (from which it has its name)' (Dioscorides, *Materia medica* 3.58).[10] Now it is rare in the region (and discussed neither by Cevasco 2007 nor Camangi et al. 2009). Nor is lovage a plant which has appeared in palynological studies from the region, although sometimes its family *Apiaceae* is recorded. Curiously, the association of Liguria with plants was maintained by some early medieval writers, including Isidore of Seville (*Etym.* XVII. ix.3) who reported that 'spikenard' (*nardus*) which may have been a type of valerian (*Valeriana celtica* or *Valeriana saxatilis*) was harvested there. Paul the Deacon (*HL* II 15) provided his own characteristically dubious plant-derived etymology: 'The second province is called Liguria from *legere* namely the harvesting of legumes, in which it is very fertile'. Although this is probably nothing more than book learning, legumes have actually been widely grown in Liguria: vetches (*Vicia* types), for example, appear regularly in pollen diagrams and the common lentil (*Lens edulis*) has even been found in prehistoric contexts where plant seeds (as opposed to pollen) are rare in Liguria.

More practical documents such as charters do contain references to environmental features, and some sense of the land and its contemporary nature in a few places is possible (see below 29–30 for the activities of the monastery of Bobbio and Figure 2.2). Although this information is mostly generic, it does have the advantage of being located sometimes to specific places (see Montanari 1979). Even so environmental archaeology remains the only convincing way to access fundamental ecological shifts which can be linked to other early medieval evidence. A good starting point is Prato Spilla, a high site in the Emilio-Tuscan Apennines (1,300–1,700 m asl about 15 km east of Pontremoli), which has produced a radio-carbon-dated pollen diagram (reproduced in Lowe and Watson 1993 from Lowe et al. 1994; Davite and Moreno 1996: 138, 142; and Cevasco 2007: 201) which shows that significant change took place during the Lombard period from a system of pasturing in woodland (*saltus*, a Roman term) to one of pasturing in deliberately created open pastures with only few carefully managed trees (wooded meadow system or *prato-pascolo alberato* in Italian) (Davite and Moreno 1996: 139; Moreno and Poggi 1996; Grove and Rackham 2001: 210; Cevasco and Moreno 2009).[11] The pollen record shows a marked increase in grasses (*Gramineae*), in beech and in daisy-like plants (*Compositae*) (Davite and Moreno 1996: 139; Cevasco 2007: 142, 147), suggesting an economy based around the production of hay and leaf fodder from shredded and pollarded trees, which will have required the felling of existing woodland (Davite and Moreno 1996: 140). This shift in how *alpeggio* worked, taking animals to different sorts of grazing in the uplands, has been linked to a modification in the meaning of the word *alpes* to indicate a site of high summer pasture as, for example, *Alpe Adra* donated to the monastery of Bobbio by Charlemagne in 774 (see Chapter 6). Further evidence of this development is the appearance of a new sort of long-handled scythe, typical of the northern Apennines until the 1950s, which is illustrated in the 'Months' mosaic (twelfth-century) at Bobbio (Davite and Moreno 1996: 141; Cevasco 2007: 202–4). Finally, Chiara Davite and Diego Moreno have suggested (1996: 142) that the combination of the Prato Spilla data with information about hay-making in the early ninth-century Bobbio inventory of Wala and with the 'long houses' of 'Byzantine' date for housing animals at Luni might mean that a new system of transhumance from Luni up the Magra and Enza valleys was in place much earlier than has been thought for some Tuscan valleys near Lucca (see Wickham 1988).

The point can be further pursued in the Edict of Rothari issued in November 643 CE where there are hints of the contemporary existence of this sort of landscape (Everett 2003: 123–6). Chapter 300 of the Edict deals with the illegal cutting of trees, including beech trees but *fagus* the Latin word for beech is not used. The Lombard word *hisclo* appears instead glossed in the phrase *hisclo quod est fagia* (seemingly close to modern Italian *faggio*).[12] Ch. 349 deals with pigs eating beech mast (*isca*),[13] and Ch. 350 with pigs damaging a meadow (*pratum*). Put these three chapters together and the result is a wooded beech meadow. Ch. 358 adds a bit more anecdotal information about hay-making:

> No one shall deny fodder (*erba*) to those who are travelling, except in the case of a meadow still unreaped or cropped (*prato intacto*) at the time. After the hay or crops have been collected, he whose land it is may protect only as much as he can defend with his enclosure. But he who presumes to remove

Figure 2.2 View of Bobbio in 1892.
Source: Margaret Stokes, *Six Months in the Apennines* (London, 1892), p. 192.

the horse being used by a traveller from the stubble (*stupla*) or from that pasture where other animals were grazing, shall pay an eightfold composition for that horse on account of the fact that he presumed to move them from an arable field which had already yielded its crops (which is called *fornaccar*) (my translation; see Fischer Drew 1973: 122).

The derivation and meaning of *fornaccar* has perplexed linguistic scholars (Everett 2003: 126); it seems possible that it might just refer to the use of controlled fire to clear pasture after reaping, which is known in this region by the dialect term *fornaci* (Cevasco and Moreno 2009: 105).

As we have already seen, there is evidence that controlled burning was used near Lago Bargone to create the landscape of heaths and grassland which still exists there today, although as a pretty large chronological span for this development has been proposed, significant changes could certainly have occurred between then and now. But at other sites, especially Moglia di Casanova/Casanova di Rovengo (1,050 m asl) and the nearby Pian delle Gròppere (1,250 m asl) in the Val Trebbia, a more precise early medieval chronology has been possible. Pollen analysis has suggested that significant change to the early medieval landscape took place along the Aveto-Trebbia watershed, a major route between the coast and interior over a long time period (Moreno 1990: 104–22; Maggi and Campana 2002; Pearce 2002; Calandra 2002; Destefanis 2002b). This change from a wooded even forested landscape to a more open landscape was created by the use of fire, clearance and grazing. Of course, the pollen evidence can be hard to relate to surviving written evidence, where this exists, although the Lombard legal evidence remains suggestive.

Casanova di Rovengo describes a series of sites, including Moglia di Casanova (Guido et al. 2002a and 2002b; Cevasco 2007: 76–9, 93–4, 152–9) and Moggia di Pian Brogione (Branch et al. 2002).[14] The peat bog of Moglia di Casanova is 1,100 m asl and the pollen found at this site has been studied by Cruise (1990, supported with radiocarbon dates although some of the chronology has now been revised by Nick Branch, results reported in Cevasco 2007: 156–8). Cruise's pollen diagram suggested that grains including rye (*Avena*) were being cultivated in clearings in woods of silver fir in the Bronze Age. It also showed that alder was in expansion until the early medieval period when it was drastically reduced (Cevasco 2007: 155). This was associated with an increase in hazel and *compositae* pollen making it possible that wooded meadows were introduced here too in the fifth and sixth centuries (Cevasco 2010: 131). It could be that 'alnocultura' was adopted at this time, namely a technique in which alder trees were planted to improve soil fertility by fixing nitrogen to produce better-quality fodder. This is now a well-documented practice in modern times; and it seems from pollen records to have taken place in the distant past. At Casanova, a progressive decline in alder pollen has been observed but this in fact might mean the existence of short rotation coppicing cycles (Cevasco 2010: 133). Branch's re-assessment of the material does however propose a clear medieval phase of pasture/grazing, indicated by the decline of willow, juniper and the increase of *Plantago lanceolata*. Similar results have been observed at Lago Riane (Aveto valley, nr. Santo Stefano): again probably an alder cycle in association with a beech wooded meadow system (see Prato Spilla).

Recent archaeological investigation at nearby Pian delle Gròppere (1,250 m asl, local name for the site also known as Pian dei Furnàsci indicative of burning) has suggested that a more open, meadow landscape can be dated from the period c. 640–770 CE, because of evidence of temporary cultivation in the form of clearance still visible as piles of stones (*cumuli di spietramento* or cairns) in the current landscape (Guido et al. 2002b; Paltineri 2002; Cevasco 2007: 76–80, 188–90). There were three of these piles, each around 3 m in diameter. The site, known as Cugno Martizzo to prehistoric archaeologists, has previously evidenced middle Palaeolithic jasper-working. In 2000 one of the piles of stones was excavated, and a significant amount of charcoal from juniper (*Juniperus communis*), beech and silver fir was found at the base level which was radiocarbon dated to 640–770 CE (Guido et al. 2002b: 117). It has been suggested that these stones represent what was left over when the land was cleared and that the charcoal may have been produced as fertilizer, although the exact connection between this evidence and the practice of *ronco* is still open to speculation (Paltineri 2002: 85). Given the date of this evidence it is, once again, interesting to observe in Rothari's edict (ch. 148) the suggestion that fire needed to be carefully controlled: 'He who makes a fire beside the road should extinguish it before he goes away and not leave it negligently' (Fischer Drew 1973: 76).

Mogge di Ertola (1,100 m) is a complex wetland site in the Aveto valley with a deep chronology of about 9,000 years (Guido et al. 2002a; Maggi and Campana 2002; De Pascale et al. 2006: 117–21; Cevasco 2007: 41–4; Menozzi et al. 2007; 'Zone Umide' 2009). Long before the Roman period a water basin was transformed into a peat bog, seemingly by the use of a stone dam structure which has not yet been dated, and later the deliberate deposition of a layer of clay on top of the peat layer (dated 210 BCE to 130 CE) may have been intended to drain the bog (Menozzi et al. 2007: 4). Directly on top of the peat, there was evidence of burning (from charcoal) which indicates a dry period in the basin's history (also radiocarbon dated to 250–540 CE [Menozzi et al. 2007: 3]). Pollen from the period 770–1160 CE (again radiocarbon dated) included a high percentage of herbaceous plants and other anthropogenic indicators (Menozzi et al. 2007: 6) and this continued. In a recent study of non-pollen palynomorphs (organic micro-fossils) at this site, the section of the core which it has been possible to radiocarbon date to 770–1160 CE has low tree pollen, although both chestnut and walnut seem to have been on the increase suggesting human activity (Menozzi et al. 2010: 508). Several weeds including sedges (*Cyperaceae*) and true grasses (*Poaceae*) which are associated with human activity also increased. Coupled with certain sorts of micro charcoals and dung indicators, this has suggested a stable period of management and 'the presence of livestock, with grazing in an already established grassland, periodically managed with fire' (Menozzi et al. 2010: 510). Finally, as a sharp decline in alder pollen was coupled with increasing cereal pollen in this earlier medieval period it has been speculated that the system dubbed 'alnocultura' was in use here too (see above). After the medieval period, the landscape changed once again to become more wooded, with more alder and hazel and less beech.

The main advantage of this site over many others is that the documentation of past human 'activation' practices covers a very long period making it possible to demonstrate that the degree of change undergone by vegetation cover here in the early Middle Ages was unusual in the long-term perspective (Menozzi et al. 2007: 1). It really was a 'moment' of significant change in upland land management when an open pasture environment was deliberately created. Why it happened then is open to speculation as, although the Roman and early medieval history of this area has been recently surveyed (Calandra 2002; Destefanis 2002b), the evidence remains limited if suggestive, as there is at least some evidence of Roman occupation here unlike in many other Ligurian valleys inland ('Zone umide 2009'). Intriguingly at Mogge di Ertola itself in the levels dated 210 BCE to 130 CE and 250–540 CE, two fragments of Roman bricks were found, one dated by thermo luminescence to 228–299 CE. It has been reasonably suggested that these are remnants of kilns. It is significant also that along with two known inscriptions from Salsominore (mid-first-century BCE, Calandra 2002: 21; Destefanis 2002a: 117) and Cattaragna (Destefanis 2002a: 117, 2002b: 27) and some Roman period pottery from Francosu near Santo Stefano d'Aveto, roof tiles (*tegoloni*) have been found in Crescione (Casanova di Rovengo) and a brick-making furnace at Villa, along the River Granizza (Destefanis 2002b: 28, although the evidence for the latter is simply an excavation report published in 1940 and the finds are now lost). Although this is not a lot, it is *something* as it points to the presence of people who could have been involved in the creation of this new landscape. Although securely identified early medieval sites are fewer still, in addition to the environmental evidence from Pian delle Gròppere and Mogge di Ertola, six burials of this period were apparently found in a stone slab grave in 1890 at Boschi 6 km northeast of Mogge di Ertola (Destefanis 2002a: 117–18, 2002b: 28) and some fragments of a defensive wall at Gambaro, loc. Castellaro near Santo Stefano d'Aveto (Destefanis 2002a: 118 attributed to the early medieval period). Once again this suggests human presence in and around Casanova at the right time, and the contrast with earlier periods is marked.

From the eighth-century landholding in the Aveto valley is documented by a handful of early charters from the monasteries of Bobbio and San Pietro in Ciel d'Oro, Pavia, the earliest dating to 714 (Destefanis 2002a: 77, 2002b: 25). However, although these texts are in some degree technically problematic when considered alongside the broad date ranges suggested by radiocarbon and other scientific dating methods, these shortcomings are less problematic for the overall thrust of the argument than they might first appear. The earliest charter (714 CE) is a putative grant by King Liutprand to the monastery of S. Pietro; it is probably a forgery of the twelfth century, although most scholars seem to be overly lenient towards it (Richter 2008: 95–6). It claims that the king donated a large estate at *Alpem que dicitur plana* (now Alpepiana) and its detailed bounds are given (Destefanis 2002b: 27) which imply that Bobbio already owned nearby. The bounds encircle an area some 20 km across west/east and 10 km North/South. The first detailed record of land owned by Bobbio in the area dates to 747, a grant by King Ratchis (Destefanis 2002b: 28; Richter 2008: 94–6). This document sheds some light on local land management, referring to a mill at Gambaro, a wood (*silva*) with marked trees (see the chapters in Rothari's Edict – a text known at Bobbio – dealing with this practice known as *teclatura*),[15] and woodland officials called *silvanus* and *waldeman* (see Wickham 1994).

Later documents shed further light on local land management. In the diploma issued by Louis II for Bobbio in 860 reference is made to a 'plane tree to which a metal plaque is fixed' (*platanus in qua clavus est fixus* possibly *Platanus orientalis* but more likely *Acer campestre* or a similar tree) being used once again as a boundary marker (Destefanis 2002b: 31; Richter 2008: 95). Inventories from Bobbio evidence a sizeable amount of pig-grazing, including on its Ligurian properties (below 115–19), mini-ecosystems which were presumably based largely on oak woodlands and their acorns on which the pigs were fed seasonally (see Rothari again). The famous ninth-century inventory of the nunnery of Santa Giulia in Brescia also explicitly linked woodland to the number of pigs that could be supported, as that measure was used as the way

to calculate the size of woodland (Montanari 1979: 35, 232–3, 1994: 12). Other
Bobbio documents refer to cereals (rye at Alpepiana in the twelfth century)
and to hay meadows (returned in cartloads by tenants). The monastery's
pastures also clearly produced cheese, most usually from the sheep pastured
alpeggio-style at *Alpe plana, Alpe longo* and elsewhere (Destefanis 2002b: 33). In
general, terms these documents evidence a mixed-use economy well adapted
to risk management but unfortunately specific practices are not locatable to
specific sites using this material.

The sites of environmental archaeology discussed so far have demonstrated
what plants can tell us about past human activity. By implication some sites
tell us about animals too, the herds of cattle and flocks of sheep that travelled
the upland valleys from one pasture to the next, which sometimes left behind
physical evidence of their presence (as dung, or as seeds of grass species
trapped in their feet). The extremely long history of transhumance in this
region certainly shows as much (see above 20). Equally, it is very likely that
animals were as vital a part of early medieval economies, which even the few
written sources show (Montanari 1979: 222–53 [domestic], 254–76 [wild],
277–95 [fish], 1994). Strabo of course had mentioned Ligurian sheep, their
milk and hides (or fleeces) in the context of pastoralism, but not other animals.
Diodorus had said more:

> They are continually hunting, whereby they get abundant game and
> compensate in this way for the lack of the fruits of the field . . . Some of
> the Ligurians, because of the lack among them of the fruits of the earth,
> drink nothing but water, and they eat the flesh of both domestic and wild
> animals and fill themselves with the green things which grow in the land, the
> land they possess being untrodden by the most kindly of the gods, namely,
> Demeter and Dionysus (i.e. they have neither grain nor wine). The nights
> the Ligurians spend in the fields, rarely in a kind of crude shanty or hut,
> more often in the hollows of rocks and natural caves which may offer them
> sufficient protection.[16]

As already seen, Diodorus wanted to bring out the 'primitive' nature of the
locals, but setting that aside he made some valuable points: both domestic and
wild animals were eaten, the latter hunted in abundance. Early medieval written
evidence from this region ought to reference sheep, other domestic and wild
animals, and hunting.[17] The Bobbio charters and especially the inventories

certainly mention domestic animals and yet, although these are linked to named estates or farms, the information is still too generic: *olivetum dominicum in Adra, de quo exeunt ad partem dominica oleum per bonum tempus librae CL* ('the monastery's olive grove in Adra, from which in a good year 150 *librae* of olive are returned') in the 883 inventory does not tell us much of itself about how this olive grove was managed (Castagnetti et al. 1979: 151). But for more concrete evidence from specific sites archaeology is the best guide. In 1990, a survey of Iron Age Apennine pastoralism (Giannichedda and Mannoni 1990) argued that archaeological finds of animal bones, artefacts associated with animal production and vernacular buildings for their shelter suggested that the *castellari* of Camogli, Uscio and Zignano, and Praxelli di Rossiglione were all *alpeggio* sites. Monte Zignago, site of a thirteenth/fourteenth-century village, provided substantially greater evidence of more elaborate pastoral activity. But from this range of evidence it is of course not possible to posit continuous pastoral activity at any of these sites across the early medieval period.

For the early medieval period the different sort of approach taken by species history, now a topic of much interest for several disciplines including Italian medieval archaeology, may provide more evidence (Clark 1987; Baker and Clark 1993; Baker 1994; Salvadori 2003; Valenti and Salvadori 2006). Wetland sites tend not to preserve bones because of high soil acidity, so in Liguria osteological evidence typically comes from lower altitude sites often near or on the coast. Domestic animals of some species are generally easier to identify archaeologically; wild pigs or boar can be particularly difficult to distinguish from the domestic article, although some wild animals – various sorts of deer are a case in point – are relatively more recognizable. Several archaeological sites have provided useful information about the key animal species exploited by humans in Dark Age Liguria. These seem to have been sheep, goats, cattle, pigs and deer. Sites relevant to debates about the animal archaeology of the area include Castel Delfino (mostly late medieval), Filattiera (MS), Luni, Sant'Antonino di Perti (De Vingo 2011), Savona (Priàmar), and Genoa itself (Andrews and Pringle 1978). These sites have been of some importance in wider-ranging syntheses which have tried to understand the ways in which animals were part of early medieval diets. In the past, animal bones have tended to be seen in terms of production and consumption debates. More recently methodologies derived from surveys and excavations of early medieval villages

sites in Tuscany (of mostly ninth- and tenth-century date) have questioned
this approach, to take a possibly more sophisticated look at who ate what in
such villages and how what they ate might be related to the time periods in
which they ate it (Valenti and Salvadori 2006). This research has argued that
the 'best' cuts of meat especially of beef were found in the 'best' houses, whereas
the poor ate the worst cuts; that pork was only found in a very limited range of
cuts, implying that pork shoulders were used a form of payment by peasants
to their lords; and that hunting (especially for deer) becomes recognizable
archaeologically in stone buildings from the eleventh century, and seems
to have been associated with the seigniorial aristocracy, and not at all with
peasants (Valenti and Salvadori 2006: 183–7). The evidence of Castel Delfino
(near Savona) and Zignago fit into the latter category, but most of this evidence
is dated after the eleventh century. Other sites in the region do provide some
early medieval evidence about animals, notably Genoa (discussed in Chapter 5)
and Filattiera (MS), in northern Tuscany in the Magra valley.

'Filattiera' describes a complex of sites in the Lunigiana which have been
excavated over a long period (Bullough 1956; Biasotti and Giovinazza 1982;
Cabona et al. 1982, 1984; Giannichedda 1998; Giannichedda and Lanza 2003;
Christie 2006: 439; Greppi 2008: 55–9; Banti 2009). At 212 m asl it is much
lower in altitude than the upland mire sites and consequently its archaeology is
different; open area excavation has been possible, with finds of a varied nature.
These have usually been much more securely datable to the early medieval
period and evidence what Neil Christie has dubbed a 'low-status or working
rural community' (Christie 2006: 439). The environmental finds have been
particularly interesting. Pigs for example were consumed at fifth/sixth-century
Filattiera aged 2 to 3 years (Giannichedda 1998: 196–7), whereas very much
younger ones were found on the archbishop's table in tenth-century Genoa
(Cesana et al. 2007). The presence of pigs at Filattiera implies a woodland
economy, perhaps where the animals were grazed in oak woods on acorns in
season. However, excavations here have also suggested that oak was in decline
compared to chestnut at this time: maybe these pigs ate chestnuts too, as was
certainly the case within living memory in this region. Filattiera also turned up
many seeds of wheat, barley, foxtail millet (*Setaria italica*, around 50,000 seeds
from a sackful carbonized when a hut burnt down in the early sixth century),
material which also included chestnut, and some peach stones, walnut shells
and grape pips from pressings, what Giannichedda has called 'everyday

pleasures' (1998: 198–212; Giannichedda 2003). The presence of foxtail millet is particularly interesting as it is often planted now for hay and silage (it both germinates and grows fast), but is also edible and quite healthy. This plant does not tolerate water-logging. This site shows clearly that late Antique economies here were mixed, adaptable and did not make much use of locally grown wheat (see Horden and Purcell 2000: 201–9).

Late Roman sites like Filattiera – and also Gronda (Davite 1988) and Porciletto (Melli et al. 2006) – can be interpreted in various ways. Looked at from the perspective of modern, highly urbanized western societies they can seem extremely poor; indeed Tiziano Mannoni argued this case very strongly in the early 1980s (Mannoni 1983b). They can seem like good evidence for 'catastrophic' interpretations of the end of the Roman world. But a change of perspective can make all the difference: compared with prehistoric *castellari* they do not seem especially poor but rather they seem typical of much older habits and ways of life to be found across upland Europe at relatively isolated rural sites. Lastly, it is vital to note that all excavated archaeological sites are at some level atypical because they have been excavated. The more 'successful' sites are almost certainly those which still exist – the current network of villages and hamlets – and which have not been excavated. These patterns of settlement, especially the dynamic relationship between hilltop and other sites, are the subject of the next chapter.

Notes

1 Strabo, *Geography*, 4.6.1: translation from *LacusCurtius* http://penelope.uchicago.edu/Thayer/E/Roman/Texts/Strabo/home.html (accessed 15 June 2012). The barley drink was presumably beer.

2 Diodorus, *Bibliotheca historica*, 5.39: translation from *LacusCurtius* http://penelope.uchicago.edu/Thayer/E/Roman/Texts/Diodorus_Siculus/5B*.html (accessed 15 June 2012).

3 Post-medieval Liguria has been very intensively studied: Balzaretti et al. 2004; also Watkins 1993; Krzywinski et al. 2009: 104–13; Cevasco 2007 (reviewed by Balzaretti 2009); Cevasco 2010 and above all the many works of Diego Moreno, notably 1990 and 1997b.

4 Palynology is the study of pollen grains as found in excavated sites. Linkage of these grains with dating evidence can provide crucial evidence of former plant cover. Anthracology is a cognate study using carbonized wood remains rather than pollen. It is particularly important in this heavily wooded region.

5   *Ronco* refers to the clearance of woodland to provide land for temporary arable
    cultivation; *alnocultura* describes a system of cultivation of alder trees to provide
    leaf fodder.
6   Shredding involves the stripping of young leaves from trees using a metal tool to
    provide fodder, especially at times of year or in places when grass or hay are scarce.
7   Excellent discussions of this and other wetland sites can be found at the 'Le zone
    umide' website: www.dismec.unige.it/zum/index-en.html (accessed 20 March 2012).
8   Controlled burning has long been a relatively less labour intensive way to clear
    steep terraced sites of unwanted vegetation.
9   A statistic arrived at from research by the Laboratorio di Geomorfologia Applicata,
    Università degli Studi di Genova: www.geomorfolab.it/pagine/chI_siamo.htm
    (accessed 22 June 2012), a partner in the transnational ALPTER project 'Terraced
    landscapes of the Alpine arc', www.alpter.net/ with some Ligurian results at www.
    alpter.net/Large-scale-analysis-of-Ligurian.html?lang=en (accessed 22 June 2012).
10 Later known to Carolingian scholars as *libesticum*, lovage was included in the
    Carolingian *Capitulare De Villis*, Plan of St. Gall (*lubestico*) and the 'Little Garden' of
    Walafrid Strabo (*libisticum*) and appears to have been grown on some Carolingian
    royal estates (e.g. Asnapius). But its presumed connection with Liguria had been
    forgotten by then.
11 The terms used to describe such a system by historical ecologists vary and include
    Savannah and 'trees without forest' (Grove and Rackham 2001: 190–216).
12 Fischer Drew 1973: 111 and Azzara and Gasparri 1992: 83 both translate as beech.
13 For *isca* Fischer Drew 1973: 349 gives 'mast', whereas Azzara and Gasparri 1992: 93
    give 'meadow' (*pascolo*). It is not clear what this word means but it may be related to
    hisclo which clearly did mean beech.
14 Pian Brogione is most interesting as the site of a seventeenth-century chestnut
    grove at the altitudinal limit for that species (Cevasco et al. 2010). At the moment
    no early medieval presence has been detected at this site.
15 This has now been documented archaeologically for this period by Dreslerová and
    Mikuláš 2010.
16 See note 2 above.
17 I am very grateful to my doctoral student Robert A. Hearn for much discussion
    on Ligurian hunting which was very important across the region in the modern
    period. For more details see Robert Hearn's website at www.roberthearn.moonfruit.
    com/# (accessed 09 September 2011).

3

Villas, Villages and *Castra*

Inland high wetland sites prove that residues of ancient pollen are an effective way to understand the dynamic relationship between people and their environment over the long term (Montanari and Guido 2006). Although it is difficult in every case to weigh up the exact importance of human activities within these complex past ecosystems, analysis of plant remains can reveal how early medieval humans managed the land in comparison with their Prehistoric and Roman forebears, even though there are still relatively fewer sites with early medieval pollen in Liguria. Human management of vegetation cover must also be related to a wider history of settlement which is the theme of this chapter. Prehistoric Ligurian settlement took the form of small-scale dispersed sites with low populations (Maggi 1999). Late Bronze Age settlement tended to be around watersheds, on hilltops (*castellari*), caves relatively near the coast or associated with important passes such as the Passo dei Giovi which linked Genoa and the Po plain. Dispersed settlement does not necessarily result in ineffective social organization as Maggi argued, although using the written evidence of the 'Polcevera tablet' (*sententia Minuciorum*) dated 117 BCE rather than archaeology to make his point (Maggi 1999: 63). This famous bronze artefact unearthed in Isola, near Serra Riccò (Polcevera valley) in 1506 shows that the local people – called *Viturii* by the Roman senate – who lived in scattered settlements in the middle of the Polcevera valley apparently without any 'capital', managed nevertheless to defend themselves in a major property dispute against the *Genuates*, the inhabitants of urban Genoa (Giannattasio 2007: 134–5). As we shall see, early medieval Ligurian settlement organization was more similar to this dispersed pattern than to the more nucleated and more urbanized Roman landscapes often presented as 'the norm'.

The chapter draws mostly on archaeological research and a few brief reflections on that discipline are appropriate before proceeding. Archaeology is not good at reconstructing past political events – such as the dispute between the *Viturii* and *Genuates* – because it cannot provide sufficiently precise dates. Nor is it immune to generalization which glosses over the lives of real past people: pollen samples for example are more inscrutable than objects which were once handled again by a real person (see Giannichedda 2006). Indeed, while archaeologists like to believe that their evidence is less compromised than historians' written sources (Moreland 2001, 2010: 37–74; Francovich and Hodges 2003; Kulikowski 2007), they could make more explicit distinctions between different types of archaeology and how effectively each restores the distant past to us (see Pearce 2011). For historians – not all of whom think that the 'past speaks for itself' (Sherratt 1993: 127) – archaeological investigation can provide a direct physical connection to people who lived centuries ago, even in the supposedly 'dark' ages.

In Liguria some stray un-contextualized finds of this sort help to bring this period to life. A Lombard bronze frying-pan from Rossiglione (Stura valley) conjures up images of dark-age omelettes (Giannichedda 1993) or a similarly dated short axe from Langasco (Polcevera valley) the sounds of woodland work (Carpaneto 1975: 13; De Vingo and Frondoni 2003: 33). The Langasco axe (of 'barbuta' or 'long-bearded' type) was a typical woodland tool used to work timber rather than fell trees. It was found detached from any meaningful archaeological context but perhaps similar foresters' tools might have been used to maintain a wooded-meadow system of the kind found at Mogge di Ertola in this period or some other sophisticated management practice. This axe can also be linked to the seventh-century Lombard laws which deal with the marking of trees with notches or cuts to indicate woodland boundaries (*Ed. Roth.* 238–41), the practice known in Latin as *teclatura* and to the Lombards as *snaida*. These activation practices must also have required the use of axes or similar metal tools.

Stray finds are really the equivalent of the tangential anecdotes so often found in early medieval narratives and absence of context is a real problem for any survey of settlement change in Dark Age Liguria. Not all sites are equally well-studied and the quality of their evidence is thus variable. Prehistoric Liguria has, as was clear in the previous chapter, been substantially studied over a longer period and some studies have the time-depth to reach into early medieval times; these are particularly meaningful contexts. But Liguria has not often figured much in general surveys of archaeological work in early medieval Italy and it is therefore quite hard to pull it all together in a way which does not do a disservice to the specifically *archaeological* nature of the work on which a survey necessarily relies. There has not been, for example, any large-scale multi-period survey such as those for South Etruria, the Biferno valley or San Vincenzo al Volturno in the Molise, and so the results of those surveys do not make appropriate comparisons for Liguria. A paucity of large open-area multi-period excavations of village sites also makes meaningful comparison with other sites problematic. Seemingly perfect comparative material from several well-known and highly significant sites in neighbouring Tuscany, notably Montarrenti, Poggibonsi and Scarlino (Valenti 2000; Francovich and Hodges 2003: 68–70, 77–80) is not really appropriate. These are crucial sites in debates about settlement change, the formation of villages and *incastellamento* because they have been excavated in great detail and cover the whole period c. 600–1000. While on the face of it good comparators for Liguria topographically and climatically there is only one similar Ligurian site – Corvara near Beverino (SP) – and this is anyway much smaller and less thoroughly excavated. The Tuscan sites have no appropriate Ligurian comparisons therefore but probably because the right sort of excavations have not yet been carried out.

Turning to the many excellent excavations have been undertaken in Liguria, it is clear that much more notice has been taken recently of Dark Age levels than used to be the case. Of sites covering time periods similar to those documented by pollen samples, the most important is probably the Arene Candide, a series of caves near Finale on the western Riviera studied since the nineteenth century. These caves were shown by Brea in one of the earliest properly documented stratigraphic excavations to have been occupied from the fourth-millennium BCE to the first-millennium CE, and he documented early medieval levels dated to the sixth century (Bernabò Brea 1946; see Maggi et al. 1995; Maggi 2004). Finds included amphorae, glass stem beakers and soapstone (*pietra ollare*) artefacts (Christie 1995: 313; Bernabò Brea 1946: 33–5, 253–5) which, while demonstrating engagement by 'cavemen' (Christie 1995) with urban markets into the seventh century (Murialdo et al. 1998: 236–41), did not stop Tiziano Mannoni (1983b) from categorizing the Arene Candide as one of his 'poor' late Roman settlements. More recently Neil Christie has argued that late Antique reoccupation of caves and rock shelters here and at the sites of Le Marie and Pollera also near Finale, was not necessarily 'second class' settlement because permanency was advantageous (1995, 2006: 477–8). This is convincing as Dark Age inland sites were certainly not very permanent and displayed levels of culture that were easily as poor.

Roman coastal settlement

Caves and open-hilltop sites were not favoured in the Roman period when settlement was much more focused on the coast itself and on the valley floors which led inland to the Po plain, an area of much greater population. While inland upland Liguria was relatively untouched, Roman impact elsewhere was much deeper with the coast revealing more and more archaeological evidence for the profundity of their presence. The *Barrington Atlas* is the best general guide to Roman settlement patterns (Talbert 2000), and Maps 39 (*Mediolanum*) and 41 (*Pisae*) make clear how little we really know for certain from written sources about most Roman sites across the region (see Mannoni 1983a; Milella 1989).[1] Some existing routes were developed, especially the *Via Postumia* from Genoa to Piacenza built 148 BCE up the Polcevera valley (Bianchi 1996; Cera 2000: 24–50), the *Via Aemilia Scauri* (from c. 107 BCE) which ran along the coast westward from Pisa, via Luni and Genoa to Piacenza, and the *Via Julia Augusta* along the western Riviera (from 13 BCE). Romans consistently favoured coastal sites including Albisola, Anzo di Framura, Camogli, Chiavari, Genoa, Lavagna, Luni, Moneglia, Portofino, Portovenere, Savona, Sestri Levante and Vado Ligure, which are all definitively documented (Gambaro 1999; Spadea and Martino 2004).[2] They also settled at *Libarna* (Serravalle Scrivia) in the Scrivia (Petracco Sicardi and Caprini 1981: 59, 67), and in the Staffora, Vara (Vezzano) and Magra (Passo del Bracco) valleys. Settlements at higher altitudes were fewer, but included Bobbio (Trebbia), Bedonia (Taro valley, Emilia-Romagna) and Cairo Montenotte (Bormida valley). The *Barrington Atlas* maps places which still exist today demonstrating in these cases the long-term importance of the Roman push in favour of nucleation and of the exchange networks, roads and road stations (*mansiones*) and rivers needed to maintain a nucleated landscape in this region.

The Barrington maps do not show change over time, and there were many changes in the later Roman period. Some were 'natural' such as climate change, or may have seemed 'natural' at the time such as changes to the coastline and the silting up of rivers including the Centa at Albenga. But as Roman land reclamation is well-evidenced in some places including Genoa and Vado human impact must also be kept in mind (Carobene et al. 2006, 2009). Changes in settlement have long been part of debates about the end of the Roman world, and Liguria is no different in this regard. The extent of depopulation and discontinuity in urban settlement are important and dealt with below. But the most diagnostic issue is probably what happened to villas, luxury or otherwise (see Ripoll and Arce 2000; Francovich and Hodges 2003: 31–50; Dyson 2003: 13–35, 89–97; Wickham 2005; Christie 2006: 430–7, 406–2; Brogiolo and Chavarría Arnau 2008; but less important in Decker 2009).

The principal Roman villas now known in Liguria are shown in Table 3.1. Each complex overlooked the beautiful coast presumably not only for aesthetic reasons but also to tap into pan-Mediterranean exchange networks for luxuries. None lasted beyond c. 400. Some sites continued as large farms including Albisola (4 km NE of Savona) where a church dedicated to St Peter was built and a burial ground for private funerary use developed c. 500 (De Vingo 2010a: 80). The third-century villa near Sanremo (Bussana, loc. Foce) may be associated in some way with the early phases of the nearby church of San Siro (Medri 2006). At Quiliano (4 km east of Savona), the church of San Pietro in Carpignano was built inside a small villa (Marcenaro and Frondoni 2006: 72–3; De Vingo 2010a: 80). This pattern of Christianization of former villa sites reflects what happened in other parts of Italy to similar-sized villas during the couple of centuries after c. 400 (Brogiolo 2001). By contrast, a small *villa rustica* at Lusignano near Albenga probably supplied the Roman town with fresh food and it may have been occupied well into late antiquity as was Albenga itself (Massabò 2004: 180–3). In eastern Liguria, the villa at Varignano (near Portovenere) underwent substantial alteration during the fifth and sixth

Table 3.1 Roman Villas in Liguria

Location	Date	Type
Albisola Superiore	Imperial period	Large residence and farm
Ameglia, Bocca di Magra	1–4 CE	Villa with baths, high status buildings and decorations
Albenga, Lusignano	1 CE to late antiquity	'villa rustica'
Portovenere, Varignano Vecchio	1 CE	'villa rustica/maritima'
Sanremo, Bussana	2nd CE	Productive site
Sanremo, Bussana loc. Foce	3rd CE	With baths

centuries, and was then abandoned (Christie 2006: 436). There are likely to be other villas waiting to be discovered along this striking coast, which must have appealed to Roman elites in the same way as the Bay of Naples did.

Mid-slope inland sites

Debates about villas are very well-known to scholars and these few Ligurian examples add little that is new (Dyson 2003; Christie 2004: 39–102, 2006: 428–37). Less well-known are late Roman small-scale rural sites although what happened here was, when viewed in the light of early medieval settlement patterns, arguably as important in the long term (see Decker 2009 and Grey 2011 for fascinating new insights on this issue). There are several significant sites in or near Liguria including Corti (near Albenga), Savignone (Scrivia valley), San Cipriano and Costa Bottuin (near Trensasco, Polcevera valley), Porciletto (Sturla valley) and Gronda and Filattiera (Magra valley). Apart from Filattiera, all came to light in rescue excavations but together they form a thought-provoking group. In the settlement hierarchy proposed by Francovich and Hodges in their survey of the end of Roman villas (2003: 33–6), these sites were most like small farms (e.g. Porciletto) but some (e.g. Corti) were more like *vici*, small farming villages (Patterson 1991; Arthur 2004: 105–9; Christie 2006: 437–42; Decker 2009: 33–48; Moreland 2010: 116–58). As none of these sites was in use after c. 600, they reveal how Roman presence ended in the Ligurian countryside.

Corti, in the hinterland of Pietra Ligure and within the *municipium* of Albenga (Massabò 1999, 2004), was the most substantial of these sites and specialized in processing animal and agricultural products presumably for markets in Albenga (De Vingo 2010a: 82). Olive oil production, probably for export as at villas near Luni and Varignano, stopped during the third and fourth centuries when pottery vessels evidence the importation of oil from elsewhere. Between the fifth and ninth centuries the site became increasingly marshy. It only returned to agricultural use from the tenth century. Recently, this chronology has been confirmed at Pietra Ligure (c. 1500 m from Corti) in cores taken from the beach which have conclusively shown that between seventh to ninth centuries chestnut pollen predominated here, with little evidence of cereals and especially of olives (Arobba et al. 2007: 91). If by then cereals, vines and olives were apparently marginal in this landscape this finding fits well with hypotheses about changing climatic conditions in this period as we shall see.

Savignone loc. Refundou (Figure 3.1) is a mid-slope (490 m asl) site overlooking the River Scrivia (Figure 3.2) where rescue excavations documented a small number of dry-stone walled and thatched houses extending about 30 m across (Fossati et al. 1976; Casteletti 1976; Cagnana 1994: 170). Several hundred kilos of re-used Roman roof tiles (*tegoloni*) were found, the use of which remains unclear (Mannoni 1983b: 262). There was no local pottery but, perhaps surprisingly, imported ceramics were present either regionally produced fifth/sixth-century *ceramica grezza* paralleled at Ventimiglia and Luscignano in the Lunigiana or imported *terra sigillata chiara* D and African amphorae of fourth/fifth-century dates (Fossati et al. 1976: 315–20). These imports caused puzzlement among archaeologists as such

IN THE FIELDS AT SAVIGNONE.

Figure 3.1 In the Fields at Savignone in 1878.
Source: Alice Comyns Carr, *North Italian Folk* (London, 1878), p. 142.

Figure 3.2 Elizabeth Fanshawe, Sketch of the Val di Scrivia, 3 June 1829.
Source: In author's possession.

pottery – used even for common cooking pots – was deemed inappropriate
to the 'elementary level of life' observable from the structures and plant
remains (Fossati et al. 1976: 325; Cagnana 1994: 170). Comparisons with
more recent peasant dwellings in this region may however help to explain
this apparently paradoxical collection of furnishings.[3] The few carbonized
plant remains evidenced rye cultivation and tree cover of silver birch, elm
and field maple with little oak, hazel or chestnut (Casteletti 1976), not
dissimilar to present vegetation cover. Additionally, two coins were found,
one a coin of Theodosius I (379–395) (Fossati et al. 1976: 314). Refundou
was probably occupied throughout the second- and first-centuries BCE then
abandoned until the fourth-century CE when it was active until c. 500; later,
the site became agricultural and was not reoccupied until modern times, even
though it is near the current village site.

Buildings similar to those at Savignone were found at: San Cipriano nr.
Pontedecimo (Polcevera valley), situated on an east-facing slope at 314 m asl.
Roof tiles produced in the suburbs of Genoa itself were again found (Cagnana
1994: 169–70; De Vingo and Frondoni 2003: 84). A single low dry-stone-walled
building was excavated with a wooden superstructure supporting a straw roof,
a beaten earth floor with a broken tiled floor in the centre. A hoard of 40 bronze

coins, the most recent dated 364–378 CE helped to date the fire which destroyed the building and caused its abandonment. About ½ km NE of the current village of San Cipriano, the church of San Michele di Castrofino (probably from *castrum finis*, a fortified site which was later part of the Byzantine *limes*) preserved a possibly eighth-century burial stone of Sabatinus, a deacon, and his parents who seem to have 'Germanic' names (De Vingo and Frondoni 2003). Not far from here at Trensasco (Costa Bottuin, a few kilometres south of Sant'Olcese, GE), a single late imperial building was discovered again with a floor of crushed tiles which might have been the hard core for a wooden floor as at Savignone and San Cipriano (Maggi 1992: 53–85). This site turned up quite a bit of fourth-century pottery, again mostly imported. Porciletto (250 m asl) is in a hamlet near Mezzanego (Sturla valley) about 10 km from Lavagna on the coast (Bianchi 1996; Melli et al. 2006). Now the area is characterized by relatively sparsely distributed hamlets, so it is interesting that scattered finds here have suggested Roman rural settlement (Mannoni 1983b: 260–1).

Comparison is worth making with two other late Roman sites bordering Liguria in the east. In the 1970s at Gronda di Luscignano (Massa, 450 m asl), east of Aulla in the upper Aulella valley, a small fourth- to sixth-century village and early medieval cemetery (c. 15 graves) were uncovered on top of an earlier village site (Davite 1988). The graves were poorly preserved; the only dating element being a single coin of Otto II. Pottery of fourth- to sixth-century date (Davite 1988: 401) and comparable with material from Savignone, San Cipriano and Filattiera, was used to date the site although some of the proposed dates at this site have been questioned (Christie 2006: 439). In contrast, Filattiera-Sorano (Lunigiana) is much more thoroughly excavated owing to its fame as the likely location of a fortification mentioned by the Greek author George of Cyprus c. 610 CE: *Surianum; kastron Soreon* (*Descriptio orbis Romani*, n. 550) (Bullough 1956; Cagnana 1994: 174).[4] Hilltop defensive works have been uncovered nearby at both Castelvecchio and Monte Castello (c. 800 m asl) which bear some comparison with Monte Barro, north of Milan. Below at Sorano on the valley floor near the River Magra excavations revealed a village which existed between the first and sixth centuries CE, with houses built of timber and river cobble (Giannichedda 1998). Ceramics were mostly of local production and functional, but some connections to coastal ports were evidenced in the third century with the presence of imported pottery. Although new buildings were made at the end of the third century, the village declined during the sixth century with one burned house producing some carbonized foods (this interesting botanical data was discussed above 32–3). Filattiera was probably a type of *vicus* (Christie 2006: 439). It is notable that in the nearby church of San Giorgio there is the epitaph of 'Leodegar' (dated 752) made from Luni marble which was once in the parish church of Santo Stefano (Banti 2009).[5] Its existence is an important evidence for evangelization here in the Lombard period (see 76–7 below).

Mannoni (1983b) argued that urban dwellers impoverished by the third-century urban crisis across the Empire were forced to return to rural subsistence sites in the hills such as these which he termed 'stazioni a tegoloni' (1983b: 254, 'roof tile sites'). They shared many features being mid-slope at around 300–500 m asl on the sunny side and potentially adapted to modest cereal production. There could be other explanations for this apparent shift particularly that 'roof tile' sites were in effect continuously occupied because the evidence for continuity is likely to be under nearby currently occupied sites. *Tegoloni* probably provided a layer to assist drainage or simply to build a firm platform for construction on a sloping site as presumably hard core was bought in then as it would be now. More recently, Paolo De Vingo and Alessandra Frondoni (2003: 32–3) set out a revised settlement sequence in which late Antique people repopulated the mid-slopes inland from Genoa and made use of pastures at higher sites, a pattern which continued throughout the early medieval period until the eleventh century when the valley bottoms were settled and monastic buildings constructed with castles on higher sites. The mid-slope sites were predominantly mixed woodland, with a limited presence of beech, rye and chestnut (poorer foods nutritionally than some cereals) and display adaptation to environmental conditions as much as reflection of social situation (De Vingo and Frondoni 2003: 33).[6] The fact that cereals were not apparently much grown even though it was *possible* to do so may be a fact of wider cultural significance in the settlement history of the entire region.

Each of these sites brings us closer to early medieval people and where and how they lived in this region. The settlement history of the Genovesato just outlined is typical of Liguria as a whole: coastal villas and inland hamlets were replaced by coastal *castra* and inland villages (see Francovich and Hodges 2003). Explanations for when this shift happened and why are probably complex, and certainly still open to debate particularly at the micro level

(Arthur 2004; Provero 2007). The presence of churches at or near many of these sites is obviously an indication of continuing commitment to and investment in settlement. Indeed church sites may be particularly important as they might help to bridge the gap between the wealth of late Antique settlement archaeology now emerging and the hilltop archaeology characteristic of the late tenth century onwards, for, in this region, the on-going research problem is the lack of rural sites with eighth- and ninth-century levels. We can conclude that the late Antique inland sites just considered do not tell us when nucleated villages were 'founded' in Liguria, as 'founded' is an inappropriate word for what was a much more evolutionary or indeed piecemeal process (Valenti 2000; Francovich and Hodges 2003; Guglielmotti 2005; Wickham 2005; Brogiolo 2006; Cheyette 2008). The problem will only be resolved by more extensive excavations at currently occupied village sites, obviously a contentious matter in Liguria as there is only one published excavation of a nucleated village: Corvara (SP) near Beverino in the lower Vara valley, dated late tenth century but not earlier (below 131–2).

Fredegar and the Lombard conquest

Coastal sites have caught the attention of historians much more than inland late Roman farms and increasingly archaeologists are studying them too. The key starting point for historians is the statement made by Fredegar writing in the 660s,[7] that the Lombard king Rothari reduced the coastal *civitates* to villages (*vici*) as part of his conquest of the region:

> Rothari went with his army and took from the Empire the coastal cities of Genoa, Albenga, Varigotti, Savona, Oderzo [in Friuli...] and Luni. He ravaged and destroyed them and left them in flames; and the inhabitants, stripped of their belongings, were seized and condemned to servitude. He ordered that these cities should be known as villages in future; and he raised their walls to the ground. (Fredegar IV, 70–1; Krusch 1888: 156–7; my translation)[8]

These five places were the principal late Roman settlements on the coast; so it is significant that Genoa is listed first implying a centralized function for it, almost as the capital of the area in his eyes. The other sites, listed west to east, have each been investigated by archaeologists so Fredegar's statements about fires and demolition can be tested. Archaeological research on the coast has gone much further though with important excavations at Ventimiglia, Vado Ligure, Finale, Noli, San Fruttuoso and other sites including the islands Bergeggi, Gallinaria, Gorgona, Tino and Tinetto. Given the amount of research available, these coastal sites allow us to test hypotheses about continuity and discontinuity at early medieval urban sites (Brogiolo and Gelichi 1998; Pavoni 1988; Ward-Perkins 1997; Whittow 2009), and they serve to introduce this chapter's final section about the militarization of hilltop sites as part of the Byzantine defence of the province against both the Goths and the Lombards and the later connections, if any, which these places may have had to proto-castle sites which appeared on the scene towards the middle of the tenth century.

Archaeological research at Albenga, Varigotti, Savona and Luni in the seventh century questions the veracity of Fredegar's record and again raises issues about appropriate comparison. Albenga and Luni are both substantial Roman archaeological sites, whereas Varigotti, a sparsely inhabited promontory, and Savona, a large town unlikely ever to be thoroughly excavated, are not. Being so different now can these places be realistically compared now in the way Fredegar did then? Roman Albenga (*Albingaunum*) was a significant town inhabited throughout late Antiquity as recent excavations show. Why this should be when other sites on the western Riviera declined dramatically at the same time is still unclear, but the continued presence there of the Byzantine military was probably crucial (Gardini and Murialdo 1994: 168–9; Christie 1990: 241, 250; Greppi 2008: 10–12). Its walls were famously restored in c. 416 by Constantius as recorded by a surviving stone inscription (Mommsen 1877, V: 7781) and verses of Rutilius Namatianus describing them (Mosca 2004; Christie 2006: 290). Tzittanus *comes et tribunes* there in 568, is interesting both for his evident political role at the moment of the Lombard invasion and his Armenian name (Brown 1984: 53–60). The presence of a bishop of Albenga in 451 (Cantino Wataghin 2000: 217) also helps to explain the town's success but, as important Christian structures have been preserved from earlier, a long-lasting process of Christianization can be posited (Gambaro and Lambert 1987: 203–6; Massabò 2004; Marcenaro and Frondoni 2006: 89–129). The cathedral and adjacent baptistery were probably built on the site of the former Roman forum (Marcenaro 2006). The cathedral has fourth-century remains underneath and the famous baptistery – dated between the mid-fifth and the early sixth century – has preserved the most important Christian mosaics of the region, including a controversial inscription, as well as several early tombs, including a Lombard-period one. Indeed later additions to the baptistery in the eighth century including a carved window and an *arcosolium* tomb (Russo 2003: 76), clearly show the building still in use or at least restored *after* the supposed destruction by Rothari.

Two early funerary churches were outside Albenga's walls: San Vittore (fourth/fifth century) and San Calocero (fifth century, perhaps older). Recently, another font at San Clemente (fifth/sixth century) has been found in excavations at the Roman baths. These church remains are linked to a corpus of 33 late Roman inscriptions (Mennella and Coccoluto 1995: 86–141). Most recently, within a programme of underwater archaeology to plot Roman port sites along the Ligurian coast, Isola Gallinaria off the coast from Albenga has been studied (Spadea and Martino 2004). The port of Albenga is at the moment impossible to understand archaeologically because of a large amount of sediment deposited by the River Centa in the last 2,000 years; but ceramic finds at Gallinaria have demonstrated its continued use as a safe harbour until at least the fifth century (Spadea and Martino 2004: 267–8).

'Varigotti' (Comune of Finale Ligure) refers both to a settlement right on the coast and to the spectacular promontory of Punta Crena overlooking it. Studied extensively by Nino Lamboglia, there has been much recent work at this Byzantine coastal fortified site protecting the harbour (Valabrega 1986; Christie 1990: 250–1, 2006: 368–9, 372; Marcenaro and Frondoni 2006: 82–3; Greppi 2008: 12–14). In situ remains, supposedly Lombard decorative elements in the church of San Lorenzo Vecchia on the mainland (especially a reworked Roman sarcophagus, now in the museum at Finale), and inscriptions from nearby locations as well as a fragmentary seventh-century one recovered from excavations inside the church, all suggest some sort of continuity. San Lorenzo – now largely late medieval – is on a prominent site overlooking the promontory and is likely to have earlier origins (Frondoni et al. 1997: 104). Recent excavations have not found Byzantine structures because of past disruption of the stratigraphy (Frondoni et al. 1997) although earlier some Byzantine pottery and burials were found (as reported by Milella 1989), also not properly stratified. Was Varigotti a *civitas* then? Lamboglia argued a common-sense 'yes' by linking Paul the Deacon's phrase *civitates et castra Romanorum* and the prologue to Rothari's Edict with Varigotti's strategic position commanding the coast and its hinterland, but his opinion has not been entirely borne out by recent archaeology. Varigotti is better seen in relationship to nearby Perti, a much more impressive and much-better excavated site at a greater altitude, discussed below.

Savona is also known archaeologically. The site known as Priamàr was earlier regarded as a Byzantine *castrum* built on top of the pre-Roman *oppidum* but despite some evidence of structures and burials of that period, caution is advised as significant disturbance was created when the later medieval fortress of Priamàr was built. Late Antique Savona was closely linked with nearby Vado (*Vada Sabatia*), as Vado's population probably relocated to the Priamàr hill then (Christie 1990: 252). Vado's large corpus of inscribed stones suggests however a fairly dramatic decline at the site from the mid-third century on, with archaeologically demonstrable fifth-century difficulties (Christie 1990: 251–2; Mennella and Coccoluto 1995: 72–85, docs 33–9), which may have had been caused by the silting up of local rivers and changes to the coastline (Carobene et al. 2009). Recent excavations have suggested a more complex situation as a large necropolis existed here from the end of the fourth century which continued in use for about 300 years (Greppi 2008: 17, 104; Varaldo 1996; Lavagna and Varaldo 1997). During the seventh century some homes were built over the graves, and it may be that this phase was short-lived with a contraction observable mid-century linked to Rothari's conquest (Greppi 2008: 18). In the eighth and ninth centuries this site – a presumed early Roman villa with a seventh- to ninth-century burial area (De Vingo 2010a: 83) – was reoccupied and stone built properties erected, which may be connected with reference to a *castrum* here in 887. This development is clearly observable outside the fortified area may represent Paul the Deacon's settlement of *Saona* (*HL* II 16). In 864, Bishop Stradelbertus of Vado attended a Milanese synod and a fragment of carved stone decoration presumed to be from his cathedral at Priamàr has survived, which is evidence of some continuing activity (Marcenaro and Frondoni 2006: 69–71).

Luni is better-known archaeologically than any of Fredegar's other sites because it was completely abandoned by the medieval period (Ward-Perkins 1981; Lusuardi Siena 1985, 2006; Delano Smith et al. 1986; Christie 1990: 254–5; Gardini and Murialdo 1994: 162; Gambaro 2003). It had been an important if comparatively small – about 1 sq km – planned Roman provincial walled town with houses, a theatre and forum (Frova 1977), and was occupied in some parts until the Byzantine withdrawal (Ward-Perkins 1981; Campoltrini 1989), with continuity across the fourth to sixth centuries at some church sites (Ward-Perkins 1984: 52). Yet as elsewhere (e.g. Albenga) the Roman monumental public buildings were plundered for stone and even demolished, the streets stopped being maintained and new buildings of wood were built on top of Roman stone structures (Wickham 2005: 674). Luni 'died' in the seventh century which might link with Fredegar's view of the Lombard conquest, although interesting arguments have been put forward recently for a more structural and less political collapse which owed much to changing climatic conditions (Fazzini and Maffei 2000). Luni's early medieval cathedral of S. Maria at the northwestern edge of the town on top of earlier Roman domestic accommodation later used as an early Christian burial ground, has been excavated to reveal an impressive sixth-century Byzantine floor mosaic as well as a ninth-century crypt (Ward-Perkins 1984: 73; Lusuardi Siena 1985, 2006; Christie 2006: 75, 95–6) and the existence of a bishop here from the fifth century certainly seems to have resulted in some limited building at that time.

While Fredegar's idea that the Lombards destroyed Imperial *civitates* might have some support from archaeological evidence and may actually have happened, Fredegar's account has also had a malign influence on archaeologists when they discuss seventh-century phases of their sites. Fredegar, writing in another region entirely, is unlikely to have had any direct knowledge of the Ligurian coast or of Rothari's activities there (Collins 2007: 50), and curiously omits several sites which he might have noted including Ventimiglia, Vado Ligure, Finale, Noli and San Fruttuoso. Fredegar tends not to be mentioned when *these* sites are discussed, suggesting a certain circularity of argumentation. For the western Riviera, Noli is key with important finds in the last few years which have completely changed established views of its history (Christie 1990: 251; Gardini and Murialdo 1994: 175; Marcenaro and Frondoni 2006: 76–81; and especially Frondoni 2007). The site of Noli – probably George of Cyprus' early seventh-century *Neapolis* – has material covering the whole of the early medieval period at three main sites: via XXV Aprile; the church of San Paragorio; and the ex-Ferroviale (Di Dio 2006; De Vingo 2010b). Early medieval Noli probably developed on the coast not in the nearby hills as was earlier thought as a 'quasi-urban' settlement (Frondoni 2007: 20). San Paragorio church was built in the early eleventh century but excavations underneath have uncovered a sixth-century baptistery with an *arcosolium* tomb in the church dated first half of the sixth century, later re-used for the tomb of *Domina Lidoria* as her funerary stone now dated sixth/seventh century was found there (De Vingo 2010a: 91). Adjacent excavations have located the early medieval village/town which survived until a fire in the ninth century, possibly caused by a Saracen attack (Frondoni et al. 1997: 102). Almost all the burials found were single adults without grave goods, and probably fifth- to sixth-century date (De Vingo 2010a: 88). Crucially, this site was in continuous use from the end of the sixth century until the tenth century. Especially interesting is the mid-eighth-century C14 (+/- 120 years) date for a collapsed, burnt house, as this can be perhaps linked to the Lombard conquest. The wood used in these buildings as green timber was silver fir (*Abies alba*), a species thought to have been extinct in this region by this time. Noli shows how important micro evidence can be for macro interpretations as this site has – for its current excavators – turned on its head the old hypothesis of a move from coast to hilltop in the wake of Rothari's conquest. Yet the possibility remains that Fredegar's account of what happened on the Ligurian coast was about right: maybe Noli survived and other sites did not because Rothari did not destroy it but did destroy them.

Nearby at Finale Ligure excavations at Finaleborgo (Murialdo 1988; Palazzi et al. 2003) and Finalmarina (Marcenaro and Frondoni 2006, 83–5) have revealed a late antique/early medieval baptistery which might be the original parish church of San Giovanni Battista, dateable from amphorae types Keay VII (central Tunisia, mid-fourth/early sixth century (Spadea and Martino 2004: 264). The burial of an infant *Paula* here is recorded in an inscription dated 517 (De Vingo 2010a: 90). In Finale's hinterland the former church of San Cipriano at Calvisio has eighth-, tenth- and eleventh-century phases, but nothing earlier (Marcenaro and Frondoni 2006: 87–8). Further west, Ventimiglia (Roman *Albintimilium*) has also been much studied (Lamboglia and Pallares 1985; Gambaro and Lambert 1987: 206–8; Christie 1990: 249; Mennella and Coccoluto 1995: 142–9, docs 74–7, who have even here blamed Rothari for this town's collapse). Ventimiglia apparently entered a crisis at the start of the fifth century. Earlier Roman settlement was on the flat coastal strip, and is documented by inscriptions and excavations. These have found that the theatre was in a state of decay as early as the mid-fourth century (Christie 2006: 222), with burials around it c. 450, and houses within in the sixth and seventh centuries (Christie 2006: 224–6). There were burials of this period on the main *decumanus* which cut through fifth-century and later cobbling on the older Roman surface. Further remodelling and repairs were evidenced into the Lombard period (Christie 2006: 236–7), providing some parallels with Luni. Yet, although Fredegar doesn't mention Ventimiglia, because George of Cyprus does mention its existence in the early seventh century is still likely. Some have argued that this must mean that the Byzantines moved up the hill, to the site where the medieval settlement was to be. At the moment evidence after this period is patchy: the first reference to a diocese here is 680, when Bishop John was at the Roman synod; the current cathedral, baptistery and nearby church of San Michele, are all tenth/eleventh century; and there are very few inscriptions of this period, especially when compared with earlier survivals.

The coastal sites of the eastern Riviera are currently less well-known than the western ones, but have recently had more attention (Christie 1990: 253–5; Gardini and Murialdo 1994: 160–2; Marcenaro and Frondoni 2006: 19–36). In the early 1990s both Neil Christie's and Gardini and Murialdo's surveys of regional archaeology had little to report, now the area around Portovenere (*Portus Veneris*) has been studied as part of the *Soprintendenza* programme of underwater excavations (Spadea and Martino 2004: 256–9). Tino and Tinetto, islands just off Portovenere, have remnants of some of the earliest Christian buildings in Liguria, probably connected with early eremitic monastic practice here although precise dating is elusive (Gardini and Murialdo 1994: 161–2; Marcenaro and Frondoni 2006: 28–31). The Portofino peninsula has also been studied, including Portofino (*Portus Delphini*) itself, nearby San Michele di Pagana and the abbey of San Fruttuoso di Capodimonte (near Camogli). Ceramic evidence suggests that the latter site was first occupied in the sixth century, but attempts to push back the history of the existing church before the tenth century are not convincing (Gardini and Murialdo 1994: 162).

There is no doubt that excavations show that most coastal settlements recorded in the Roman period continued to be important into the seventh century and that some of them continued to be occupied after that, especially Noli and also Albenga. Plentiful ceramic evidence has enabled exchange networks to be plotted in some detail. Although the study of pottery is specialized (see Milella 1989; Reynolds 1995; Wickham 2005: 728–41 for Italy) and difficult to compress without significant distortion, the two key points are that (a) fine wares continued to be traded across the Mediterranean to coastal Liguria until the seventh century and (b) after this, new types of pottery (locally or regionally made and distributed inland probably via river transport) appeared, such as the *vacuolato* (spotted) types in northern Tuscany (and the Magra and Vara valleys) and 'testi' (flat terracotta cooking vessels) found in the same period and places. Imported fine wares including African Red Slip and other sorts largely from North Africa and the western Mediterranean came into western Liguria especially Ventimiglia and Albenga but also Perti and into Genoa well into the seventh century (625 or even 660; Brown and Christie 1989: 392), which shows that long-established pan-Mediterranean exchange networks continued to function at some level, although the quantities involved were greatly reduced which is certainly important (Wickham 1998). Much less found its way east, although such types continued to be imported to Luni until the seventh century (Gandolfi 1998).[9]

Very little of this sort of luxury pottery seems to have found its way inland at this period, and the economic distinction between coast and interior was clearly a real one in this respect (Wickham 1998: 286–9). As this had long been the case it may not 'mean' much in terms of real change over time. The presence of pottery, whether locally made, regionally made or sourced from further afield, at 'poor' inland sites has caused much debate as scholars seem perplexed that people who apparently lived materially impoverished lives in most other respects had decent earthenware to cook with and to eat off. Locally or regionally produced pottery (*ceramica commune*) was certainly produced at Ventimiglia and Albenga, and used in Genoa (Scuole Pie and Mattoni Rossi sites) (Biagini et al. 1998; Olcese 1995; Lavagna 1998 (Savona common wares); Maffeis and Negro Ponzi 1995 (common wares). The artefacts were mostly cooking pots and basic table wares. What pottery use meant to many of these communities remains unclear (Maffeis and Negro Ponzi 1995) but Mannoni (1983b) argued that these types evidenced a subsistence economy, an argument supported by the appearance of the 'testo' in eastern Liguria, a form specifically designed to make use of chestnut-based foods, long-associated with mountain poverty and inwardness in more modern times. More recently studies of the *vacuolata* types in this 'area show that these were produced in northern Tuscany and diffused north-eastwards in the Magra and Vara valleys but rarely further into Liguria (Giannichedda and Quiros Castillo 1997: 382). The meanings of this sort of local ceramic network need further research. Lastly but crucially, it is still the case that Lombard-manufactured pottery is extremely rare in Liguria, which suggests that exchange with the Lombard parts of Italy was always rare something unlikely to have been the case if the Lombard 'conquest' had had a real impact at ground level. It has only been found at Perti – a characteristically stamped pot dated c. 610–643 of Piedmontese production (Mannoni and Murialdo 2001: 356–9; De Marchi 2003: 19), and perhaps also at Vado.

These regional ceramic patterns fit well with what is known for other parts of the western Mediterranean (Wickham 1998: 285–6). By the end of the sixth century coastal economies were ceasing to reach inland (Wickham 1998: 287; Marazzi 1998), but the impact of the Lombard invasion had yet to be really felt. The almost total absence of Lombard pottery types from Liguria is surely significant and supports the view that by the eighth century economies across Europe were principally characterized by extreme regionalism (Wickham 2000: 346). In this respect at least Fredegar's assessment was correct: Rothari's conquest did not suddenly integrate Liguria with *Langobardia*. Although eighth-century pottery in this region as elsewhere is still difficult to identify and date with certainty, and furnished burials cease, recent excavations at Noli have shown some coastal vitality in that period. Inland, some vitality can also be observed at some hilltop sites, to which the final part of this chapter is devoted.

Hilltop sites

Hilltop sites have been thoroughly covered by Neil Christie, a specialist in this area (Christie 1990, 2006: 331–48). In Liguria as in most other parts of Italy, hilltop settlement has been very important historiographically as well as historically (Brown 1984: 42–5; Wickham 1988; Brown and Christie 1989: 392–4; Francovich and Hodges 2003: 61–74, 99–102; Provero 2007: 157–61; Wickham 2009: 517–19). Historians have considered why people moved to hilltop sites at certain times and abandoned them at others; if a widespread move to the hills took place in the late Roman period; how the Byzantine defensive network of forts (the 'limes') functioned and what happened once the Byzantines left; if there was a hiatus after the Byzantine withdrawal until the next round of well-documented hilltop living in c. 1000; and the roles *castra* played in the development of powers of territorial lordship by local aristocrats.

Hilltop settlement was likely to be important across Liguria in the early middle Ages given the nature of the terrain but it was obviously encouraged by the Byzantine state's development of a local defensive network intended to protect their coastal interests from inland attack (Christie 2006: 372–80; Bakirtzis 2010: 354–5). Both Procopius writing about the Gothic Wars and George of Cyprus in his 'Description of the Roman World' (c. 600–610) recognized this. Although George's exists only in a ninth-century version perhaps incorporating later additions (Gelzer 1890), it is a useful snapshot of Liguria as seen from far away at a time fairly close to Rothari's invasion. George noted Luni (n. 534 in his list), Ventimiglia (n. 537), Genoa (Γενούη, n. 538), Portovenere (n. 624), Taggia (n. 625) and Albisola (n. 626) (Gelzer 1890: 28, 32); a different group of coastal sites to Fredegar's but intriguingly similar to known Roman villa sites. George also recorded *kastron Soreon*, Sorano, near Filattiera in the Lunigiana. *Kastron* described a fortified place which led Donald Bullough to suggest Byzantine origins for the surviving *castrum* at Filattiera (Bullough 1956), which subsequent excavation at Castelvecchio and Monte Castello (800 m asl) has proved correct (Cabona et al. 1982, 1984). The relationship of Sorano to the nearby hilltop sites is still not absolutely clear although excavation has confirmed its abandonment by the end of the sixth century (Giannichedda 1998). At Monte Castello more than 100 m of walling of a large castle has survived, which existed from the mid-sixth century to the mid-seventh century (C14 date), later than Sorano. A large single-floor dry-stone-walled building (20 m × 8 m) of uncertain function was put up at this time but soon abandoned after the Lombard conquest (Giannichedda 1995: 533). The nearby tower of San Giorgio is probably of tenth-century date and the parish church of Santo Stefano was recorded in 990 as a stopping place between Luni and Pontremoli in the itinerary which reported the journey of Sigeric incoming archbishop of Canterbury to Rome to receive the *pallium* from the pope (Ortenberg 1990: 199). Both suggest later re-occupation of the area.

Sant'Antonino in Perti near Finale is the most important excavated Byzantine *castrum* in Liguria. Like Filattiera it was not a major fortress but guarded a subsidiary route and unsurprisingly therefore it was ignored by both George of Cyprus and Fredegar. It had probably already been inhabited in the late Roman period as the local church of Sant'Eusebio preserved the earliest Christian inscription from Liguria dated 362, although there is no other certain evidence for a fourth-century church here (De Vingo 2010a: 84–5). The excavations produced a wider assemblage than normal for a military site including two flutes, women's clothing and fishing equipment in addition to tools, weapons and glasses which demonstrates both cultural sophistication and likely year-round occupation (Murialdo 1985, 1998; Bonora et al. 1988; Mannoni and Murialdo 2001; Bianchi 2006–7; Christie 2006: 374–8; De Vingo 2011). Crucially, there was no violent destructive layer which might be attributed to Rothari's activities, and some evidence that Perti continued to be occupied after the Lombard invasion.

What happened to these Byzantine hilltop fortifications in the eighth and ninth centuries remains unclear as no evidence has been forthcoming from Filatteria or Perti or from excavations at later medieval defensive sites such as Castello di Andora (Varaldo et al. 2003, a Roman site), Molassana (Mannoni 1974), Salino (*Castronovo*; Milanese 1978), Corvara (Cagnana and Gavagnin 2004; Cagnana et al. 2008) and Zignago. By the year 1020 or thereabouts – the end of the period covered by this book – clear archaeological evidence suggests that people were definitely living again at this type of site, a confirmation of something charter evidence has long suggested. An ever-clearer picture of this complex phenomenon (known in Italy as *incastellamento*) is emerging for both Liguria and neighbouring Tuscany which shows that territorial organization, local political jurisdictions and 'feudal' powers which were increasingly centred on castles or defended hilltop villages (Wickham 1988; Benente 2000; Valenti 2000; Ricci 2002, 2007; Francovich and Hodges 2003; Calcagno 2004; Guglielmotti 2005, 2007b; Provero 2007: 157–61). The political aspects of this are explored further in the next chapter. Here the material aspects of settlement history are examined, in particular what hilltop living was actually like in inland Liguria at this time.

The 'formation' of medieval territorial jurisdictions is indicated in documents, mostly charters, by words such as *finis* ('boundary'), *territoria* ('territory'), *vallis* ('valley') and *plebs* ('parish'), terminology most recently studied by Paola

Guglielmotti who has concluded that even though these words all occur in
tenth-century charters in this region their presence does not suggest fixed
identities on the ground, something which did not happen until the eleventh
or even twelfth centuries in most places. What *territoria* meant in the tenth
century therefore is still unclear, but it was not a village and the hamlets under
its jurisdiction (nowadays a *comune* and its *frazioni*). Fortified hilltop sites also
appear in charters as indicated by *castrum*, notably Molassana in the Bisagno
valley documented from c. 900 (Belgrano 1862: 148–9, 161–2, 173–4, 199, 204–5,
209–11, 233–4, 236–3, 243, 248, 257–8, 271–2, 275). Molassana was highlighted
by Mannoni (1974: 15–17) but excavations of the castle in 1968–84 did not
find early medieval levels. As he pointed out, local place-names such as *villa
Molaciana* and *S. Siro emiliano* suggest a late Antique past for the various small
dispersed settlements nearby. Even so, the small scale of the castle site (700 msq),
the absence of houses within its walls and field survey of the surrounding hamlets
suggest that the current settlement pattern was genuinely established in the tenth
century rather than before (Mannoni 2000: 73). Crucially, the same group of
charters record the construction of a water mill (*molendino*) at Molassana in
either 956 or 971 (Belgrano 1862: 209–11), noted subsequently in 986, 988 and
992 (Belgrano 1862: 173–4, 275, 205; Origone 1974). Other mills are reported in
charters produced by Genoese bishops who appear to have been re-organizing the
local landscape in the interests of increasing production, especially of chestnuts.

In addition to more conventional economic, political and social explanations,
climate change may also have prompted this shift in settlement patterns
(Christie 2006: 487–91). As already discussed, Fredric Cheyette has developed
the argument that movement from lowland to hilltop sites observable across
upland Europe during the early medieval period may be attributed more to
changing climatic patterns than to changes in the nature of lordship (Cheyette
2008: 155–64). As weather got colder and wetter, people relocated to drier
sites and developed a more silvo-pastoral economy (Cheyette 2008: 150). It
is possible that Perti and other Ligurian hill sites evidence this phenomenon
as does the silting up of rivers at Albenga and Luni. The residential culture
observed at Perti may mean that whole communities and not just soldiers lived
at militarized hilltop sites because living at lower levels became impossible
and similarly impoverished 'roof tile' sites may evidence a very rational and
considered response to damp conditions because broken tiles were ideal to
drain increasingly sodden mid-slope sites. Cheyette goes so far to suggest that

the 'poor' foods produced and consumed at such sites were unable to support the level of population that Roman cereal production had and this explains why the Dark Age rural population became smaller and more dispersed. However, this seems simplistic as predominantly subsistence cultures do not necessarily have to be equated with poverty and low populations, as in Liguria a carefully controlled 'chestnut culture' did support an early modern population much greater than that of cereal-eating Roman times.

The formulaic phrases describing land-use in local charters allow this culture to be explored further as precise site-specific examples of careful land-management designed to cope with unreliable harvests are documented. Although a systematic study of this evidence does not yet exist,[10] even a cursory glance shows that sufficient formulaic variation is apparent to permit 'realistic reading' of this evidence (above 22). The many micro-toponyms for specific woodland sites suggest that people were actively managing such sites as why else would they have names in this sort of documentation. Chestnuts, for example, are presented in two ways in the Latin: *castanea* (the tree, including specific named trees) and *castanetum* (a chestnut plantation or chestnut wood, again sometimes named), although the plural (*castaneti*) is more common (see Montanari 1979: 296–301). At Bavari in 952 we find a *castaneto de colloreto* and a *castanea baronciasca* (recorded also as *castanea budosclingna*) (Belgrano 1862: 161–3), yet in 965 these appear simply as *castanetis* in an apparently unspecific list (Calleri 2009: 2–3). The next year a *castanetum* is referenced alongside a fig orchard (*ficetum*) and the bounds described: 'up to the pine tree then to the small bridge, then lower down to the lord's meadow, on the other side to the *costa de luimare* descending to the ditch in the gravel'. This was to be 'worked and improved' (*laborare et excolere*) (Belgrano 1862: 144–5). In 994, two *castaneti* are named: *castaneto in fontaneclo* and *castaneto de lo tordo* (Belgrano 1862: 177). Just occasionally there is much more. In a contract drawn up in November 1006 between Martin a resident of Gallaneto (Comune di Campomorone) in the Polcevera valley and the monastery of Santo Stefano in Genoa, there is startling detail about how such trees were managed as well as the more usual expectations put on tenants by their monastic lords (Calleri 2009: doc. 21, 36–8). Martin had:

> to prepare the ground (*pastenare*) for chestnut trees and cut and improve (them) and to put in domestic chestnut trees where appropriate so that after ten complete years have passed they should return thence every year half of

the chestnuts that have been collected there and two good silver pennies and
take those pennies to the monastery and the chestnuts to the aforementioned
place Gallaneto (my translation).[11]

Pastenare (*pastinare* in classical Latin), translated as 'prepare or dig the ground',
was usually applied to fruit trees often with the implication of taking new land
into cultivation. *Excolere* usually means 'to improve' and is linked to *colere* ('to
cultivate' but also 'to graft', which might make more sense if they were trying
to improve the fruit quality of 'wild' trees). In earlier charters dated 965 and
1005 which deal with Gallaneto, chestnuts were mentioned generically as
castaneti (Calleri 2009: doc. 1, 3–2 and doc. 19, 33–4), but in the latter case also
associated with figs.

Fruiting trees are mentioned in many charters, often generically as 'fruiting
trees' (*arbores fructiferis*). Although chestnuts were commonest, fig, olive
and more rarely apple orchards appeared (respectively *ficetum*, *olivetum* and
pometum). Other trees include oaks (a *robor grande* on one occasion, more
commonly *roboretum* 'oak wood' but also *cerretum* 'turkey oak wood'); willows
(*salicetum*) and rarely pines (a single pine tree, *pinus*, as a boundary marker).
Woodland (*bosco*) appeared as did *ronco* describing a site where trees have
been cleared to create arable. References to cultivated or cultivable land were
significantly fewer, indicated as *terra laboratoria*, *terra arabile*, and often in
lists alongside meadow (*pratum*) and pasture (*pascum*), and on one occasion
'grass' or 'hay' (*herbis*). The other commonly recorded land use is *cannetum* (a
reed-bed) and likely to refer to the giant reed (*Arundo donax*) still grown here
today. Occasionally, there is precise reference to uncultivated – but useful –
land: *gerbis* (see modern Italian *gerbido*) and *brunetis* (heathland), mostly
likely meaning tree heather (*Erica arborea*) still common here. Although
putting all these terms together prevents a more profound site-specific analysis,
nevertheless it does indicate land use similar to much of what is observable in
less urbanized parts of the region today.

Reference to cereals is relatively rare in these documents and remarkably a
similar pattern has been noticed at a series of archaeological sites, including
Pietra Ligure and Albenga (Arobba et al. 2007: 91). While this coincidental
observation might be due simply to a selective sample of sites where by chance
cereals simply were not grown for whatever reason, this cereal absence in
Liguria seems more likely to be real potentially supporting Cheyette's argument

that wetter and colder climate meant fewer and poorer quality grain harvests. It is likely that peasant farmers and their lords were practical people who grew what was most sensible to grow where they lived and so if they moved to the hills, the chestnut was a much better bet as a staple food than wheat. As archaeological evidence shows many hilltop sites seem to have depended on chestnut flour and the foods that could be made from it not merely bread but also polenta – the Genoese *panissa*. The appearance of mills which greatly facilitate the production of flour from the dried, hard chestnuts in these very charters is unlikely therefore to be coincidence. Reading the different sorts of evidence together therefore, it seems likely that the production of chestnuts was not simply subsistence but also locally – maybe regionally – commoditized: chestnut flour was storable and tradable in just the same way as grains were. If these and other products of fruiting trees were sold for profit, then this would help to explain the interest of outsiders such as monasteries of Bobbio, Santo Stefano and San Siro in these otherwise seemingly remote sites.

Conclusion

Writing the history of currently occupied villages is evidently harder than dealing with abandoned ones and for this reason it is unwise to read back from current to past settlement however tempting this method may seem. Similar problems bedevil urban sites where the continuously settled parts of towns are hard to dig up. Precise dating of domestic rural 'vernacular' architecture is difficult but, in the absence of archaeological investigation of existing village sites (such as the Tuscan examples already referred to), this is the only means we have to estimate the age of the existing settlement network under which it is highly likely early medieval levels are to be found (De Maestri and Moreno 1980). Excavated sites may have been abandoned and never resettled because they were always 'marginal' for successful settlement or in the case of *castra* were so closely linked to political events that once the political context changed they lost their purpose. Complete understanding of past rural settlement patterns in wet mountainous regions really does require open-area archaeology on the 'Tuscan model'. In Liguria only the archaeology of western coastal settlements especially Noli comes close to this type of investigation. The relative absence of

Roman and early medieval period sites along eastern coasts and in the whole of the interior has led to some speculation that there simply wasn't much Roman or early medieval settlement here, as Paola Guglielmotti (2005) implies by opening her book on Ligurian settlement with the tenth century. Nevertheless, the crucial work remains that of Tiziano Mannoni who first tried to explain the *absence* of seventh- to tenth-century rural sites (1983b: 264). His blanket characterization of early medieval rural sites as 'poor settlements' whose inhabitants had left towns because of economic crisis to live lives of subsistence in the countryside still has some merit, even though too little is known about the *urban* poor in the Roman period for a like-with-like comparison to be properly sustained. Dark Age Ligurian homes in the countryside were certainly of 'poor' construction and appearance with little comfort, although the availability of imported pottery in some places suggests occasional participation in wider exchange networks (Cagnana 1994). All the houses surveyed by Cagnana were of local construction rather than 'imported Germanic' styles using local materials with no need for specialist workers which says much for the self-sufficient, adaptable and even creative nature of these communities (Cagnana 1994: 172). Subsistence (or 'sustainability' in current usage) is not necessarily a bad thing as it could be a more secure lifestyle than dependence on the vicissitudes of a complex and distant Mediterranean-wide exchange system. Subsistence farmers almost certainly led better lives in their 'poor' homes than those who worked in the grim sixth-century mines at Monte Loreto (Castiglione Chiavarese) where, at the site of the oldest copper mines in western Europe (c. 3500 cal BC), a series of dry-stone structures dating to the Byzantine period may have housed those extracting copper or iron ores (Maggi and Pearce 2005: 68).

Terms like 'poor', 'impoverished' and 'low-level' are obviously relative and material poverty was equally characteristic of inland Ligurian valleys until a generation or so ago and of the prehistoric sites discussed in Chapter 2. It is also lazy to impose modern metropolitan attitudes on these rural communities (Lagomarsini 2004), and phrases such as Giovanna Petti Balbi's 'Apennine marginality' and 'the countryside adopted a subaltern role' though understandable do not explain how such disparities arose in given societies and what mechanisms maintained them. In fact, the completely opposite view that coastal settlements depended for most of the early medieval period on the products of the mountains to survive in the disintegrating Mediterranean economy of which they were a part is as plausible. If the coast was central and the interior marginal – *if* it was – then the reasons are most likely to be found at the political level, which is the subject of the next chapter.

Notes

1 The place–name evidence for Roman settlement in Liguria should not be ignored: see Petracco Sicardi and Caprini 1981: 9–30, with a glossary of all place names of classical origin to the sixth century in the region at 31–82.

2 Some of these places have Pre-roman names, for example Moneglia (*Monilia* in Latin; *muneğa* in dialect) recorded in the *Sententia Minuciorum* (see Petracco Sicardi and Caprini 1981: 63).

3 Several houses I have visited in Colli di Valletti and Porciorasco near Varese Ligure (SP) displayed great contrast between the structural fabric and level of comfort and the presence of objects from around the world.

4 George of Cyprus wrote his history of the eastern Roman world c. 610 in Greek. It begins with Italy.

5 The inscription was moved in modern times. The churches are a few hundred metres apart.

6 Scurtabò (Vara valley, 666 m asl) is another mid-slope site which demonstrates the importation of late Roman Mediterranean amphorae. It has not yet been excavated, but is discussed at 126 below.

7 'Fredegar' refers to an early Frankish chronicle probably composed in Burgundy c. 660 by an otherwise unknown author. It is one of the most important sources for earlier seventh-century history.

8 Collins 2007: 50–1 plausibly suggests that Fredegar's information on Italy may have come via diplomatic missions between the Franks and Lombards.

9 There is some disagreement about the amounts of later pottery coming into this region. Paul Roberts (1995) argues convincingly that there was less African fine ware than is often thought, notably at Ventimiglia (317–8) and Luni (22, 73, 321–6), although he agrees that African Red Slip was relatively abundant at Perti (320).

10 I hope to produce such a study at a later date. Montanari 1979, the classic discussion, only rarely took note of Ligurian evidence.

11 *pastenare de castaneas et taliare vel et scolere* (sic. *excolere*) *et inserire de castaneas domesticas ubi oportunum fuerit usque at decem anni etspleti* (sic. *expleti*) *et rendere debeant exinde per unumquemque anno de castaneas, que ibidem colecta fuerit, medietatem et argentam denarius bonos duos dati et consignati ipsi denarii at eodem monasterio et ipsas castaneas ic super locum Garsaneto.*

4

Political and Religious Change

A small bronze tablet (38 × 48 cm) with 46 lines of Latin text was discovered by a peasant ploughing his field at Isola near Serra Riccò in 1506. Known as the 'Polcevera Tablet' (or *sententia Minuciorum*) it is the iconic document of early Genoese history, despite being as much about the Polcevera valley as about Genoa (Giannattasio 2007: 134–5). Dated 117 BCE, it records a legal judgement made in Rome about a dispute between the inhabitants of Genoa (the *Genuates*) and those living mid-valley, including the *Langenses* and *Viturii*. Particularly informative regarding common rights to pasturage (*compascuo*), it has become the most important text in an on-going debate about the extent and nature of initial Romanization in this part of Liguria (Häussler 2007). As suggested in the last chapter these 'tribes' (the rather dismissive term most often employed by historians) were at some level political communities, perhaps brought together by the external challenges posed to long-established customs and practices by the people of Genoa and its immediate hinterland (Maggi 1999). The judicial text conceived social organization in the area in terms of groups of peoples mapped on to a specific quite confined and carefully defined territory. As there is no mention of Liguria within the text it is probably the case that individuals at this time thought of themselves as Genoese or 'Vitrurians' or 'Langascans' not as Ligurians or even as Romans.

Roman narratives of Romanization present a highly rhetorical characterization of the *Ligures* ('Ligurians') and their region. They focused on the coast with Strabo (4.6.1) for example, selecting only Genoa ('the emporium of the Ligures'), *Vada Sabatorum* (Vado Ligure) and Albenga for comment. Strabo did not use the word 'Liguria' for the latter was not an administrative division recognized by the Roman world then. By the time of Augustus Romans imagined a 'greater Liguria' called 'Region 9' (*Regio IX*), created c. 7 CE. This was conceptualized as the territory of the *Ligures* and extended from Nice in the West to the Magra in the

East, but went much further inland than now to encompass Turin, Vercelli and Milan (Christie 2006: 66). By the time of Diocletian in the late third century that province had been renamed 'Emilia and Liguria' and was dependent upon Milan which had just become the official capital of the western empire. By the absolute end point of the Roman occupation in the early seventh century when these earlier divisions had long since disappeared, the Byzantine state might have administered a 'maritime province of the Italians' (*Provincia Maritima Italorum*) recorded by the sixth-century geographer known as 'Anonymous of Ravenna' which extended to Tuscan coastal sites, although its existence has been questioned as there is no evidence for provincial governors (*iudices*) in Liguria at this time who would have run it (Brown 1984: 13, 43; Christie 2006: 372–3). The Lombard 'conquest' in the 640s brought into being a territory which was roughly the shape and extent of the modern region, possibly the most profound consequence of that supposedly cataclysmic event.

During the long period just described from the beginnings of Roman interest in the region to their departure centuries later religious identity remained diverse across Liguria as in the Empire at large. This diversity continued long after the initial 'Christianization' which can be dated here to the fourth century. Small Jewish communities, for example, are recorded in Genoa and Luni as late as the sixth century and exposure to the ideas of Islam might have been possible from contact with Arab traders and raiders in the ninth and tenth centuries and probably before. As in north-western Italy as a whole the local process of Christianization seems to have been slow with the exception of a few coastal locations where Roman culture was more deeply embedded (Cantino Wataghin 2000). The earliest definite reference to the Christian religion in Liguria is as late as 362, a fragmentary scratched inscription on a Roman tile found during excavations under the church of S. Eusebio at Perti in 1979 (Mennella and Coccoluto 1995: 77–8, doc. 34; Cantino Wataghin 2000: 217; Marcenaro 2006: 23). The tile, one of those covering a tomb, memorialized Lucius who died during the consulship of Claudius Mamertinus and Flavius Nevitta and its brief words were preceded by a Constantinian-style Christogram and followed by a simple cross demonstrating his Christian belief. As the first record of a bishop of Genoa is dated 381, it is probably fair to see the later fourth century as the time when Christianity started to flourish in the region.

From that point until its elevation to an archbishopric in 1133, Genoa was a diocese dependent on Milan and although it was probably always the ecclesiastical centre for the region there is little sense of any particularly distinctive Genoese (or indeed Ligurian) expression of Christian identity at this time. Indeed this is something which proves difficult to observe at most points in the period as cultural manifestations of Christian practice – baptisteries and the mosaics which decorated them for example – were almost always strongly influenced by Milanese taste and custom. As in other Italian regions fourth-century Christian practice here is documented almost exclusively by funerary inscriptions, burial customs and the archaeology of sacred buildings (Christie 2006: 80–9, 174–81). The corpus of Ligurian Christian epigraphy is small and expresses entirely conventional Christian pieties. About one hundred inscribed stones of fourth- to seventh-century date have been recorded and around a third of these (33) are from Albenga (Mennella and Coccoluto 1995: 86–141), with most of the rest from other sites on the Ponente including Ventimiglia (Mennella and Coccoluto 1995: 142–9), Savona, Vado, Finale, Varigotti, Perti and Noli (Mennella and Coccoluto 1995: 72–85). Genoa and places further east have preserved far fewer, which confirms that this was a less Romanized area.

At Albenga which continued to flourish in the fifth-century inscriptions can be linked to substantial contemporary Christian buildings including the recently excavated church of San Calocero on a hill just to the south of town (Massabò 2004: 151–9) and the cathedral with its fine mosaic-decorated baptistery (Figure 4.1), one of the oldest in northern Italy (Massabò 2004: 76–83; Marcenaro 2006: 41–68; Christie 2006: 134–5). Another early baptistery has recently been unearthed at the site of the Roman baths/San Clemente which is now in the flood plain of the Centa (Massabò 2004: 98–117). In 451 a bishop of Albenga is recorded as present with those of Genoa and the other Ligurian suffragans at a Milanese synod, which suggests that the see was probably the most important in western Liguria then. Even a century later, as the Lombards were invading the Po plain, several impressive inscribed monuments were produced in Albenga including in 568–71 those of Honorata 'most illustrious and pious woman' of the senatorial class and her Armenian husband Tzittanus 'count and tribune' (Mennella and Coccoluto 1995, n. 43; Marcenaro 2006: 16–17; Brown 1984: 53–60, 75), Donatus

(Menella and Coccoluto 1995, n. 44), and in 597 that of Maurianus (Mennella and Coccoluto 1995, n. 45). Each of these records formulaic if genuinely felt public displays of Christian faith by the rich and powerful which are not in any way distinctively Ligurian.

Figure 4.1 Albenga baptistery in 1911.
Source: Frederic Lees, *Wanderings on the Italian Riviera* (London, 1912), opposite p. 126.

The buildings which such inscriptions helped to adorn are worth closer attention, the baptisteries above all as these document the progress of conversion to meaningful Christian practice and belief, and the amount of time, money and effort put into them by the local political class (Cantino Wataghin 2000: 225–9; Christie 2006: 133–6). St Ambrose built one of the most influential of early western baptisteries in terms of its design and style at the end of the fourth century next to the cathedral of Santa Tecla in Milan (Milburn 1988: 204–6; Christie 2006: 133). Restored by Bishop Lorenzo in the mid-fifth century, its octagonal form became popular elsewhere in the archdiocese including Liguria. The main phase of baptistery building in northern Italy was the fifth to sixth centuries and in Liguria significant examples can be found at Albenga, Capo Don di Riva Ligure (where the octagonal font was part of a small church complex),[1] Finale, San Paragorio at Noli (Figure 4.2), and intriguingly at the ruined inland site of Libarna, built on the site of the theatre. The famous intact Albenga baptistery follows the Ambrosian octagonal plan and as entire amphorae were used to build its roof to lessen its weight it can be accordingly dated to the last quarter of the fifth century (Massabò 2004: 78). The early sixth-century mosaic in one of the niches advertizes to viewers the relics held there: Saints Stephen, John the Evangelist, Laurence, Nabor, Felix and Protasius and Gervasius, a classic Milanese line-up (Massabò 2004: 81–2; Marcenaro 2006: 55–68). The imagery, colours and techniques used in its design closely reflect those at San Vittore in Ciel d'Oro adjacent to the basilica of Sant'Ambrogio in Milan (Marcenaro 2006: 64–5). Even after the Byzantine departure there is evidence that the building continued to be cared for because several highly decorated eighth-century pierced window-coverings (Figure 4.3) and an imposing *arcosolium* tomb which employed re-used decorative slabs of the same period have survived to this day. The recent discovery of another font at the church of San Clemente itself built into the ruins of the earlier Roman baths and constructed from rubble there caused some excitement as it too has been dated between the fifth and sixth centuries, and appears also to be of Ambrosian design (Massabò 2004: 107–13). Whether these baptisteries were centrally financed with Milanese money or by locally active Christian communities as an earlier generation of local historians somewhat romantically argued, there seems little doubt that their existence along the entirety of the western coast confirms this

Figure 4.2 Noli in 1908.
Source: Gordon Home, *Along the Rivieras of France and Italy* (London, 1908), p. 219.

as the most populous, economically viable and culturally innovative part of Liguria in the final decades before the Lombards arrived in Italy.

Perhaps *the* crucial event of Christian history in the region was the arrival of Bishop Honoratus of Milan in Genoa in September 569 in flight with his clergy to escape the invading Lombards, at least if Paul the Deacon's eighth-century account of this journey can be trusted (*HL* II 25). It completely transformed the profile of the Genoese see within the region for the Milanese bishops represented one of the most powerful and distinctive regional churches in the late Antique West. Soon after the letters which Pope Gregory the Great exchanged with successive bishops of Genoa – including Laurence between 590 and 593 and Constantius between 593 and 600 – provide much more detail about the Genoese church than hitherto available (as discussed in the next chapter).[2] Gregory himself noted in April 593 that many Milanese clerics and aristocrats had settled in Genoa to escape the barbarians, although it is odd that he did not say a little more about the traumatic history which had brought them and their bishop there. Gregory's letters reveal failings in local Christian practice especially among priests and those of lower clerical rank who fell far short of Gregory's high moral expectations.

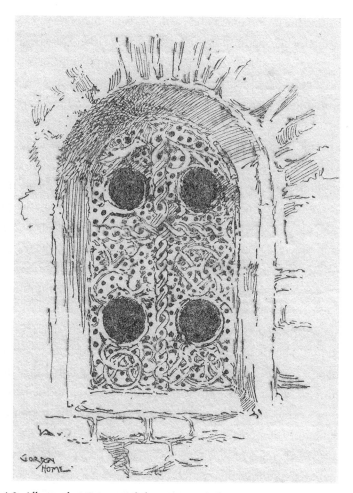

Figure 4.3 Albenga baptistery, eighth-century window cover.
Source: Gordon Home, *Along the Rivieras of France and Italy* (London, 1908), p. 207.

This theme emerges strongly in Gregory's correspondence with Venantius bishop of Luni between 594 and 603, most of which deals with managerial problems in the latter's church. In May 594 Gregory wrote to Venantius about Christians who were being enslaved by Jews near the city (*Reg.* 4.21). He explained that while they should continue to work for their Jewish masters on their estates – places which may have been like the *vicus* of Filattiera – they should not be enslaved as slavery was wrong. In September (*Reg.* 5.5) Gregory advised that 'Your Fraternity must go to the island of Gorgona (off the coast from Livorno) and investigate what has been brought to us concerning the ex-priest Saturninus'. Gorgona had its own Christian history as a site for early monastic practice like many off-shore Mediterranean islands as Gregory surely knew. A disapproving Rutilius Namiatanus who had probably not converted to Christianity implied that monks were there already as early as 416: 'For lately one of our youths of high birth, with wealth to match, and marriage-alliance equal to his origins, was impelled by madness to abandon mankind and the world, and made his way, a superstitious exile, to a dishonourable hiding-place (Gorgona). Fancying, poor wretch, that the divine can be nurtured in unwashed filth, he was himself to his own body a crueller tyrant than the offended deities' (*De reditu suo* Book I, lines 515–26). A desire to buttress monastic practice with the support of the holy dead may explain why the relics of Saint Julia of Corsica (martyred c. 439) were brought here, or so Gregory believed (Pergola 1999: 16–17).[3] The pope continued the correspondence about Gorgona in November (*Reg.* 5.17) saying that Saturninus could after all run the monasteries at Gorgona and Capraria, which suggests that Venantius had indeed gone there and found everything in order. However, further up the coast at Portovenere, he insisted that Jobinus, deacon and abbot, was removed from office and had to do penance. In this same letter Gregory intriguingly noted that the copy of his own *Pastoral Care* sent with it should be passed on to the Irish monk Columbanus – who might therefore have already visited this region prior to his foundation of the monastic community at Bobbio c. 612–13 – and that another copy was being sent separately to Venantius presumably as a guide for how he ought to be running his church.

Venantius was certainly an active bishop as by October 597 (*Reg.* 8.5) he had in Gregory's words 'founded a convent within the city of Luni, in your own House, for nuns, as a mark of your devotion, and you desire to have it consecrated in honour of St Peter . . .'. Gregory's detailed instructions for how to go about doing this shed very interesting light on what a small suburban convent in this region could be like at this time. Perhaps inevitably disputes arose around the nunnery, a common early medieval pattern, and in January 599 (*Reg.* 987) a nun called Adeodata complained – as nuns often did – about her mother Fidentia's attitude towards her and Gregory wrote to support her advising Venantius to do the same. In February–April (*Reg.* 9.115) he went as far as sending an abbess to Venantius for this convent and again made it very clear that Venantius should support her and the nuns. As late as May 603 not long before he died, Gregory (*Reg.* 13.31) notes that an enquiry into complaints made about Bishop Deusdedit successor to Constantius at Milan/Genoa, was to be undertaken by Venantius (see also *Dial.* 3.9) which demonstrates the importance of the see of Luni and his personal moral standing.

Gregory's correspondence has been used many times to write the early history of Ligurian monasticism but even so its nature remains obscure (Penco 1955, 1956, 1961; Pistarino 1979; Polonio 1997, 2002, 2007). Martin of Tours (d. 397), one of the iconic figures of western monasticism, had travelled through the region on his way to the island of Lèrins and is thought to have stayed on Gallinaria, the island 2 km off the coast at Albenga (Penco 1961: 73–80), but secure archaeological confirmation of this is still lacking even though there have been recent excavations there. Ancient folkloric traditions regarding eremitic life along the entire coast still impress some historians but again there is little firm archaeological evidence to support them where that evidence could reasonably be expected. Pope Gregory's letters do show that holy men and women were following monastic rules in the region, notably at Venantius's nunnery where the bishop had provided everything needed to support ten nuns, including a chapel, its silver plate, and a farm near the River Magra (*Reg.* 8.5; Martyn 2004: vol. 2, 505; Polonio 1997: 88). Unfortunately what became of this institution is unknown once Gregory's letters come to an end in 604. Curiously, there is a lack of other reliable evidence for local monastic institutions from then until the early tenth-century charters which deal with the property interests of Genoese foundations of Santo Stefano and San Siro (below 105–7), with the exception of San Caprasio at Aulla probably in existence in the eighth century although traditionally believed to have founded in 881 by Adalbert of Tuscany (Arslan et al. 2007; Giannichedda et al. 2003, 2011). The most powerful monastic institution at that period was probably Bobbio, located at the northern boundary of the region in the Trebbia as it had benefitted from substantial Lombard and Carolingian patronage. It developed property interests in Genoa itself by the middle of the ninth century and more generally across eastern Liguria as the result of further royal patronage as is discussed in the next two chapters (below 98–101, 115–19). The other important monastic foundation was San Fruttuoso di Capodimonte, near Camogli on the eastern Riviera (Bonora 1986; Davite et al. 1986; Frondoni 2005: 24–35). According to traditional accounts which cannot be supported with contemporary evidence the relics of San Fruttuoso a bishop of Tarragona martyred in 259, were transferred to Capodimonte in 711 by Prospero, one of his successors as bishop when the latter was in flight from an Arab attack. But there is no archaeological confirmation of this eighth-century date as recent excavation has confirmed the tenth century as the period of the foundation. The tenth-century history of this community is briefly discussed in the next chapter.

Returning to Gregory's correspondence with Venantius this is interesting not simply for the light it sheds on the practicalities of church management but also for its underlying sense of impending moral panic which can be linked to the wider structural changes occurring in the later sixth century. The dramatic lessening of pan-Mediterranean exchange was not just an economic phenomenon but was also experienced as the winding down of Graeco-Roman cultural hegemony on this particular Mediterranean shoreline or putting it another way as 'the end of civilization' (Ward-Perkins 2005). Liguria was still – just – part of that globalized world and investment in *castra* such as Perti shows how much the Byzantine state was prepared to spend to keep it and the other fortifications in its *limes* going (Balbis 1979; Schreiner 1997; Schwarcz 1997; Origone 2000).[4] Similarly the large, costly buildings of Christian worship still being constructed on the coast especially at Albenga most likely with a combination of public and private money evidence the same sort bullish attitude on the part of some in the ruling class. But other evidence, especially the letters of Cassiodorus, suggests that some sense of political unease or even dissent may have operated at a specifically regional level in Liguria throughout the sixth century, not just at its end. In 507–508 the Ostrogothic king Theodoric wrote to all Goths and Romans at Tortona regarding a local fortification (Barnish 1992: 14–15). In 508–512 he wrote to the local *Saio* Wiligis: 'Let Ravenna return to Liguria the supplies it usually receives from there', as these were needed to support the court and the people (Barnish 1992: 30; Burns 1984: 178–9). In 533–537 Cassiodorus wrote to the Ligurians 'You report yourselves to be oppressed in the matter of weights and measures' (Barnish 1992: 156–7) and further complaints about tax collectors were reported when Cassiodorus wrote to the governor of Liguria (Barnish 1992: 165–6). The following year (538) he wrote to Bishop Datius in Milan regarding famine and the need to maintain the granaries in the context of a revolt against Gothic rule in the region.

Similar tales of regional woes are reported by Procopius in his *Gothic Wars* where he noted that the Ligurian landscape was being rapidly militarized in the face of battles in the Cottian Alps: 'there are numerous strongholds . . . garrisoned, as had been the custom for many years, by many of the noblest of the Goths, who resided in them with their wives and children . . . (and) by falling suddenly upon some of the fortresses in the Alps, they captured them and made slaves of their inhabitants, and a large number of these captives, as chance would have it, proved to be children and wives of the men who were serving under Uraias. For most of these men were natives of these very fortresses'. Procopius does not name any of these sites but surely one of them was Perti (Christie 2006: 360). A sense of the importance of Liguria to the Byzantine state and also of the practical difficulties in keeping control of it from such a distance comes out most clearly from the Procopius' account of Belisarius' activities in the region:

> And with them was also Fidelius, who had been made praetorian prefect. Since he was a native of Milan, he was regarded as a suitable person to go with this army, having as he did some influence in Liguria. They set sail, accordingly, from the harbour of Rome and put in at Genoa, which is the last city in Tuscany and well situated as a port of call for the voyage to Gaul and to Spain. There they left their ships and travelling by land moved forward, placing the boats of the ships on their wagons, in order that nothing might prevent their crossing the river Po'. (Dewing 1919: vol. 3, 386–7)

Both Cassiodorus and Procopius give the impression of a province just about hanging on to its ancient roots during the first decades of the sixth century. When the Byzantines finally gave it up the consequences for local elites were bound to have been grave. The first consequence was clearly political: a sudden shift in the external focus of power from south to north was caused by Rothari's successful conquest. The second was theological for Rothari was an Arian Christian: the fundamental tensions provoked by the arrival of the Lombards can be clearly felt in Gregory's letters, and in the moral decay which both he and Venantius seem to have believed was infecting their church. The third was directly economic: the end of the Mediterranean-wide exchange probably caused a food crisis in which radically fewer cereal imports might have provoked yet another flight to the hills of the sort posited by Mannoni for the third century. Set this culturally traumatic Lombard incursion alongside the cold and incessant rain of a significantly worsening climate, the disappearance of distantly traded creature comforts and the prospect of being ruled by a heretic king and we can surely sympathize with the fears of some sixth-century Ligurians.

Lombards in Liguria

Paul the Deacon writing in the 780s had noted that the invasion of the cities of northern 'Liguria' by the Lombard king Alboin had caused Honoratus bishop of Milan to flee to Genoa in 568. Having successfully invaded Milan, Alboin 'then took all the cities of Liguria except those which were situated upon the shores of the sea' (*HL* II 25, Foulke 1907: 79). We do not know the details of why Alboin did not press on to the coast but it is most likely that the well-staffed Byzantine *limes* was effective in stopping him. Rothari's successful invasion of the Ligurian littoral 150 years later changed the administrative geography of the region for good, and was probably a more significant moment of political discontinuity than the 'end' of the Western Roman Empire in the mid-fifth century had been. Contemporaries certainly thought so. If Fredegar presented a rather apocalyptic view we now know that it may have some support in recent archaeology. Later sources concurred including Paul the Deacon who, while correcting Fredegar's earlier mistake in attributing Friulian Oderzo to Liguria, recorded that:

> King Rothari then captured all the cities of the Romans which were situated upon the shore of the sea from the city of Luni in Tuscany up to the boundaries of the Franks. Also he captured and destroyed Oderzo a city placed between Treviso and Cividale. (*HL* IV 45; Foulke 1907: 199–200)

Given how important this cataclysmic series of events seemed to these two historians, it is frustrating that neither text precisely dates Rothari's victories. The modern consensus is that they happened between 642 and 644 (Christie 1990: 229, 231 and 235; Capo 1992: 524–5; Pavoni 1992: 107; Jarnut 1995: 56). The promulgation of Rothari's law code or 'edict' in November 643 provides one fixed date in this king's otherwise date-free history but because of the lack of dated events for the rest of his rule it is hard to relate it to other facts of the king's reign. Very probably however, there was a connection between the timing of the edict and Rothari's wars against the Byzantines as its prologue speaks of the need for Lombards to defend themselves and their homeland against their enemies (Azzara and Gasparri 1992: 12). Further, if Rothari issued a written text of Lombard law as part of the process of conquest of Liguria, this raises the intriguing possibility that Liguria was also intended to be subject to Lombard legal customs from 643 onwards. As there is no contemporary charter documentation from the region it is not possible to be certain about this, but it is worth pointing out that Rothari's code drew on earlier Justinianic legislation which held currency in Byzantine Liguria and that this might have helped to make palatable a putative Lombard take-over of a formerly Byzantine area.

The new administrative status of Liguria remained unclear however. Possibly it became a duchy although the evidence for this is slight (Hallenbeck 2000: 69). More likely it never became a formalized duchy like the other conquered regions of Friuli, Tuscany, Benevento and Spoleto. The issue has to be raised because of a surviving eighth-century funerary stone (175.5 × 72.4 × 8.5 cm) and inscription dedicated to Audoald 'bold and warlike who under the kings held the duchy of Liguria (*Liguriae ducatum tenuit*)' who 'vanquished enemy camps' (*hostilia castra*) (Everett 2003: 72, 258–60; also http://sepolture. storia.unipd.it/). Unfortunately, this inscription like Fredegar's and Paul's brief accounts of Rothari's conquest cannot be certainly dated as there is only an incomplete dating clause on the stone. Of the possible range of dates raised there by the combination of date (7 July), indiction (first) and the reference to 'kings' plural, the year 763 seems most plausible as then Desiderius and Adelchis were ruling, and in recent memory there had been plenty of opportunity for a warrior to show his prowess to help these kings put down various rebellions against them. This scenario is made more likely because the stone was found in the royal capital of Pavia and was almost certainly manufactured there, rather than in Liguria. The little that we know of Audoald's personal history as a warrior therefore perhaps implies that the title of 'Duke of Liguria' was bestowed on him as a personal honour. He would not in these circumstances have ruled a duchy with territorial identity.

Lombard's cultural influence in Liguria was equally inconclusive: there are no definitely Lombard graves from the region and only minimal finds, most nobably some distinctively Lombard pottery from the Perti excavations interestingly of *early* seventh-century date, which makes it possible to envisage that a local shift in cultural orientation from North to South may already have been underway *before* Rothari arrived on the scene. This is so little however that it is much more plausible to argue that Liguria was not really ruled by the Lombards at all in any meaningful sense at any point. One object often regarded as 'Lombard' but in fact probably not so confirms this impression of Lombard weakness. This is another inscribed funerary stone of a certain 'Leodegar' erected in 752 during the reign of King Aistulf (Banti 2009). It survives at Filattiera-Sorano in the middle of the Magra valley.

> Leodegar regardless of the cares that protect life, in this place tore down pagan idols of various kinds and carried to Christ the prayers of those who were leaving the faith. With smiling face and with great generosity he distributed food to the destitute and food from his table to needy pilgrims. Every year I gave the necessary tenths, I founded for the church a hospice dedicated to the Father dispenser of grace for the love of Christ I built the basilica of San Martino where, in devotion to the Holy One, he chose his body to be buried here and made a dowry of all his goods and handed over his body to the earth; his spirit contemplates the heavenly truth. He lived in peace on this earth a period of ten times four Olympiads, with the addition of two decades (46 years: Banti 2009: 825). He died in the fourth year of the reign of Prince Aistulf (i.e. 752) (my translation).[5]

As Leodegar is most likely a Frankish rather than a Lombard name and his chosen saint was Martin – a Frankish favourite – it was probably a Frank rather than a Lombard who evangelized this part of the Magra valley if the claims made by the text about Leodegar's life can be believed (Banti 2009: 819–20). The physical stone itself is interesting. Made from Luni marble – probably re-used *spolia* from the decaying Roman city (Giannichedda and Lanza 2003: 85) – its epigraphy has been directly related to Lombard 'court' quality by Ottavio Banti which suggests high-level, possibly even, royal patronage. Its dedicatee may have been in the Lombard royal circle, and his activities in the valley at some level known to Aistulf. Although speculative this is thought-provoking given that Audoald's stone is of similar quality and relates to the same region at a similar time. The stone's location at Filattiera is also important as that village was on a major pilgrim route along the Magra valley which connected the Po plain to Rome. The dedication of a church there to St Martin is further evidence of the slowly evolving cultural and religious orientation northwards which had been proceeding for centuries in this region.

Attentive reading of these eighth-century sources helps to pinpoint the territorial changes which may have taken place during the transfer from Lombard to Carolingian hegemony over the region. Referring to the same valley as Leodegar's stone the document which records Charlemagne's donation of land to the papacy in 774 (*Liber Pontificalis, Life of Hadrian* ch. 41) reports one of its boundaries as: 'from Luni with the island of Corsica to Sorano then to Mount Bardone that is in Berceto' (Bullough 1956: 15).[6] Sorano is the very place in which Leodegar's inscription was displayed and Hadrian's *Life* therefore evidences both its function as a way-station on an important route and perhaps also as a boundary marker for the eastern edge of Liguria. In 772 a Lombard royal diploma had mentioned the *fines Surianense* ('territory of Sorano') confirming this possibility. Paul the Deacon writing a few years after Charlemagne defeated the last Lombard king but for a Lombard audience expressed a clear concept of the territorial extent of 'Liguria' in his Lombard history. In *HL* II 15 he reported that 'The second province is called Liguria. . . . In this are Milan and *Ticinum*, which is called by another name, Pavia (*Papia*). It extends to the boundaries of the Gauls'. In II 25 he added that 'Alboin . . . took all the cities of Liguria except those which were situated upon the coastal strip'. In *HL* III 23 he described Venetia and Liguria as 'regions of Italy'. Paul's Liguria was on the face of it the old Roman 'Region 9' but in fact he knew that the situation in his own time had changed as in his description of Liguria as a 'province' (using the old terminology employed by his late Antique sources) he in fact assigned Genoa, Acqui, Savona, Bobbio and Tortona to the 'Cottian Alps', which implied that Milan and Pavia were in Liguria 'proper' (Christie 2006: 69). Especially noteworthy here is Paul's listing of the monastery of Bobbio alongside Ligurian towns as this indicates the important role which he believed it to have in the area.

Conclusion

Despite yawning gaps in our knowledge which make it impossible to write a traditional continuous narrative history of political and religious life in Liguria between the end of Roman rule and the ninth century it is possible to highlight several key themes by way of conclusion. A specifically

Ligurian political or religious identity is hard to find at any point in the early medieval period, although there are occasional hints of it after the Lombard 'conquest', most tantalizingly the reference to Audoald 'Duke of Liguria'. It is not surprising that the possibility of Ligurian autonomy should have been raised during the Lombard period as that state was noticeably weaker than either the Byzantine or Carolingian Empires. Before Rothari arrived on the scene Liguria had been a far-flung backwater in a huge sprawling state. After the Lombards disappeared to be replaced by Carolingians Liguria returned to political marginality despite being of some interest to some of those rulers, as we shall see in the next chapter. Genuinely game-changing political events such as the total withdrawal of the Byzantine state from the region or the invasion of the heretical Lombards generated just enough documents to show that such geo-political shifts outside the region did periodically impact on politics within it. However, as the evidence of political activity within Dark Age Liguria is almost entirely the work of highly sophisticated outsiders such as Cassiodorus, Procopius, Gregory the Great and Paul the Deacon, it will always be impossible to see things from the perspective of insiders. Usually we don't even know who they were. Yet the fact that documented political activity in Dark Age Liguria tended to take place at sites also documented in Roman times is a strong argument for continuity rather than discontinuity in the political outlook of local elites and of those outsiders by and for whom our evidence was written.

External documentation also sheds some light on the bureaucratic administration of the region at several points in time. Letters written in the sixth century by Cassiodorus and Gregory the Great tried to sort out administrative problems which had arisen because their world no longer had a single agreed secular authority. Therefore we should pay special attention to the complaints of locals to Cassiodorus about unfair taxation and the worries which Gregory expressed about corrupt Ligurian clergy as these concerns hint at the possibility of internal political dissent and divided political loyalties. In contrast belief in the universal religion of Christianity indirectly evidenced by funerary monuments, burials and church buildings but never directly documented locally by narrative texts such as contemporaneous saints' lives developed slowly and was initially confined to the western coast. Christianity eventually drew the region firmly into the orbit of the city of Milan and its increasingly powerful archbishops. But even this could not straightforwardly engender a sense common purpose in this region because of the fundamental theological differences thrown up by the 'Three Chapters' controversy and the heretical adherence of many Lombard rulers (Chazelle and Cubitt 2007: 5–7, 12–14, 243–64).

Taking all the evidence cited in this chapter together does not add up therefore to a single unitary narrative of either political or religious development in Dark Age Liguria and, while neither early medieval politics nor religious practice is completely obscure in this region, our knowledge of them is so fragmentary that historians ought to stop writing narrative histories which pretend that an uncomplicated story of regional development and progress is possible and which present Dark Age Liguria as a rather dull overture to subsequently more dramatic acts which climaxed in the exciting proper history of the Crusades (Pavoni 1992; Epstein 1996; Airaldi 2010).

Notes

1 Riva known in late antiquity as *Costa Balenae* was the site of a Roman road station (*mansio*). The earliest church (San Siro) was built on top of this. In 1988 an impressive stone a metre-and-half high was found here memorializing Maria an aristocratic woman (Mennella and Coccoluto 1995: 119–21). The most likely date for it is the first half of the seventh century.

2 Martyn 2004 is an excellent English translation of Gregory's letter collection, the *registrum*. I have cited them using his numbering by book and letter: *Reg.* 4.21. Markus 1997 is essential.

3 Her relics were transferred to the nunnery of San Salvatore in Brescia in 762 at the request of King Desiderius and Queen Ansa. As Brescia was part of the arch-diocese of Milan this translation may imply continuing ties between the Milanese church and the Ligurian coast at this period.

4 Christie (2006: 372) suggests that 2 *nummeri* (1,000 soldiers) were stationed in Liguria, including Genoa.

5 The shift between the third and the first person in this text is not uncommon in this period and indeed helps to demonstrate its authenticity.

6 The monastery of Berceto may have had Frankish connections as it is traditionally thought to have been founded in King Liutprand's time by a Frankish bishop of Reims passing through the area on a visit to Rome (although the source is late, the late ninth century *Vita Moderamnus*).

5

Genoa

Genoa's past is better documented than anywhere else in the region. Historians mostly present Genoa as central to Ligurian history and everywhere else as peripheral, a representation which distorts a more complex and diverse past. The surviving written evidence for the early medieval town although better than for other parts of the region is still not especially impressive and again prevents a sustained narrative of 'what happened' in Genoa between the fifth and the eleventh centuries from being written. Historians have rarely given proper consideration to archaeological research in the city even though this is essential for this period. Although the archaeology of large towns is always problematic and in Genoa many potentially important sites have been destroyed by later development and much of the historic centre will never be excavated, even so some remarkable new discoveries have come to light in recent years, especially at Castello and the Porto Antico. One of the most startling discoveries has been a 9 m wall near the Acquasola Park and associated residential remains which have pushed the dateable occupation of Genoa as far back as c. 2300 BCE. Later, a necropolis existed by c. 400 BCE and its excavation has established links with Greek culture, including early evidence for wine-drinking. Genoa already had a port then and important excavations of it have been underway for some time (Carobene et al. 2006). The first written reference to Roman *Genua* is in Livy (205 BCE), where the name meant 'knee' or 'mouth' in reference to its distinctive topography (Petracco Sicardi and Caprini 1981: 52). Later writers were interested in Genoa's maritime business and Strabo who examined *Genua* and the region in some detail pronounced it 'the *emporium* of the Ligures' in an early reference to its trade (Strabo 4.6.1; 5.1.3).

Archaeology at Castello and Porto Antico

Excavations at Castello (50 m asl) of the complex site of the pre-Roman hilltop *oppidum* (Piazza Santa Maria di Passione) discovered occupation of the fourth-century BCE, Etruscan inscriptions and amphorae demonstrating western links with Provence and Marseilles (Milanese 1987). By c. 250 BCE Genoa was certainly a part of Mediterranean-wide trade networks and remained so until c. 640 CE at least. However, local and regional coarse wares suggested that dealings with the interior hinterland and the Po plain – accessible via the Polcevera valley – also took place. Further explorations of *Genua* show that both Italian and North African pottery was coming into the town in the early Imperial period (Milanese 1993; 1995). Overall, archaeology suggests that the Roman town was small, on the typical grid plan and near – or possibly right on – the waterfront. It is now the heart of the 'historic centre' with the cathedral of San Lorenzo on its northern edge. A significant settlement shift from the hill of Castello to the flat land down by the port (*porto antico*) took place during the Roman period as shown by the surviving grid pattern of streets (the *vicoli*), and these two sites are therefore important in debates about continuity/discontinuity over the long term (Figure 5.1).

Genua had few monumental Roman buildings and early medieval levels have been therefore more valued here than in many other Italian towns (Mannoni and Poleggi 1976; Gardini and Milanese 1979; Poleggi and Cevini 2003: 17–26). At Castello the date of presumed late antique abandonment remains unclear but the *oppidum* had probably been resettled by c. 700 as of ten early medieval burials uncovered there one was of a young man adorned with beads who probably lived there then (Gardini and Melli 1988: 174). These were near a considerable section of eighth-/tenth-century walling which had two towers (Andrews and Pringle 1978; Christie 1990: 253), and Poleggi has argued that this was part of a continuously walled circuit from the Carolingian period (Poleggi and Cevini 2003: 24–5, 29); but this circuit is not evidenced elsewhere archaeologically. The hill certainly became the bishop's official residence when a large (11 × 11 m) rather squat stone tower-house with massive walls 0.8-m thick was erected in c. 980–1050 (Miller 2000) and a rich episcopal lifestyle was suggested by the remains of many pig roasts of the choicest cuts and a substantial luxury ceramic assemblage (Cesana et al. 2007).

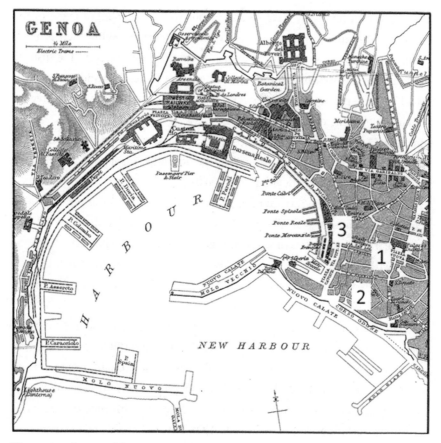

Figure 5.1 Centre of Genoa. 1 = Cathedral. 2 = Castello. 3 = Porto Antico.
Source: Black's, *The Riviera* (1898)

Recent archaeological investigations of the port have proven extremely interesting (Carobene et al. 2006). Excavations to a depth of 3.5 m below the sea at Portofranco uncovered artefacts and environmental evidence across the 2,000-year period 1000 BCE–1000 CE. The deepest levels of sedimentary deposition had preserved pottery from across the Mediterranean coming into Genoa long before residence at Castello had begun and by the time of Strabo's *emporium* large amounts of amphorae confirmed the port's significant role in exchange. A level of very stony material contrasting completely with previous layers of fine sand suggested that a dramatic change had occurred between c. 200 and c. 600 CE, dates arrived at by C14 dating of plant remains (Carobene et al. 2006: 296). The seventh- to ninth-century deposits of fine sand above this were the result of increasing amounts of silt from the Bisagno and Polcevera rivers,

and deposition here may have resulted from structural changes made to the
harbour at this time as the sea was clearly very shallow then. While there is much
material yet to be assessed, preliminary results therefore indicate the historic
harbour was less well maintained during most of the early Middle Ages than
for a long time previously. The *Via Postumia*, the first Roman road in the region
which was to a degree maintained in the Dark Ages, significantly linked Genoa
directly to Aquileia (the northernmost port of the Adriatic) via the Po plain and
was perhaps used for the onward transportation of goods landed at Genoa by
land to larger Roman towns (Mannoni 2004b: 276).

Evidence of commercial buildings and settlement near the port has also
been found. Right next to the port (via Mattoni Rossi) dry stone, wood and
beaten earth homes were in use from late Antiquity into the early medieval
period with rooms later used for burials (Gardini and Murialdo 1994: 163–2).
Similar finds have come from Piazza Matteotti (Palazzo Ducale) and Piazza
Scuole Pie (Porto Antico), and evidence of late Antique economic activity
even closer to the shore has been discovered at via Gramsci, under the current
portico over-looking Piazza Caricamento (Macchiavello 1997). One two-storey
property with substantial mortared walls was most probably some sort of
warehouse rather than residential (Mannoni 2004c: 238). This set alongside
written evidence does suggest that the port was active in some degree for at
least some of the Dark Ages (below 99–100), but on a greatly reduced scale.

Excavations of other parts of town give a similar impression. Genoa's early
ecclesiastical geography and especially the origin of Genoa's early cathedral (or
cathedrals) is hotly debated. In the 1960s the standard view was that the earliest
Italian cathedrals were to be found outside city walls and only later re-located
inside. Genoa conformed to this pattern with two early cathedrals: San Siro
a short distance outside the (presumed) walled circuit and San Lorenzo just
inside. More recent excavations suggest that San Lorenzo was in fact the only
cathedral from the start. Research at San Lorenzo has focused on the origin
of the current building and how archaeological sequences there might relate
to the 'other' cathedral of San Siro (Macchiavello 1997; Di Fabio 1998, 2003).
In San Lorenzo's cloisters early medieval dry stone and beaten-earth-floored
buildings allied to some burials were uncovered similar to those at via Mattoni
Rossi (Gardini and Melli 1988: 172–3; Gardini and Murialdo 1994: 164). More
importantly, under the current cathedral a 2-m section of perfectly preserved

stratigraphy covering the late republican to the post-medieval period was revealed in the 1960s (Gambaro and Lambert 1987; Cagnana 1998). This had three main phrases. (1) Probably agricultural fields, with more than 100 fragments of amphorae of mostly Mediterranean production dated late second-/early first-century BCE and a dump for broken commercial containers although late first-century domestic table wares were also evidenced. (2) A large building with a high quality tiled floor of the Augustan period which was in use for over a century. (3) Cellars above this floor, and evidence that the building was destroyed in the late fourth/early fifth century CE after which there was again an agricultural layer. It has been proposed that in the late fifth/early sixth century 'a building with cultic purpose' was erected (Gambaro and Lambert 1987: 251) and that the current eleventh-/twelfth-century building lies directly on top of this, meaning that no early medieval phase for the cathedral would be found. Twenty years after the initial investigations a reconsideration of the finds, especially the pottery, confirmed the sequence originally proposed. Results from level 3 were confirmed in 1975 with an excavation in Piazza San Lorenzo (Gardini and Milanese 1979) which showed in the fourth/fifth centuries a contraction of the inhabited area which became 'largely rural' (Gambaro and Lambert 1987) although why this could not have been an urban garden is not entirely clear. A cemetery which is assumed to have existed here because of nineteenth-century finds of late Antique sarcophagi was also attributed to this phase but no evidence of a full-scale necropolis was found in either excavation.

The church of San Siro is also not far from the *porto antico* but peripheral to the Roman settlement and outside the line of the presumed early medieval walls. It is much less well known archaeologically than San Lorenzo and altered much more since the medieval period. Although long regarded as the first Genoese cathedral nothing archaeological will take San Siro back to the fourth century and the first written record of a bishop of Genoa (Macchiavello 1997: 22–3 and below 88–9). Gregory the Great referred to it as *in Genuensi urbe . . . ecclesia beati confessoris Syri*, so at the least a church dedicated to Syrus existed in the late sixth century when other written sources suggest that several bishops were buried there (below 95). However, as no excavation has been made underneath the present church its early state remains uncertain. In 1987–8 studies in the cloister and near the bell tower unearthed a sixth-century sarcophagus and nearby some other burials suggested a late antique cemetery (Macchiavello 1997). However, finds from Via Gramsci (also extra-mural) have demonstrated that this area was not exclusively funerary at this time and have suggested that it may have been more central to the late Roman settlement than has usually been thought.

Between 1968 and 1971 a rescue dig was carried out at the via San Vincenzo site (Bellatella et al. 1989), which was in the suburbs until the end of the nineteenth century, and now c. 300 m due east of Brignole station. An 11-m section of Roman road was found together with some walls of medieval date (Bellatella et al. 1989: 363, 379). In layers immediately on top of the Roman road finds included pottery and coins as late as the fifteenth century. In association with the road seven inhumations of children inside North African amphorae were uncovered, three of which dated to the late fifth/early sixth centuries, and one (tomb 2) a neonate dated late sixth/early seventh century. The road surface however seems to have stopped being maintained in the late fourth century and an agricultural layer covered it in the tenth century. The excavators suggested that intense use of this road in the fourth/fifth centuries could be explained because it was the initial stretch of a network which connected Genoa with Milan via the *Via Postumia*. In their view, its abandonment and the 'ruralization' of this part of town was suggested by the burials (near another burial site for adults at vico San Vincenzo). However, when set alongside other burial sites in Genoa these may just as well indicate continued settlement and use of the road network (Gardini and Melli 1988: 160). Three burials at vico San Vincenzo unfortunately only broadly dateable to the sixth/twelfth centuries may be linked with the burial stone and inscription dedicated to the subdeacon Sanctulus (493/494 CE) originally from the church of Santo Stefano (Mennella and Coccoluto 1995: 63–5), while 16 tombs near Piazza Annunziata (the demolished church of Santa Sabina) – a mix of adults and children – 'not earlier than the sixth century' may be linked with the Greek inscription of the solider Magnus of 591 found there. These graves were mostly of the pitched tile type ('a cappuccina') but some were slab graves, possibly of the Lombard period (Christie 1990: 253). Putting all this together there is now clear evidence for continued occupation of parts of Genoa into the early sixth century, and perhaps beyond. The handful of coins found (Arslan 2005: 64) as a result of these various excavations support this picture, as does the fact that as at Luni North African amphorae were found in levels as late as the mid-seventh century (above 48–9).

Early medieval 'Genoese' sculpture

The small corpus of early medieval sculpture preserved in Genoa has been another area of considerable debate. Objects span the entire period and have been seen by most art historians as suggestive of a thriving 'pan-Mediterranean culture' in the city (Dufour Bozzo 1987; Di Fabio 1990; Frondoni 2003, 2005; Marcenaro and Frondoni 2006: 39–66). However, as the origin of these sculptures is controversial it has to be wondered how many of them are in fact Genoese (Russo 2003). The earliest dates traditionally given (e.g. by Frondoni) for the earliest Dark Age stone sculpture made in Genoa are sixth century. A decorative relief, now in the Sant'Agostino museum was argued by Russo (2003: 73) not to be Genoese. Two sarcophagi may have been made in Rome, but Russo suggested the one from San Lorenzo to be from Genoa, or at least re-worked there, although the other from the abbey of Boschetto has no contemporary context so its origin is uncertain. A relief from Cogoleto (mid-sixth century?) was probably worked locally by an itinerant workman from a Byzantine context. Although these four objects might help to conjure up the appearance of the final phase of the Byzantine town they do not add reliably to our knowledge of that culture.

In contrast objects attributed to the seventh-to-ninth centuries are potentially more significant, given the relative lack of other sorts of evidence from Genoa in this period. Although no inscribed stones survive from seventh-century Liguria (Russo 2003: 75) a sarcophagus from the church of Santa Marta probably dates to that period (Frondoni 2005: 18) and interesting parallels for its design can be found in southern Italy at the same period. More important is a small capital decorated with acanthus leaves still in situ in the former crypt of Santi Nazario e Celso, now beneath Santa Maria delle Grazie, in the Castello district. This has been dated stylistically to the early seventh century perhaps meaning that the crypt is of the same date (Poleggi 1973: 28; Cavallaro 1993: 34; Marcenaro and Frondoni 2006: 58). A similar capital (now lost) was found in nineteenth-century excavations at Santo Stefano (Marcenaro and Frondoni 2006: 56). The survival of these architectural fragments at least allows some speculation that church decoration of some quality can be dated to what is otherwise a poorly documented period in Genoese history.

The church of Santa Maria di Castello which is very close to the site of the tenth-century bishop's house at San Silvestro, has preserved several interesting artefacts although none appear to be in situ now. Thoroughly surveyed in the early 1970s (Poleggi 1973), the church's foundation has been traditionally attributed to the Lombard king Aripert in 658 on the basis of a charter dated 1049. While such a pedigree has little to recommend it, the survival here of a carved screen dated to the late eighth- or early ninth-century and of some limited excavations has raised the possibility of an early medieval origin for this church (Poleggi 1973: 107; Cavallaro 1993: 38). The screen has close stylistic parallels with contemporary sculpture from the monastery of Bobbio. Santa Maria also has many re-claimed and re-used mostly late Roman architectural features (Poleggi 1973: 89–109), but it is uncertain where these objects, some of them very impressive columns, came from. As they seem to have inspired ninth- to eleventh-century copies in the same church they were probably there by then. There is also a lunette depicting two kissing doves of tenth- or eleventh-century date (Poleggi 1973: 91, 108). Perhaps the most interesting object is a plaque (37.5 × 36 cm) with a Kufic inscription (Figure 5.2) dated on palaeographical grounds to 'before the eleventh century' (Amari 1873; Poleggi 1973: 101–2). This reports verses 187–8 of the III Sura of the Qur'an which are often inscribed on columns and stones in mosques. Although a report of its reappearance in 1859 during restorations of a part of the building dating from before the twelfth century is useful (Amari 1873: 633), it will never be known for certain when this object arrived in this church. Whatever the real history of this object it certainly raises the possibility of interesting cross-cultural contacts.

All the objects so far discussed may support the view that Genoa remained linked to a pan-Mediterranean artistic world if only in a minor way throughout its Dark Age. A group of tenth-century objects of clearer provenance have been thought by some to evidence the 'transformation of the city' between the late ninth and early eleventh centuries, an extreme claim even though they are certainly high-quality sculpture (Cavallaro 1993: 34). A bas-relief made of white Greek marble from the Benedictine monastery of San Siro (foundation charter dated

Figure 5.2 Kufic inscription, Santa Maria di Castello, Genoa
Source: Amari 1873.

1007) represents a peacock about to eat a grape, a well-known representation of Christian salvation in the contemporary Greek world (Frondoni 2005: 17–19; Marcenaro and Frondoni 2006: 50–1). Close parallels with Byzantine styles c. 950–1000 especially as practiced in Constantinople, have suggested that it was possibly imported from there then. It has been argued that Ottonian money paid for this work as part of the monastic renewal which Bishop Theodulf is presumed to have initiated (Dufour Bozzo 1987: 63–6). However, as this artefact is once again no longer in situ it could have been imported at a later date when Genoese connections with Constantinople are more certain.

A more significant group of c. 30 carved capitals came from the now-demolished monastic church of San Tommaso at *Caput Arenae,* a prominent site in the west of the city overlooking the port. Presumed to have come from the cloister, one group is more refined stylistically and made from eastern marble, while another group is less refined and made of marble from the Apuan Alps, and so probably of local manufacture (Di Fabio 1990). They were most likely commissioned by monks of Greek origin or ones who knew about Byzantine artistic traditions and it again is possible that Ottonian patronage was involved as in the year 999 Empress Adelaide seems to have made a donation to the monastery (Uhlirz 1957; Frondoni 2005: 18–19, 20–3). There are close stylistic parallels with the monastery of San Fruttuoso near Camogli explored below in the context of charter evidence.

All told the surviving material culture of early medieval Genoa is quite modest when compared with what exists elsewhere in Italy (see Brogiolo and Gelichi 1998) and in other parts of the Mediterranean. But it is not negligible, and clearly there is much more to come from archaeological investigation of the port in particular. Material evidence demonstrates that some sites were occupied over long periods, especially the Castello hill, probably because they could be supplied by the Mediterranean wide exchange networks of which Genoa was a part. Castello was also an easily defensible site (Figure 5.3). Clearly some people were living in some parts of Genoa between the fifth and seventh centuries but after then there is a gap in archaeological evidence of occupation until the end of the tenth century, which may tie in with a period in which the port silted up in part due to climate change. The corpus of sculptured stones in some respects fills this gap, although the problematic attributions must be kept to the fore. Genoa could therefore have been the 'gateway community' (see Hodges 1982) for the interior, the crucial outlet on the Mediterranean for the Po valley in the way that Comacchio was for the Adriatic especially as the written evidence, not quite as feeble as is sometimes made out when compared to these material survivals, tends to suggest the same thing.

Gregory the Great's Genoa

If early medieval Genoa has a justified reputation with archaeologists for being poorly documented especially in comparison with many other urban sites in Italy (see Brogiolo and Gelichi 1998; Gelichi 2002; Christie 2006: 183–280), historians

Figure 5.3 View of Genoa from the East, c. 1880.
Source: Photograph in author's possession.

have often dismissed this period altogether with Steven Epstein characterizing its history then as 'practically nothing' (Epstein 1996: 12–15). While the surviving written evidence is sparse it is also fascinating. The first significant texts are Cassiodorus' letters (*Variae*) which have to be approached cautiously (Barnish 1992: xxxiii). Cassiodorus reported two letters which King Theodoric wrote directly about people certainly resident in Genoa. The first dated 507–512 was addressed to 'all Jews living at Genoa' and sent in response to a request from the Jewish community there to make alterations to, and possibly to expand, their synagogue (*Var.* II.27; Barnish 1992: 34–5; Epstein 1996: 13; Urbani and Zazzu 1999: ix–xi, 1–2; Christie 2006: 34). The king specifically allowed them 'to add a roof to the ancient walls of your synagogue' but prevented them from 'adding any ornament, or straying into an enlargement of the building' as they seem to have requested. Theodoric added, after criticizing their beliefs at the outset that 'I cannot command your faith, for no-one is forced to believe against his will'. In a second letter (c. 511) the king confirmed to the 'Jews of Genoa' (*Iudeis Genua*) their ancient privileges (*Var.* IV.33). These are tantalizing references as where the synagogue was and what it looked like is unknown, as is the size of this Jewish community.[1] But it was not unique in sixth-century Liguria for in May 594 Gregory the Great wrote to Bishop Venantius expressing dismay that Christians were being enslaved by Jews right under his nose in Luni itself (*Reg.* IV.21), which was against Justinianic law: 'no-one should possess or own a slave whether Christian, heretic, pagan or Jew' (*Codex* 1.10). If we discount the veneer of Christianity these few references suggest that Genoa still retained a multi-religious character in the sixth century: this Jewish community could have been there for a very long time given what archaeology tells us about pan-Mediterranean exchange networks. It seems not to have lasted however as the next reference to Genoese Jews is as late as June 1132.

By Gregory the Great's time the Genoese church had been linked politically with Milan in a more direct way than hitherto. The earliest record of a bishop of Genoa can be dated to 381 when Diogenes was at the Council of Aquileia called by Ambrose of Milan (Cantino Wataghin 2000: 217). In 451 Bishop Pascasius had attended a Milanese synod with other Ligurian suffragans. In 430 two Genoese priests Camillo and Teodoro had sent questions about theology to Prosper of Aquitaine. In 569 however Bishop Honoratus of Milan went to Genoa, a crucial event in the history of the relationship between the two cities provoked by the arrival of the Lombards in Milan as we have seen (Picard 1988: 73–5; Navoni 1990: 84). Honoratus fled to the safety of Byzantine-controlled Genoa which really was secure as excavations of contemporary *castra* such as Perti and Filattiera part of the lines of forts known as the *limes* have shown. Although Paul the Deacon's unique account of this event was brief and written down over two centuries later (*HL* II 25, above 68), Genoese historians have made a great deal of it arguing, for example, that the new bishop and the Milanese elite who accompanied him (for whom there is actually little or no evidence either) founded a Genoese church dedicated to Ambrose, the Milanese saint par excellence, just North of San Lorenzo despite there being no archaeological evidence for a sixth-century phase of this church (Poleggi 1973: 30 and Navoni 1990: 84). Nor is anything else known of Honoratus: even the site of his burial is disputed some giving Noseda, near Milan (Picard 1988: 59), others Noceto, near Camogli. His successor Frontus is equally obscure (Picard 1988: 75).

Gregory's letters by contrast do provide useful information about the Genoese activities of the Milanese bishops he corresponded with, although he obviously provides a one-sided and possibly even personal view of Genoa during his pontificate. At this time, Milan and Genoa effectively operated as a single diocese as the Milanese bishops and clergy remained in Byzantine territory (Picard 1988: 74). Laurentius, who became bishop of Milan in 573 probably the year in which King Alboin was poisoned placing his wife Theodelinda in a position of considerable power (Picard 1988: 76), ended the rift with Rome over the Three Chapters affair but was unable to return to Milan because of continued hostility to the Lombards and their Arian practices (Chazelle and Cubitt 2007: 111–12). In 585 the 15-year old Merovingian king Childebert II addressing him as Patriarch in a letter of surprisingly sophisticated Latin (Wickham 2009: 173) asked for his assistance against the Lombards, whom he was fighting on behalf of the Byzantine emperor Maurice, which suggests that Laurentius at Genoa had access to resources (especially troops) brought in by sea from other parts of Byzantine-controlled Italy, which would not have been the case had he been in Milan. Gregory's letters to Laurentius while fairly mundane reveal that the Milanese church (and by implication now the Genoese too?) held land in Sicily which it was keen to exploit (Pasini 1991) and again, connection by sea would have made this possible.

Laurentius' death in 593 is recorded in three of Gregory's letters (*Reg.* 3.29, 3.30 and 3.31). It provoked some dispute about his successor and perhaps even suggestions that the local clergy should return to Milan. Gregory considered the election of the new bishop in three letters he wrote in March–April 593 to Milanese clerics (*Reg.* 3.26, 3.29, 3.30; Markus 1997: 142–3). As was customary, procedures were to be overseen in person by the papal representative a sub-deacon called John, who administered papal land in the region (it would seem), for which evidence now no longer survives. 'It is therefore necessary for you set out for Genoa' Gregory wrote to John, suggesting that he was concerned about the possible outcome. In March (*Reg.* 3.26) Gregory was writing to Magnus, a priest in the Milanese church who seems to have been influential saying that he thought that bishop Laurence had wrongly excommunicated him. Clearly he was trying to heal some deep rifts.

Constantius (593–600) was elected Laurentius' successor and a larger number (14) of Gregory's letters to him have survived (Markus 1997: 134–42; Chazelle and Cubitt 2007: 111–4). These are supplemented with other letters to Bishop Venantius of Luni (seven, above 69–71) and three to the Lombard king and queen, Agilulf and Theodelinda, then living in Milan. A succession of letters (*Reg.* 4.2; 4.3; 4.4; 4.33; 7.14) about the Three Chapters show how Gregory tried to win over Agilulf and Theodelina via the mediation of Bishop Constantius. In the course of these (4.2) reference was made to *nobilissimi* ('the very noble') in Genoa who subscribed to a doctrinal statement issued by Constantius: these 'could well denote senatorial exiles in Genoa' (Brown 1984: 166) although this is all we know about them.

Gregory wrote to Constantius about apparently more mundane church business, mostly concerning the moral laxity of clerics at Luni, Portovenere, Ravenna, Brescia, Como, Milan and possibly Genoa itself, as he did to Venantius of Luni. These seem to show that the diocese of Milan was in melt-down hardly surprising, given the combination of an ideological rift around the 'Three Chapters' and the uneasy political situation which the arrival of the Lombards had caused and that Constantius at Genoa was finding it difficult to maintain control over it from so far away. Genoa was many days journey from Milan and Gregory seems to have sensed that Genoa and the littoral might easily slip from imperial control. In 594 he urged Constantius to help Venantius to conduct an enquiry into bad clergy at Luni (*Reg.* 4.22); to deal with similar problems in Brescia (4.37); and to enact the deposition of several priests and abbots, including Jobinus formerly deacon and abbot in Portovenere (5.18; Martyn 2004: 336–7). In 599, Constantius was urged to deal with more rebellious clerics in Como, problems which had arisen from a property dispute (9.187). A particularly interesting letter was sent to Constantius in August 599 (9.235; Martyn 2004: 708–9) which recorded that an old, blind man called Philagrius had complained that 'agents of your church occupied a field containing his vineyard'. Gregory wanted Constantius to restore the property if it was proven that the church did not in fact own it. Philagrius had also claimed that he was 'being compelled to pay just as much as the other inhabitants of the city of Genoa are paying' which makes clear that the vineyard being taxed was in Genoa rather than Milan as most editors suggest. He added that the church of Tortona mid-way between Genoa and Milan was unjustly 'holding' his son-in-law Maurus in some relationship of dependence with obvious consequences for his daughter and grand-children left at home. Constantius was advised to deal himself with the bishop of Tortona to bring the matter to a humane conclusion.

These letters reveal that the arrival of the Milanese bishop in Genoa had brought the town and its inhabitants to the attention of the pope in ways which would almost certainly not otherwise have been the case. Local political equilibrium seems to have been fractured when the Milanesi arrived with some locals – the 'very noble' and Philagrius the man with a Greek name – perhaps taking their chance to complain about a heavy-handed church expropriating their land. Or was Gregory's reading of the situation correct that some clerics were dishonest and misusing church land for their own and their families' gain? The Milanese impact on Genoa was also in part physical. While local tradition is probably wrong in claiming that the church of Sant'Ambrogio was founded by Constantius who was later buried there (Picard 1988: 80; Navoni 1990: 85; Polonio 1999: 2), other bishops – Laurentius, Deusdedit and Asterius (immediate successors of Constantius) – significantly chose San Siro for their resting place in Genoese tradition the *basilica apostolorum* (Picard 1988: 76; Di Fabio 1998: 16–17, 25). San Siro also appears in one of the stories in Gregory's *Dialogues* (IV.55), which reports that Valentinus, an official of the Milanese church reputedly 'extremely dissolute', was buried in the city (*urbs*) of Genoa 'in the church of the blessed confessor Syrus'. If anything therefore San Siro was the Milanese church in Genoa at this time. If St Syrus's burial here had attracted *ad sanctos* burials in the fourth to sixth centuries and if this church was the site of the earliest cathedral (from 381 CE) unsurprisingly incoming Milanese gravitated to it. But all this remains impossible to document archaeologically and the early church is obscure, apart from the later survival of the peacock sculpture already discussed (Frondoni 2003 for recent excavations).

Before Gregory died late in 604, he exchanged a few not especially cordial letters with Deusdedit, Constantius' successor (*Reg.* 11.6; 11.11; 12.14; 13.31). Deusdedit elected by the Milanese clergy from among their number in September 600, 'set out for the city of Genoa' in October (11.14) which proves that he resided in Milan along with other clerics even though it was under Lombard control ('collaborators' in Gregory's view perhaps). Once Gregory's letters cease Genoa is plunged back into literary oblivion; we do not even know when Deusdedit died. Luckily, his successor Asterius was known to the Anglo-Saxon historian Bede as *genuensis episcopus* (*HE* III 7, 'of Genoa' *not* 'of Milan') as he consecrated Birinus first bishop of the West Saxons in 629 (Polonio 1999: 3):

At that time, the West Saxons, formerly called Gewissae, in the reign of Cynegils, embraced the faith of Christ, at the preaching of Bishop Birinus, who came into Britain by the advice of Pope Honorius; having promised in his presence that he would sow the seed of the holy faith in the inner parts beyond the dominions of the English where no other teacher had been before him. Hereupon he received episcopal consecration at the pope's command from Asterius, bishop of Genoa (*Unde et iussu eiusdem pontificis per Asterium Genuensem episcopum in episcopatus consecratus est gradum*).[2]

This reference is interesting as it implies that Birinus passed through Genoa on his way to Britain (from Rome?) which has given rise to the idea that he may even have been a monk at Bobbio (Wood 2001: 39). It also suggests that Asterius was firmly established at and identified with Genoa rather than Milan. His immediate successors are obscure but tradition has it that John 'the Good' (641–659) was the bishop who finally returned to Milan after Rothari had conquered Genoa and united the old imperial province to the Lombard kingdom.

Lombard Genoa

According to Tom Brown, Byzantine Genoa lost its 'administrative functions and its economic links with other regions' as a result of the Lombard conquest (Brown 1984: 14). This is likely but it remains hard to estimate the extent of the 'conquest' of Liguria by King Rothari, given the available evidence as argued above (Polonio 1999: 3–4). While some sort of rupture took place in the short term – North African pottery appears to have stopped arriving in Liguria precisely in the mid-seventh century and Lombard pottery did not replace it – in the longer term the Genoese looked inland and especially to the north in a way that was probably new as a result of becoming part of the Lombard kingdom, in theory at least. Evidence for Lombard Genoa is exiguous however as there is little material evidence beyond the seventh-century sculpted capital from Santi Nazaro e Celso (see above) in a church dedicated to two favourite Milanese saints, and the perhaps Bobbio-influenced plaque from Santa Maria di Castello, a church traditionally associated with King Aripert. No Lombard coins or pottery have been found in Genoa, in contrast with a few sites elsewhere in the region (see above 75–6).

Once the Milanese bishops had left, the Genoese see appears to have reverted to its earlier position as suffragan. In 680, Bishop John participated in Pope Agatho's Easter council at Rome where he witnessed the record of its proceedings along with 125 other bishops 'by grace of God bishop of the holy Catholic church of Genoa', the only one of them to term himself 'catholic' pointedly distinguishing himself from what he probably perceived to be Arians at Milan (Polonio 1999: 4). Otherwise, the activities of the Genoese bishops are unknown between the mid-seventh and the mid-ninth centuries. Bede comes to the rescue again as he recorded in both his 'Greater Chronicle' (Willis 1999: 237) and his *Martyrology* (Hallenbeck 2000: 9–11) that the relics of St Augustine of Hippo were transferred from Sardinia to Pavia by King Liutprand c. 725–731 (repeated by Paul the Deacon, *HL* VI 48). There has been some speculation that this translation would have used Genoese ships and that the body travelled via Genoa up the Scrivia valley, the most direct route from Sardinia to Pavia a legend reported (or created?) by Johannes de Varagine the famous thirteenth-century bishop of Genoa (Mannoni and Poleggi 1974: 172; Pavoni 1988: 246; Polonio 1999: 4; Hallenbeck 2000: 25–6, 162–3; McCormick 2001: 516, 865). Supposedly Liutprand built a monastery at Savignone to commemorate the translation, but once again no authentic early evidence for this has survived. Other routes were possible, notably through the Lunigiana (and note the presence there of an important Lombard-period inscription at Filattiera in the mid-eighth century, above 76–7). Lastly, the most intriguing Lombard text which relates to Liguria is found on the funerary stone of Audoald, 'Duke of Liguria' (Everett 2003: 72, 258–60) (above 75). Its evidence as the record of a personal honour gains in plausibility when read alongside a reference to a Carolingian count of Genoa in 806.

Carolingians, Arabs and Ottonians

Genoa seems a place entirely marginal to the Carolingian world as the surviving evidence for it is minuscule relative to the large amounts preserved for other parts of that vast empire. Liguria was only very tenuously on the radar of Carolingian-period writers, even Paul the Deacon who noticed it a mere five times in his *Historia Langobardorum* (II 15, II 16, II 25, II 23, VI 24) although each time calling it *civitas* or *urbs*. However, taken in the round the surviving evidence for gives a more subtle impression of Genoa as a 'gateway' site of some importance from a Carolingian perspective (Airaldi 2010: 282–8). The region emerges in Carolingian sources near the end of Charlemagne's

reign with the famous account of the arrival at Portovenere of the elephant
Abul Abaz, a gift from the ruler of Baghdad, and his journey north (Hodges
1989; Brubaker 2004; Dutton 2004: 59–62), an event important enough to be
described at length by the 'Royal Frankish Annals' spread over the entries for
801 and 802. In Easter 801 Charlemagne, returning north from his coronation
by Pope Leo in Rome via Ravenna, heard about the elephant from a Persian
legate while at Pavia. By October, Issac 'the Jew' coming back from a legation
sent to the Persian court four years earlier had landed with the elephant at
Portovenere but because the weather was bad the animal spent the winter in
Vercelli. By 20 July 802, Issac, Abul Abaz and other gifts arrived in Aachen at
the imperial palace. Maybe Issac and the elephant travelled Northwest from
Portovenere via Genoa to reach Vercelli, although other routes were possible.

Genoa appears in the 'Royal Frankish Annals' for 806 when Ademar 'count
of Genoa' assisted King Pippin in his anti-Arab expedition to Corsica:

> Pippin sent a fleet from Italy to Corsica against the Moors who were
> devastating the island. Although the Moors did not wait for its arrival but
> made off, one of our men, Ademar, count of the city of Genoa (*comes civitas
> Genuae*), rashly engaged with them and was killed. (King 1987: 97)

As this is the only reference to a 'count of Genoa' it is not possible – as with
Audoald, putative 'duke of Liguria' – to establish the permanency or otherwise
of this institution, although Ademar being termed 'one of ours' may mean
that Frankish identity in this specific context and at this point in time was
reinforced by being anti-Arab. Although Pippin's fleet may have been made
up of cargo ships (McCormick 2001: 519, 892), there is no evidence for an
existing Lombard war fleet (Pryor 2003). Another expedition again defeated
Arabs on Corsica in 807. These Carolingian stories of 'Charlemagne's elephant'
(a 'status animal' in Dutton's phrase) and of King Pippin's anti-Arab war in
Corsica suggest that the early ninth-century Genoese, while probably still part
of a Mediterranean-wide network of exchange were feeling the impact of an
increasingly powerful and demanding Carolingian state.

The activities of the monks of Bobbio in ninth-century Genoa support this view.
Paul the Deacon when describing the provinces of Italy in *HL* II 16 noted that:

> The fifth province is the Cottian Alps, which were so called after King
> Cottius, who lived in Nero's time. It extends from Liguria southeast to the
> Tyrrhenian Sea; on the west indeed it is joined to the territories of the

Gauls. In it are contained the cities (*civitates*) of Acqui where there are hot springs, Tortona, the monastery of Bobbio, Genoa, and Savona (my translation).

Although Paul's description was based on the Classical Latin authors Eutropius (*Breviarium* VII, 14) and Pliny, he amended their accounts adding the monastery of Bobbio to the Cottian province and noting the contemporary late eighth-century spelling of Savona *Saona* rather than the classical *Savo*. By ranking Bobbio with these *civitates* Paul hinted at the longer term significance of new links between Carolingian Bobbio and Genoa. As the ninth century progressed, the Bobbio connection brought Genoa to the notice of the Carolingian royal family. Bobbio is first recorded with property in Genoa itself in the famous inventory of 862:

> In Genoa, the church in honour of St Peter (San Pietro alla Porta),[3] can be collected annually 10 *modia* of chestnuts, 8 *amphorae* of wine in a good year, 40 *libra* of oil; there are purchased annually for the use of the brothers 100 strings of figs, 200 citrons, 4 *modia* of salt, 2 *congia* of garum, 100 *libra* of pitch; it has 6 tenants, who work the vines and bring the aforementioned renders to the monastery. (my translation, see McCormick 2001: 634)

These properties were not in the earlier inventory made in 833–835 for Charlemagne's cousin Wala, exiled to Bobbio as its abbot, nor in the confirmation of property received from Louis II in 860 (Wanner 1994: doc. 31), which suggests that the Genoese property was acquired by the monks *between* 860 and 862, an interestingly precise finding although who gave it is not clear. The church was probably owned by the Genoese church, although it could have been in private hands. Michael McCormick has pointed out that what the monks obtained could only be had by sea in the case of the citrons (or other citrus fruit) and probably of the fish sauce (2001: 633–6). The citrus presumably came via Arab contacts not, given the history of trans-Mediterranean shipping back to antiquity, perhaps as surprising as McCormick proposes. The chestnuts, wine and olive oil are just as striking as the common trio of Ligurian products at least as far as the coast is concerned. They were all storable staples but only the chestnuts could be easily produced closer to Bobbio; the wine would have been of better quality near the coast as it still is, and the oil could only be produced here as most of Bobbio's other land was too high (and therefore too cold at this latitude) for olive production. However, as properties elsewhere in eastern Liguria are recorded as Bobbio property earlier than at Genoa maybe the Genoese operation was the central place for their collection.

On 5 June 774 Charlemagne's first diploma to an Italian recipient granted to Bobbio 'Alpe Adra', a large site now thought to be inland from Moneglia with land in the vicinity of Castiglione Chiavarese in the Petronio valley. This was subsequently confirmed in many other royal diplomas, and is described in the 862 inventory which also records upland properties in the Aveto and Taro valleys in and around Caregli (near Borzonasca), Comorga (San Colombano Certenoli), Ascona (Santo Stefano d'Aveto), Castiglione Chiavarese (supposedly), and Borgotaro. It is also likely that Bobbio monks traded their own production at Genoa as the town could have provided an outlet on the Mediterranean for production from their estates. Significantly, the church which Bobbio had rights over was San Pietro alla Porta (now San Pietro in Banchi), almost in the water right down in the port. Nearby (at Scuole Pie) the remains of several early medieval buildings of a workmanlike nature have been found, small structures of dry-stone masonry which were likely storehouses (Gardini and Murialdo 1994: 164). Presumably San Pietro – apparently never excavated – had a local priest or priests to hold services there for a population of local residents. All the properties listed in 862 were confirmed by Louis II on 2 February 865 at the request of his wife Angilberga, including *Ienua* (Wanner 1994: doc. 42), and they appear again in the inventory of 882 and subsequent lists, the longest and latest of which dated c. 1000 lists many additional properties in a final section devoted to *Terra que in Maritima esse videntur* (below 118–19).

How Bobbio's activities in Genoa related to the institutional Genoese church is intriguing as Bobbio was not the only monastery with property in the port area: the powerful, royal nunnery of Santa Giulia at Brescia also recorded its Genoese land ('5 free men, who return 240 *libras* of cheese') in an early tenth-century inventory (Castagnetti et al. 1979: 92; Polonio 1997: 90–1). Indeed, if Pavoni were correct that Milanese institutions had land in the Levante by this time, they too would have had representatives in Genoa (Pavoni 1992: 104–6). One wonders what successive bishops made of Bobbio's activities especially its ownership of a church but a stone's throw from their own cathedral of San Lorenzo. By 860 Genoese bishops again begin to be documented after years of silence and while there is no direct evidence about their attitudes to the monastery of Bobbio it is clear that the ninth-century bishops were quite active men, whose sights tended to look inland to Milan, their metropolitan. Already in May 825, the Olona capitulary issued by Lothar I to reform the North Italian church had required that Genoese clergy should study with the Irishman Dungal in Pavia, while those from Albenga, Vado and Ventimiglia should go instead to Turin, much closer (Azzara and Moro 1998: 126–7). Dungal himself probably retired to Bobbio and left his books to the community (Ganz 2004). Here potentially is an earlier Bobbio/Genoa link as perhaps the bishop's clergy actually did go to Bobbio to study and if they did, maybe the possibility that the monastery should have a Mediterranean outlet at Genoa was discussed.

Subsequent to Bobbio's appearance on the Genoese scene and perhaps not coincidentally Genoese bishops attended important meetings inland. In October 864 Bishop Peter attended the Council of Milan chaired by Archbishop Tado. In 876 Bishop Sabatinus (865–889) was at the Council of Pavia which confirmed the election of Charles the Bald as emperor. The next year Sabatinus was in Ravenna at a synod called by Pope John VIII, and the following year the pope himself was in Genoa on his way to Arles, the first pope certainly to have visited there (Polonio 1999: 5). From Genoa the pope wrote charmingly to Archbishop Anspert of Milan about his rough sea crossing. Another letter suggests that a previous embassy had been sent to King Carloman comprising Sabatinus and Anspert. As Michael McCormick has argued (2001) moving around like this is at the least evidence for connectedness and maybe evidence for economic vitality. These bishops certainly seem to be fully part of the northern Carolingian world in a way that their predecessors were not while they remained fully part of the western Mediterranean world.

Nearly all ninth-century narrative sources that mention Genoa also mention Saracens suggesting that one of the most clichéd themes in medieval Genoese history – the militant Christian republic fighting the Moors on crusade – might have an early medieval history. Things certainly did not begin well for the Genoese when 'their' count Ademar was killed on King Pippin's expedition to 'free' Corsica in 806. His powers as 'count of Genoa' are entirely unclear: this is the only reference to this office but is perhaps to be linked with the late eighth-century reference to Audoald 'duke of Liguria' as argued above. Both Audoald and Ademar are mentioned in military contexts, and it is indeed quite possible that when King Liutprand went to assist Charles Martel in fighting the Arabs around 739 (as recorded in a poem praising the virtues of the city of Milan – the metropolitan for the Genoese see) Audoald may well have gone with him (Pighi 1960). Although Carolingian sources presented Pippin's Corsican expedition as a success ('his army liberated the island of Corsica, which was oppressed by the Moors' as the Carolingian version of the Lombard 'origin legend' put it), in fact Arab attacks soon began along the Ligurian coast. A written account (*translatio*) of the translation of the bones of Saint Romolus from what is now Sanremo to Genoa has survived but is difficult to date precisely (Picard 1988: 602). The author – who was most likely writing in the late tenth century – explains that 'in modern times' Bishop Sabatinus (d. 889) moved the bones because of devastating Saracen attacks from *Fraxinetum* (in Provence). They were taken by sea by the clergy and the 'people' and reburied under the altar (which church is not specified) with an inscription composed by Sabatinus placed above which is lost. The sense of collective Genoese identity embedded in this text is interesting (even if a hagiographical *topos*) in the light of the supposed reference to the *populus* – or even citizens as some historians would have it – in the famous charter granted to the Genoese by kings Berengar and Adalbert in July 958 (see below).

Another text in the Genoese 'Book of Privileges' entitled *De sancto Romolo* and dated 979/980 relates more of the story (Puncuh 1962: doc. 8). The saint's translation was essential to a transfer of property for the document was drawn up to record the gift by Bishop Theodulf to the canons of San Lorenzo of land near Taggia and Sanremo, to restore it to them after the Arab attacks. A brief excursus explained that Bishop Sabatinus moved Romolo's bones to the church of San Lorenzo and placed them under the altar. The location – San Lorenzo – was important as this confirmed the intra-mural church as the cathedral rather than the extra-mural San Siro. The bones of St Syrus of Genoa were translated at some point to this church, although recently Nick Everett (2002) has argued that the Bobbio manuscript which deals with this is in fact about Saint Syrus of Pavia.[4] By the tenth century Syrus seems to have been regarded as the city's patron in preference to Lorenzo before being supplanted later by the familiar Saint George.

The translations of saints' relics as much as military campaigns helped to develop for some Genoese a sense of common identity in the face of adversity.

The crunch came in 934–935 when Genoa itself was sacked by Fatimid Arabs and although there is once again no strictly contemporary account, the drift of events is clear from both Christian and Islamic authors. Liudprand of Cremona writing in the early 960s with a helpfully transparent western Christian agenda, reported the following:

> ... the Phoenicians arrived there (Genoa) with a many ships, and they entered the city while the citizens were unaware slaughtering all except women and children. Then, putting all the treasures of the city and the churches of God in their ships, they returned to Africa. (*Antapodosis*, IV.5, my translation. See Squatriti 2007: 142)

Liutprand deliberately placed this information immediately after his (negative) account of the Arabs ('Saracens' to him) who had settled at *Fraxinetum* and the reference to a 'fountain overflowing with blood' at Genoa immediately before it was a typical but unsubtle literary device meant to suggest God's disapproval of the Genoese and their church. It is usually presumed that Arabs from *Fraxinetum* under the leadership of Muhammad al-Qaim Bi-Amrillah (second Fatimid caliph there) were responsible for this attack, even though Liudprand terms them here 'Phoenicians' (Miller 2000: 66).

Arab sources, as should be expected, told a different story and some historians using them have seen the attack as evidence of Genoese 'vitality' and the town a place worth attacking (Kedar 1997: 606). The one tenth- or eleventh-century Arab source – the so-called Chronicle of Cambridge written in Sicily – says simply that Abu al-Quasim sent a fleet to Genoa and captured it. There are many much later Arab accounts of which the most detailed is an account of Idrīs 'Imād al-Dīn who died in 1468 (Kedar 1997: 608–9). Kedar taking the report at face value despite its very late provenance thought its references to Genoese merchandize – especially cloth – revealed a sophisticated tenth-century economy. He connected Liutprand's 'treasures' with the linen (raw and yarn) and raw silk mentioned in the Arab account to develop an argument that trading with Arabs was well established. This view of peaceful trade may be supported by the existence of the Kufic Qur'ānic inscription at Santa Maria di Castello (above 88–9): perhaps this object had originally been in a small house mosque in the city which served Moslem traders, such as the one which

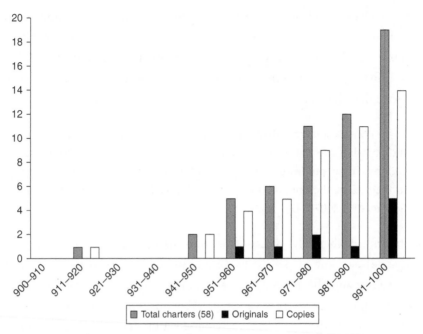

Figure 5.4 Tenth-century Genoese charters.
Source: Belgrano 1862, 1887, Calleri 1999.

survives in Toledo from this period? If so, the history of the Saracens in early medieval Genoa may as much about cosmopolitanism, pan-Mediterranean culture and economic exchange as religious hatred: the Christian monks of Bobbio obtained their hard-to-get citrus fruits and fish sauce in Genoa most probably from Arabs at the very moment when further down the coast Bishop Sabbatinus was rescuing San Siro's bones from 'Saracens'.

Liudprand's report of an Arab sack of Genoa in the early tenth century cannot be compared with charter evidence for local economic life as charters are preserved here only from the mid-tenth century. This is a late date for their appearance when compared with survivals from other parts of Italy (see Wickham 1988; Skinner 1995). A maximum of 58 documents has survived, some interpolated later, [5] and it is possible that earlier documents were actually destroyed in the Arab sack of 934–935 or maybe never existed; we cannot be sure.

Figure 5.4 shows that the number of charters rises significantly after 990. The earliest charter is a *libellus* dated 916 from the time of Bishop Ratpert about property in Bargagli (val Bisagno) (Belgrano 1862: 159–60). After this a succession of agreements appear between the Genoese church and a wide range of people from a small range of places mostly in the lower Bisagno and Polcevera valleys near the city. Most survive only as twelfth-century copies but just under 14 per cent of the tenth-century ones are original single sheets. Those from 946–981 relate to Bishop Theodulf who governed the Genoese church for more than 35 years and embarked on a 'reform' programme – if it was such – which can be compared with similar developments elsewhere in Europe (Polonio 1999: 6). His name and his reforming interests suggest he probably originated from north of the Alps (compare Ratherius of Verona active at a similar time). He revitalized religious life in Genoa especially at the extra-mural communities of San Siro and Santo Stefano documented respectively by 9 charters between 951–1000 and 15 between 965–1000, but unfortunately it has proved impossible to identify him in other charters where he might have appeared including royal diplomas or those of Bobbio. Twenty-six local charters allow the activities of Bishop Theodulf and his church to be traced year by year in some detail to the end of his episcopate in 981, and these reveal developing relationships with the Ottonian family, with local aristocrats and other owners, as well the foundation of the monastery of Santo Stefano in 965, and the creation of a community of clergy at the cathedral who may have lived in common. Three groups of documents can serve as examples of this material: those relating to San Siro; the famous Genoese diploma of Berengar and Adalbert; and the charters of Santo Stefano.

An original charter dated 951/952 records Theodulf's revocation of a previous grant of a vineyard to a priest called Silvester and re-allocation of its tithes to San Siro (ignored by Epstein 1996; Calleri 1997: 1–2, doc. 1, 1999: 57; Macchiavello 1997). The property was bounded by vines held by viscount Ydo (otherwise unknown) which extended to Castello, the first written reference to this Genoese landmark hill (Poleggi 1973: 17). The rest of the boundary clause fills in the topography of the mid-tenth-century city: 'outside the wall of Genoa in the ditch of Caderiva and the River Bisagno to the ditch of St. Michael *Caput Arenae*', a large swath of land (Filangieri 2006: 3–5). In the charter Theodulf used the phrase 'see of San Siro', and signed it himself along with a group of his clergy: Vuitbaldo, 'archpriest of the Holy Genoese Church', two deacons both called Johannes 'chief deacons of the Holy Genoese Church' (*de cardine*), and the priest John, 'of the Holy Genoese church'. The income from the re-allocated property was given to the *clerici* as a group and clearly Theodulf was building up San Siro as the leading Genoese church with a permanent staff of senior clergy to run it, manage its properties and minister to parishioners. San Siro eventually became a Benedictine monastery in 1007 under Theodulf's successor John II (Calleri 1997: doc. 9, 14–17; Frondoni 2005: 17), having been the recipient of several grants from locals in the vicinity of the Bisagno and other eastern valleys (Calleri 1997: docs 3, 5–14) and possibly from the widowed Empress Adelaide in 999 (Calleri 1997: doc. 4, 6–8).[6]

Theodulf's charter of 951–2 is as interesting as a famous document which ignores the Genoese church, the charter granted to the Genoese by Kings Berengar and Adalbert on 18 July 958 (Imperiale di Sant'Angelo 1936: 3–4; Rovere 1990, 1992: 4–6).[7] Berengar and Adalbert confirmed to the Genoese citizens their customs and prevented public officials from entering their houses and staying overnight for free (*mansionaticum*; Pavoni 1988: 244–5), with the proviso that the marquis Obertenghi (Otbert I) was to retain judicial rights there (Nobili 1993). All was done without reference to the bishop which has been taken to suggest that Theodulf was an outsider who could not command local support (Guglielmotti 2005: 22; Filangieri 2006: 3–4), a view confirmed by the charter of 951–2 where Theodulf said he was 'newly in office and ignorant of the customs of the place' (Calleri 1997: 1). Liudprand of Cremona is again illuminating for he claimed that around 960 Otbert I petitioned Otto I about Berengar and Adalbert's 'savagery' (Squatriti 2007: 220). Otto was also sought out by Archbishop Walpert of Milan, Theodulf's metropolitan, who claimed that Berengar's behaviour – he had illegally appointed Manasses of Arles to the Milanese see – had 'snatched away what ought to belong to him and his people'. Theodulf may have thought likewise and over the next few years he appears in a series of local charters which show him acquiring land of his church both inside the city but also outside in the Lavagna, Rapallo and Polcevera valleys in sites near roads of some strategic importance, including Albaro (Calleri 2009: docs 1 and 3), Bavali (Belgrano 1862: 144–5, 161–3), Molassana (Belgrano 1862: 209–10, 222–3, 233–4, 236–8, 257–8, 271–2), Pontedecimo (Belgrano 1862: 236–8) and elsewhere (Benente 2000; Guglielmotti 2007b). In parallel fashion, Otbert I also had wider interests as he was recorded in the late tenth-century Bobbio inventory as a benefactor of that monastery: *Beneficia que Aubert marchio de abbatia dedit.*

The charters of Santo Stefano record properties owned near Genoa in Albaro and a few other places which are now part of its suburbs. These documents which straddle the year 1000 are notable for contracts with locals to develop new cultivable lands for chestnuts and other fruiting trees (Calleri 2009: docs 2–28). At Albaro the properties were around the small church of San Nazaro, a favourite Milanese saint. Other Genoese churches also developed portfolios of land in eastern Liguria, notably San Giorgio in the Lavagna valley (Calleri 1997: 3–4; Filangieri 2006: 6). Here in a typical charter of exchange between the church and a certain Eldeprand San Giorgio's land was described as 'under the control of the Genoese church, sited within a wall of the city of Genoa near the church of San Giorgio' and Eldeprand's land was 'sited in the Lavagna valley, at Noali, Casa Vetere and Campo Sculdasio', and was considerably larger. Although the charter was drafted in Genoa, Liuzo the bishop's representative went to Lavagna and made the agreement in front of local witnesses and from the neighbouring Rapallo valley. Clergy representing the bishop are recorded elsewhere; for example in 969 Archdeacon Andrea represented Theodulf at the Milanese synod (Polonio 1999: 7).

Conclusion

By February 1007, when Bishop John II established the Benedictine community at San Siro, the church of San Lorenzo definitively became the only cathedral in Genoa (Filangieri 2006: 2), although as we saw earlier in this chapter that had probably always been the case. Its charters have not survived for this period, which probably makes San Siro seem more important than it really was at this time. At this point, the properties of the Genoese bishops were largely located east of the city and in the eastern coastal valleys, and this pattern continued in the following decades. Genoese episcopal influence in the western Riviera was much less perhaps as the result of those early tenth-century Arab attacks and the removal of Romolo's relics from Sanremo but also because of the strong local identity of its sees, especially Albenga. Genoese bishops never acquired comital powers as other North Italian bishops did which has given rise to the idea that Genoa was a more independent society dominated by its local, sea-faring aristocracy which came rapidly to prominence in the Mediterranean by the end of the eleventh century: but that takes us beyond the confines of this book. Instead if we return to the years around the first millennium we can voice frustration at being unable to conjure up what Genoa looked like as a town, despite the efforts of recent archaeologists. Charters and other written imply that although small it may have been quite cosmopolitan when compared with places further inland at this date. The charters foreground the activities of the bishop and his clergy, and reveal that several churches existed in Genoa by c. 1000: the cathedral of San Lorenzo, San Siro, Santo Stefano, San Giorgio and San Pietro alla Porta all supported by production from lands owned mostly to the East and Northeast of the town, some far away around Lavagna but still accessible by boat. Some of these churches – notably the monastic church of San Siro – were decorated with elaborate carved stonework which may have been imported from the Byzantine East and perhaps paid for by Empress Adelaide. But this rather rosy picture is qualified by the narrative sources which suggest that the tenth century in Genoa was a time of intense competition for political control between various groups of outsiders especially Ottonian and Arab rulers which probably caused as a side effect the development of greater local political consciousness. Even with St. Syrus' bones securely in their cathedral Bishop Theodulf and his successor John (984–1019) seem to have felt insecure; whether it was threats from Arabs, Ottonians or the local aristocracy; they may have had good reason for building their massive fortified tower house on the hill of Castello, the earliest Italian example of a bishop's house which has been archaeologically studied (Miller 2000: 66–8). At the same time – and presumably a process which helped to bring in the resources needed to build such a palace – they also extended the power of their church outside of Genoa by means of alliances based around the management of property, as evidenced by the charters. Because of this documentation local historiography has emphasized the importance of the bishop and development of a network of urban churches staffed by a growing number of clergy *de cardine* ('cardinals') who were closely linked to the cathedral and possibly even lived in common there (Polonio 1999: 6–7; Filangieri 2006). But prominent though Bishops Theodulf and John were almost nothing is known about their origins or beliefs and if their patronage of San Siro and San Tommaso suggests knowledge of up-to-the-minute Eastern artistic trends, their dealings with men and women in the countryside reveals them embedded in local politics and reliant on the interior for much of their wealth as the Genoese had so often been in the past. This subtle relationship between centre and periphery is explored from the 'peripheral' perspective in the final chapter about the Vara valley.

Notes

1 There is almost no archaeological evidence for synagogues in Western Europe before the thirteenth century in fact: Graham-Campbell and Valor 2007: 392. Ward-Perkins 1984: 244, for a synagogue converted into a Christian church (S. Paolo) in seventh-century Ravenna.

2 *Internet History Sourcebooks Project*: www.fordham.edu/halsall/basis/bede-book3. asp (accessed 25 June 2012), slightly modified.

3 On 30 July 972 Otto I confirmed Genoese property to Bobbio and a late copy of the text gives *ecclesiam Sancti Petri que est sita in civitate Ianue* (Cipolla 1918: 324, doc. XCV).

4 Picard 1988: 601 gives 'before mid-ninth century' for this *Vita S. Syri*. It is in a Bobbio manuscript, Vat. Lat. 5771 (*BHL* 7973 and *AASS* June 5) but not in any of the martyrologies and therefore is not a really old life.

5 Calleri 1999: 57–63, Appendix 1, lists all the tenth-century Genoese charters and describes their transmission histories. The principal edition is Belgrano 1862, improved upon by Basili and Pozza 1974, Calleri 1997 and 2009 for some documents.

6 Calleri reprints Belgrano's edition. The original is lost, and the entire charter is very fragmentary, and possibly suspect. There are hints in other documents of Ottonian connections with monastic communities at San Tommaso (Genoa) and San Fruttuoso di Capodimonte near Camogli. But these charters are also highly suspect.

7 The earliest surviving copy is twelfth-century in date.

6

Vara Valley

Inland valleys form a significant percentage of the land surface of Liguria, and yet their histories as valleys have often been neglected in favour of urban and coastal sites. Although several have already been discussed in this book (e.g. the Polcevera, Bisagno and Scrivia, above 40–5), in a short work it is not possible to examine the many other Ligurian valleys including those in the far west, so instead this chapter illustrates the 'valley history' approach to this period (see Wickham 1988) with a case study of the Val di Vara at the eastern border of the region (Figure 6.1). This valley is not typical of other valleys as each is different with its own unique early medieval histories: Petronio (Figone 1995), Polcevera (De Vingo and Frondoni 2003; Guglielmotti 2007b), Bisagno (Guglielmotti 2005: 28–35), Scrivia (Bianchi 1996) and Sturla among them. Nor did the Vara definitely have a valley identity in this period although the concept of a valley as a distinct place was expressed in some local documents: for example *in valle rapallo, in valle lavaniensis, in valle clavari* – respectively Rapallo, Lavagna and Chiavari – as recorded in 1031 (Calcagno 2004; Guglielmotti 2005: 30), and Lavagna was so recorded as early as 977 (Calleri 1997: 9–10). Phrases like this suggest that 'the valley' might have been a unit of political jurisdiction as early as the tenth century in this region, but Paola Guglielmotti in her study of territorial organization has rightly argued that it was not (2005: 30–1) as this politicization of valleys was a twelfth-century phenomenon. If we cannot know if people felt loyalty to 'their' valley as they often do now (see De Nevi 1988), it is likely that early medieval life experience in the Vara valley for the majority was close enough to that in other valleys especially adjacent ones with similar topography, microclimates, vegetation and so on, for it to be able to stand here as 'typical' of eastern Liguria.

For Antonio Cesena (b. 1507) writing the history of his birthplace Varese Ligure in the upper Vara valley, the Vara was indeed 'our valley' (Lagomarsini

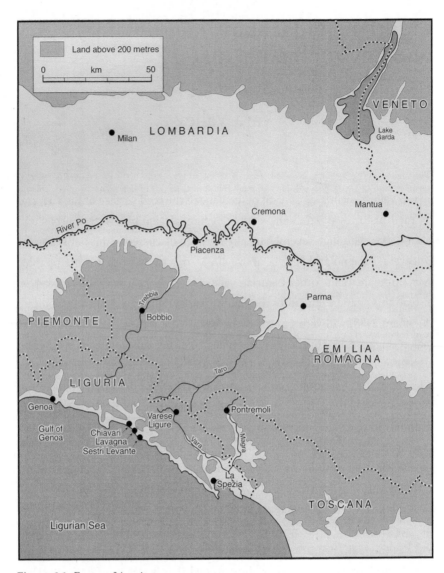

Figure 6.1 Eastern Liguria.
Source: Ross Balzaretti et al., *Ligurian Landscapes* (London, 2004), p. 2.

1993: 5) with a shared memory, all the more so once he had written it down in the mid-1550s (Balzaretti 2004). Now as then, this valley is the boundary between the modern regions of Liguria, Tuscany and Emilia-Romagna, and so routes, stopping places and passes were all important to its identity as an area of transit. In the medieval period the lower valley was within the 'Lunigiana', a cultural identity conceived as the hinterland of the Roman city of Luni (founded in 177 BCE) and later of its bishopric, although the precise origin of the term Lunigiana remains unclear (Delano Smith et al. 1986; Guglielmotti 2005, 2007a; Ricci 2002, 2007).

The Vara is a typical Apennine river flowing rapidly for most of its course in confined, steep-sided valleys with its source near Codivara ('head of the Vara') in the comune of Varese Ligure. It is prone to unpredictable and serious floods, often in October–November which can be highly destructive (as in 2011, and as recorded on several occasions in the sixteenth century by Cesena). Its lower reaches combine with the Magra which goes on to form a substantial flood plain below the hilltop town of Ameglia. The mercurial nature of the river means that there are few significant settlements on the valley floor, although the largest settlements – Varese Ligure in the upper valley (Figure 6.2) and Brugnato in the lower – are such sites which originated as later medieval planned foundations perhaps with earlier medieval antecedents (Guglielmotti 2005: 46, 59, 192–3). Most other settlement is on the mid-height slopes and spurs between 300–600 m asl, but how old these villages and hamlets are remains an intriguing question only now being answered by archaeology (see Francovich and Hodges 2003; Valenti 2000 on Poggio Imperiale at Poggibonsi). Increasingly, they seem to be mostly older than the towns of the valley floor. The over-riding vegetation of the valley – at least since the medieval period – has been beech woods at higher altitudes and chestnut woods at lower sites, which has given rise to much study of the Val di Vara's 'traditional chestnut culture' (Cevasco et al. 2010). But at some periods the hilly landscape was almost denuded of trees by intensive sheep-grazing especially at either end of the numerous transhumance routes once to be found in this area (Moreno and Raggio 1990: 201–2). As in the rest of the region therefore, the Vara valley's landscape could change dramatically as the result of human management or lack of it.

The Vara valley in our period arguably experienced a literally dark age as almost nothing has survived with which to illuminate its history then. Only a handful of significant archaeological excavations have taken place, notably at the hilltop village of Corvara (Beverino SP) and underneath Brugnato cathedral, both discussed below. Written documents from the period are even fewer, although there may possibly yet be examples waiting to be discovered in family archives.[1] This lacuna means that it is impossible to listen directly

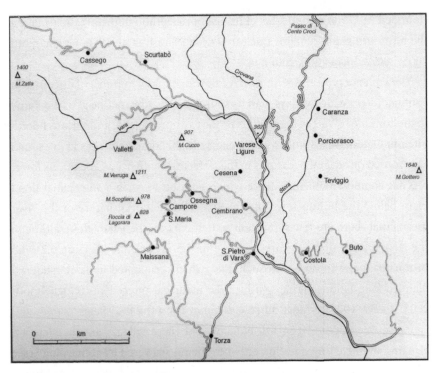

Figure 6.2 The Upper Vara Valley.
Source: Ross Balzaretti et al., *Ligurian Landscapes* (London, 2004), p. 4.

to the opinions of those who lived in the area and that outsiders' views alone
are available for the little that is known. Such indirect evidence for the early
medieval period is in fact typical of most places in most of Europe and
writing this valley's early medieval history is ironically an activity of some
methodological interest. The entire valley – as with most Ligurian valleys
excepting the Polcevera – has been marginalized in accounts of the Ligurian
past particularly the few in English. For example, when Frederic Lees visited
Varese Ligure just before the First World War he proved to be the first British
visitor to publish recollections of the place (Lees 1912: 294–8). For him Varese
was definitely 'off the beaten track', as the contemporary cliché had it (Balzaretti
2011: 455–7). Nor 80 years later did Stephen Epstein mention the valley's
relationship with Genoa, with the brief exception that in the early twelfth
century when the town of Brugnato in the lower Vara became a bishopric even
though an important Genoese document dating to 1031 firmly links the two
locations (Epstein 1996: 46). Italians have been hardly more interested and

have mostly reduced the history of this period to the history of Genoa (Pavoni 1992; Polonio 2007: 24–8; Airaldi 2010 is better). Even normally creative local historians come up with very little about this period (Tomaini 1961, 1978: 10; Gabrovec 2009: 352–61, 2011: 27–34).

Marginality has been perhaps the defining feature of Varese Ligure's entire history not just its dark-age past, and neglect by Ligurian historians is due in part to its perceived physical isolation for the Vara valley is at the very eastern extremity of Liguria bordering the Lunigiana (rather better studied; see Ricci 2002). Its liminal position near Emilia Romagna and Tuscany resulted in exposure to cultural influences rather different in character from those of Genoa and the western Riviera and so this valley provides an instructive study of a very different sort of Ligurian environment and history to theirs, just as the relationship between Lucca and the Garfagnana in Chris Wickham's *The Mountains and the City* (1988) revealed a different Tuscany to that of Florence and Pisa.

Valleys bordering the Vara are somewhat better evidenced than it is. For most of this area the interests of the monks of Bobbio – located in the Trebbia valley – provide the first significant early medieval evidence, although there has been much scholarly speculation in the absence of secure early documentation (e.g. Tosi 1992–3). A suggestive reference in Jonas's mid-seventh century 'Life of Athala' records that some monks left Bobbio after a dispute with the abbot and were exiled 'on the shores of the sea' (Book II. 1) but exactly where they went is impossible to tell, although the eastern Ligurian coast has been thought the most likely location (Tosi 1990: 434–5). The key document, however, is the grant which Charlemagne made from Pavia on 5 June 774 to the monastery of Bobbio (Collins 1998: 61–2 tentatively questions its authenticity). Having granted a wood and estate at 'Monte Longo' to Abbot Guinibaldus and his monks, the king went on to donate 'Alpe Adra' (*alpem aliquem qui vocatur Adra*), the bounds of which were described in some detail but the exact locations of which remain debatable. Unfortunately, this important text survives only in a late twelfth-century copy produced at Bobbio itself which might imply that it is interpolated precisely in respect of the boundary descriptions, as such later copies of royal grants often were.[2] There is in contrast no doubt that the monastery had possession of 'Alpe Adra' by 22 August 843, for then Charlemagne's grandson Lothar confirmed his grandfather's grant in a diploma which survives as an original single sheet. Interestingly this document reports that Adra was confirmed 'with its boundaries as inserted in the precept of our lord father of pious memory' which implies that Louis the Pious had confirmed this in a now-lost document. A further confirmation came from Louis II in 860 of 'the forest (*forestem*), called Adra with its bounds' and the use of the word 'forest' to describe Adra – rather than the earlier *alpis* – probably indicates that this property was in origin a royal hunting reserve, which could explain why knowledge of its precise boundaries was indeed important to record in writing (Wickham 1994: 155–61).

The consensus is that 'Alpe Adra' refers to a sizable block of hilly land immediately inland from Moneglia in the vicinity of the Passo del Bracco (615 m asl) (Destefanis 2002a: 66, 69–70) (Figure 6.3). Charlemagne's diploma has been seen as an important context for recent excavations at the site of the medieval hospital of San Nicolao di Pietra Colice (792 m asl near Castiglione Chiavarese, Val Petronio) by Fabrizio Benente (Benente et al. 2004: 39–41) as the current Petra Colice is the *petra Corice* recorded in the diploma. Benente equates the written record of two public roads here in 774 (if genuine) with information reported by Roman itineraries and represented graphically by the *Tabula Peutigeriana*, and has reconstructed the road system to suggest that one *via publica* linked Sestri Levante with Piacenza/Parma via Castiglione Chiavarese and the Cento Croci pass (1,055 m asl), while the other linked Casarza Ligure to the Bracco pass and the Lunigiana via San Nicolao (Destefanis 2002a: 70–7).[3] While this interpretation is possible in a general sense, archaeological confirmation of Charlemagne's text has proved elusive because excavations have not yet revealed any early medieval fabric or finds only twelfth-century and later ones. It seems premature to suppose that this was certainly the site of a *xenodochium* run by Bobbio monks therefore (Benente et al. 2004: 41). Indeed the archaeology of this hospital seems rather to support the idea that it was in the twelfth century that the detailed bounds of 'Alpe Adra' were added to the 774 diploma, as knowledge of its local topography would have increased with on-site familiarity.

However, the history of Bobbio's involvement with this area after Charlemagne's supposed grant rests on more reliable evidence, and *Alpe Adra* does indeed appear in one of the inventories for which this monastery is well-known to early medievalists. In the 'Inventory of land on the coast' (tenth- or eleventh century)

Figure 6.3 Elizabeth Fanshawe, Sketch of Sestri Levante from the Bracco Pass, 19 November 1829.
Source: In author's possession.

monastic property at *Adra* comprised one meadow (*pratum*), one estate (*curtis*), and fields, a reed bed and chestnut wood (*camporas et cannetum et castenetum*) in keeping with its upland character (Castagnetti et al. 1979: 190).[4] Curiously *Adra* had not been listed in any of the other older and more extensive inventories. During the ninth- and tenth centuries the Bobbio monks produced at least five inventories of their lands, in 833–5 (Cipolla 1918, vol. 1: 136–41; Laurent 2010: 479–85), 862 (Laurent 2010: 485–92), 883, and two undated but after 883 (Castagnetti et al. 1979: 121–92). Taken together these imply that the community acquired property at the eastern edge of Liguria and that its holdings were expanded and probably rationalized over a long time period. By the end of the tenth century, quite a lot of land had been granted out as benefices to locally powerful aristocrats including Otbert I as seen in the previous chapter (above 106). Destefanis provides a detailed discussion of the numerous sites which Bobbio may have controlled in the Ceno, Sturla and Taro valleys which connect with the Vara valley at the passes of Bocco (956 m asl) and Cento Croci (2002a: 71–3; Zironi 2004: 84). As ever, aspects of her argument depend on the identification of place-names for which several options are possible (sometimes in entirely different regions). Abbot Wala's *Breve* produced in 833–5 records land at Borgo Taro (*Turris*), Calice di Bedonia

(*Carice*), *Carelio* and *Comorga*. Marie-Aline Laurent has shown that in this text the property of most immediate use (*ad victum et vestimentum*) was that closest to Bobbio and was listed first (Laurent 2010: 482). The land in eastern Liguria was also regarded in this way by the monks. But unfortunately this earliest list does not go into any significant detail about what these properties produced or who the producers were. The 862 inventory is much more detailed in this respect and the eastern Ligurian properties are again prominent in it, in the section termed *De cellis exterioribus* as opposed to *Infra valle*, in Bobbio's own valley (the Trebbia). They are listed in the opposite order to Wala's text: *Comorga*, *Carelio*, *Carice* and *Turre*, identified by Castagnetti respectively as Comorga (San Colombano Certenoli), Caregli (Borzonasca), Calice (Bedonia) and Borgo Taro (Castagnetti 1979: 132–3, although these identifications are also by no means certain). In each case information is presented in standardized form: amounts of grain, wine, numbers of tenants and so on. Borgo Taro was clearly the most productive site of these four. Castiglione Chiavarese was listed immediately before Borgo Taro:

> In the cell of Castiglione, can be sown each year 8 *modia*, 9 *amphorae* of wine in a good year, one cart of hay, 40 *libras* of oil; there are 4 tenants, they return 4 and a half *amphorae* of wine in a good year, 41 *libras* of oil, and undertake 8 days of labour service (my translation).

This was a fairly modest set up and the same return was recorded in 883. The more interesting document is again the 'maritime inventory' and by this time (c. 1000) Castiglione is recorded as 'an estate with olives and 8 tenants' which may imply specialization in olives: even today Castiglione produces high-quality oil as the site in the Val Petronio benefits from a much warmer winter microclimate than the Vara valley a short distance away in the direction of Velva.[5] In 1998, while the parish church of Sant'Antonino Martire at Castiglione was undergoing restoration, striking (and otherwise unreported) evidence of possibly early medieval fabric was found: a well-made limestone window frame subsequently plastered over (Figure 6.4). That the style of this window could be contemporary in date with the 'maritime inventory' raises the possibility that by this time the monastery had invested in a church for those of its workers (and perhaps even some monks) living at Castiglione.

The final section of this text documents a far more extensive collection of properties than had been the case when Wala – Charlemagne's exiled cousin – was abbot, nearly two hundred years earlier. They are: Bargone

Figure 6.4 Castiglione Chiavarese, window uncovered in S. Antonino Martire in 1998.
Source: Photograph by Ross Balzaretti (1998).

(fraz. Casarza Ligure), *Bembelia, Pastano, Vausti, Florania, Francisca, Prato Monachorum, Plecleri, Adra*, Sestri Levante, *Iurnelli, Gropo*, Reppia (Nè), Lavagna (villa Floriano), *Borzone, Pontilaco, Cerelio, Campo Presbiteri, Fontana Sparsa, Campo Advenationi*, Temossi, *Alpe Tasida*, Sambuceto, *Saranta, Perlezzi, Ansaniano*, Carasco, *Treulatio, Durbula, Insula, Telamo*. Although most of these remain unidentified, some of the known places notably Sestri and Lavagna are interesting as it is possible to make connections with references to them in Genoese charters of exactly the same period (Guglielmotti 2005: 29).

At present the Vara valley has a very low population density and suffers from all the classic problems associated with drastic depopulation. In the past it was much more populous with a peak at the turn of the twentieth century.

Because of this for much of the last four hundred years at least the landscape was intensively managed for cultivation, and a substantial written record has survived for this period. A complex agri-silvo-pastoral economy developed which was based around the cultivation of chestnuts as staple food in combination with sheep farming which included annual transhumance. This form of land management may (or may not) have been similar to that of earlier periods in character if not in intensity. However, in comparison with the early modern period early medieval documents are even fewer here than for other parts of Liguria, and therefore the early political history of the region is very hard or more honestly impossible to grasp. Interestingly, medieval and early modern writers remarked on this lacuna too. For example, Antonio Cesena in the first history of Varese Ligure – certainly one of the valley's principal medieval settlements – noted that he found it very hard to find out about the town's early history for lack of written documents (Lagomarsini 1993: 43–4; Balzaretti 2004),[6] and indeed the only 'fact' he recorded about our period was the construction of what he called the 'Bridge of the Saracens' near San Pietro Vara (Lagomarsini 1993: 6). He initially wrote that 'They made the bridge known until our own days as the Bridge of the Saracens because it was made at the time when the Saracens were occupying Italy who destroyed it'. However, later he dismissed the local opinion of Saracen origins saying 'this I do not believe because I cannot see how the Saracens could ever have made a road here, since they were passing through not staying to build bridges' (Lagomarsini 1993: 44). He then explained that if they had built it, it would be very old as they were in Italy until Charles the Fat expelled them in the year 888.

Cesena's history was written in the context of the transfer of power locally from the Fieschi family to the Genoese republic after the former's famous failed rebellion of 1547. Unsurprisingly, given this political situation, roads and boundaries were one of Cesena's main concerns. Cesena recorded his notes about San Pietro's 'Saracen' bridge in an early section of his history which dealt with routes (Lagomarsini 1993: 5–6), which is a theme taken up by historians more recently who have defined Varese's history as one of 'transit' (Moreno and Raggio 1990; Raggio 1991), conditioned by regular seasonal exchange between the markets of the Po plain and those of the eastern Ligurian coast. This transitory character is, of course, typical of many mountain valley societies not just Ligurian ones: they are necessary stopping points on the way to more 'interesting' destinations. Much as Jonas of Bobbio had done when writing about Bobbio in the middle of the seventh century, Antonio Cesena conceptualized the early history of Varese and its valley as one of the gradual conquest of an initially 'wild' and unpopulated landscape. He explained how the first route into the area proceeded from Sestri Levante via Velva, Carro and Castello to Cavallanova, and then on to Buto and Caranza (Figure 6.5). Subsequently another route was made via *Castelnovo* (Castelnuovo di Salino) which then descended to San Pietro Vara on the valley floor and then climbed again via the Costa del Vegio through Teviggio to Caranza and then the Taro valley. It was in this context that the bridge over the Vara at San Pietro would have been made during the tenth century had Cesena's chronology been correct, as he himself admitted it was not. We have however no way of knowing at the moment if he was right that the bridge at San Pietro was very old, as no serious archaeological studies have been made of the old bridges of this valley. Even if his chronology is unclear, what he said about the local route ways remains interesting precisely because the earliest surviving early medieval document specifically relating to Varese also deals with routes.

The *Libellus omnium comitum de Lavania qui dicuntur filii Teodosii* was copied into the register of the archbishops of Genoa in 1147, where it is dated to March 1031 (Belgrano 1862: 290–4).[7] Although the main significance of this text is its political information about the origins of the county of Lavagna (Benente 2000; Calcagno 2004, 167–71; Guglielmotti 2005: 30; Ricci 2007), it also sheds light on more local patterns of settlement, ownership and ecclesiastical geography in the Vara valley. The *Libellus* lists properties in several valleys inland from Lavagna on the coast including parts of the Vara valley (Calcagno 2004: 171). In this period a *libellus* was usually an agreement recording conditional and temporally limited property rights in writing although it could simply mean 'a document'. The *Libellus* of 1031 is in essence a rent contract, an agreement between a local family – the ancestors of the counts of Lavagna, later the Fieschi whose demise Cesena chronicled – and the bishop of Genoa, to whom they paid a small sum of cash annually for rights over some of his land and its workforce in the area inland from Lavagna, including what became the parish of Varese Ligure (*plebs de Varia* in the text).[8] The agreement, between Bishop Landulf and Teodisius (now known as the 'First') and his legitimate sons, provides that if one of them dies without issue, the others will succeed to his portion. Its tone

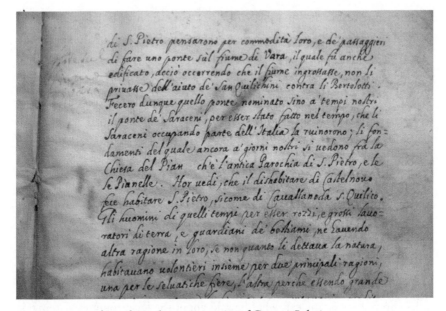

Figure 6.5 Page from the earliest manuscript of Cesena, *Relatio*.

Source: Photograph taken by Robert A. Hearn. The author is grateful to the Comune of Varese Ligure for allowing reproduction here.

suggests the existence of an earlier agreement between the Genoese bishop and Teodisius's father Ansaldo, which was being confirmed as well as extended by the new document. Teodisius and his sons took on responsibility for some of the bishop's named servile men, women and their children (*servis et ancillis cum filiis et filiabus suis*), who were at this point under the care of the church of S. Syrus (S. Siro in Genoa itself, which already had interests in this area as was seen in Chapter 5 above). These people were listed in family groups: Sempertus and his sons and daughters; Eldeprandus and Johannes, brothers with their other brothers, sisters, wives and children of both sexes; Andrea and his family; Johannes son of Lopertus with his wife and children; Andrea with his wife and children; Bernilda. Gotiza. Petrino, mother and father with their children; Johannes, Ermeza, Bruna, siblings with their children; Bernilda, daughter of Peter; Vincenzo and Alberto brothers and their children; Teuzo with his children; Aduxo, Mainucio, Mineza, Criza daughter of Altruda, siblings. These are the earliest recorded inhabitants of the Vara valley.

These people formed quite a large workforce, and at least some of them must have lived in the Val di Vara. Teodisio and his sons claimed the right to round these people up (*apprehendere*) and put them to work where they saw fit (*in servitio mittere ubi nobis opportunum fuerit*). This included rights to their newly acquired (or newly cultivated) land (*cum omni conquistu eorum*) and to the property which they currently worked for the church. Although these phrases could simply be standard forms of expression in Genoese documents of this period rather than literal statements of forced violence towards these people, it seems likely that there was little choice for them in the matter. Then another six such people are named who continued to work directly for the Genoese church. Following this, the church property over which Teodisio and his sons acquired these conditional and probably temporary rights was described in some detail. Although the exact identification of each place is not now possible, some can be identified. The order in which they are listed is also likely to be significant just as in the Bobbio inventories. Settlements were located within two types of jurisdiction – valleys (*valles*) and territories (*fines*) – and the meaning of this distinction has been much debated (see Guglielmotti 2005: 29–30). The properties are set out in Table 6.1.

Then the document which at this point becomes somewhat confused proceeds to spell out the boundaries of the properties described in a route which essentially goes from east to west in the vicinity of Varese Ligure, from Groppo Marzo on the road to Cento Croci up the Scagliana valley via Cassego to Communeglia and Codivara, as in Table 6.2.

Then a formula follows summarizing everything in general terms and stating that Teodisio's father Ansaldo held this before him which is succeeded by a generic formula describing land use: *id sunt casis, vineis, ficetis, olivetis, roboretis, aliisque arboribus fructiferis et infructiferis, silvis, campis et pascuis* . . . 'namely the houses, vineyards, fig-orchards, olive groves, oak woods and other fruiting and non-fruiting trees, woods, fields and pastures'. It is to be stressed that although this is a generic formula it is realistic in terms of the landscape of this area: everything mentioned can grow here and could have done in the time referred to by the document.

The detailed listing of the route around Varese was tested on the ground by a group of Nottingham students in March 2009.[9] Their attempt to trace it met with some success, as the listed properties essentially follow the Scagliana valley from its head to its confluence with the River Vara and the nature of the terrain in this area means that the reference to a *via publica* – a mule track in

Table 6.1 Properties listed in 1031 *libellus*

The valley behind Rapallo: *qui posite sunt in valle Rapallo, locus ubi dicitur culture vel in monte et in bocela*

In the territory of Sestri Levante: *que posite sunt in finite sigestrina*

Massasco, near Chiavari: *In mazasco vel in valle lauaniensis locus ubi dicitur zullici*

Unknown: *In levalli*

Unknown: *In carnella*

Unknown: *In cortine vel in buda*

Unknown: *Campo sabadino*

Unknown: *Roboreto cum rebus in monte presbitero . . .*

Maxena, near Chiavari: *res iuris ecclesie vestre sancti marcellini que posite est in valle clavari locus ubi dicitur macinola*

A chapel dedicated to Santa Giulia in 'Kalendo' with the tenths owing to it: *capella una que est edificata in honore sancta Julia et est constructa in loco Kalaolo . . . campo senasei, sorlana, saponico, Badalxi, Campolo, Ceredo, Besancia, Cruce, Claparia*

In another place under the jurisdiction of the plebs of *Varia* (Varese parish) the place known as *costa de castro, in casa martinasca* (Marchesano?), Scioverana, Cassego, Chinela, *casa terezanasca* (Trensenasca?), Zanega, *Kastro* . . . hamlets and tenanted houses (or farms): *In alio loco de sub regimine plebe de varia loco ubi dicitur costa de castro, in casa martinasca, Sivelana, Caxano, quellena, casa terezanasca, Zanica, Kastro . . . villis et massariciis,* with all the tithes owing

Unknown: *Silvis castanetis in loco statali que ad ipsa capella pertinent.*

Territory of Sestri: *res iuris ecclesie vestre sancti laurentii que posite sunt in finita sigestrina loco ubi dicit libriole* (Libiola?) *hoc est curticella cum capella . . .*

Table 6.2 Territory of Varese Ligure in 1031

From the rock called Nizalla: *da una parte fine roca que dicitur nizalla*

To Groppo Marzo: *da alio latere fine gropo marcio*

Descending by the stream which runs *de* gauselia: descendente *per rio qui currit*

Upon the mule track which goes from *lo capello* and Cassego: *desuper via publica que currit da lo copello et caxano*

Descending in the water of the Scagliana over the little ditch which descends from the *terricio in lignone* called *favarido*: *descendente per aqua de scablana de subtus fossadello qui descendit de terricio in lignone et ibi nominator favarido*

Unknown: *et in vineli*

Communeglia: *et in cumimelia*

Codivara: *et in caovario*

Other places: *vel per aliis ceteris locis*

---

this period and place – can only refer to a very limited number of options one of which is not far from Neofrandino and this was mapped by students on the ground. Although such work is of course speculative it does suggest that a degree of 'realistic decoding' is possible even with eleventh-century documents which describe features of a now partly altered landscape.

The fact that Varese is only documented as late as 1031 is surely a comment on the limitations of Genoese political power at this time, especially as the interests of the monastery of Bobbio are documented near here rather earlier. But it is also precisely what should be expected given the apparent lack of engagement by earlier generations with the area. There is little evidence that Romans settled in this part of the valley: recent attempts to map the Roman world) have portrayed this valley as a blank (Talbert 2000). Only the River Vara (*Boakias flumen*) is mentioned in authentic sources and even this identification is open to discussion (Petracco Sicardi and Caprini 1981: 39). It seems certain that no significant Roman road penetrated the interior, despite the views of local historians. The route of the *via Aemilia Scauri* is uncertain, with two possible routes between Luni and Sestri Levante, one via the Passo di Bracco (*in Alpe Pennina*) and the other via the Passo di Mola (*Bodetia*). Indeed in eastern Liguria the Romans seem to have stuck to the coast more than ever with documented sites at Genoa, Recco, Camogli, Portofino, Chiavari, Lavagna, Sestri, Moneglia and Anzo di Framura (although some of these identifications are speculative). Local historians have occasionally made more of this meagre evidence than seems justified (Bernabò 1988: 116–17).

Archaeological investigation of the Vara valley although still very patchy has tended to support Roman absence. There are several important prehistoric sites which are in or near the Vara valley, especially settlement at Zignago (and nearby Monte Dragnone and La Debbia) which has been studied since the 1960s (Maggi 1988). Also important are copper mines at Libiola, Gromolo valley near Sestri Levante (McCullagh and Pearce 2004; Maggi and Pearce 2005); Neolithic and Copper Age sites in Val Frascarese, not far from Castiglione Chiavarese (Figone 1995); and the jasper mines at Lagorara (Maggi et al. 1995). As seen above (19, 60), research has shown that the human activity of mining was of international significance in the Bronze Age at most of these sites but with the possible exception of Libiola there is surprisingly no evidence of Roman activity at these places. Similarly, Roman settlement remains almost completely unevidenced archaeologically although there have been some suggestive stray finds – mostly pottery and the odd coin – in the upper valley in recent years (Ribolla 1988: 106–7). In 2004 Oliver Varney, a University of Nottingham student, discovered a small Roman loom weight (210 × 240 mm) in situ in a terrace just south of the village of Porciorasco (Stora valley).[10] The set of terraces in which this find came to light might therefore have been in existence in the Roman period, although without further excavation this remains speculative especially in the light of written evidence of later agricultural use of this site (Figure 6.6). Nevertheless, this small object is certainly suggestive of Roman settlement as loom weights generally are although no conclusions can be reached about the yarn being woven from a single object (Mårtensson et al. 2009). Since 2004 another interesting local find has come to light, a small group of probably late Roman amphorae fragments discovered while ploughing a field in the nearby village of Scurtabò (Scagliana valley).[11] As this type of container was certainly not made locally but probably in North Africa this find provides some evidence of exchange in this area something which was previously unsuspected for this period (Figure 6.7). Both sites are in the comune of Varese Ligure and are at roughly the same height above sea level (Porciorasco, 559 m asl; Scurtabò, 661 m asl), a height which is similar to a number of other mid-slope sites discussed in previous chapters. Taking these two small finds together certainly suggests possible Roman period settlement in the upper part of the Vara valley and it is only a matter of time before more Roman material turns up.

A similar picture exists for the rest of the valley including those parts nearer the coast, as poorly contextualized Roman-period finds have been made at Pignone, Roverano, Genicciola, Valdonica and Ceparana, and it has been suggested that this material may evidence attempts to repopulate this part of the lower valley in the late imperial period. Elsewhere in this eastern region, there is evidence of possible Roman settlement at Statale di Ne, Porciletto di Mezzanego, Costa Bottuin di Trensasco, Monte Loreto, Rivarola, Costi (Valle Sturla) and some sites in Val Fontanabuona. These it has been suggested may indicate dispersed hamlets in the interior which further modifies the established notion that Romans were only interested in the Ligurian coast (Benente 2000: 63–4).

However, although it may be that some mass-produced products did indeed reach far beyond the coast, as sub-Roman and post-Roman archaeology is

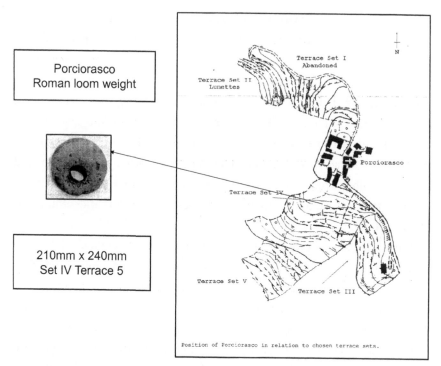

Figure 6.6 Porciorasco, Roman loom weight.
Source: Oliver Varney (2004).

Figure 6.7 Scurtabò, late antique pottery.
Source: Photograph by Ross Balzaretti.

equally deficient across the Vara valley it is hard to set these finds in any proper context. The most interesting site might potentially be the current castle at Varese where, in the reports of the excavations and restoration carried out in the 1960s suggestions were made that traces of an earlier, possibly Byzantine period fortification were found (De Negri and Mazzino 1964; Tomaini 1978: 24). Local historians are inclined to connect this with the nearby Monte dei

Greci ('Mountain of the Greeks') to come up with a very far flung outpost of the Byzantine defensive system of the early seventh century.[12] While this is not impossible the evidence presented is certainly slight as the 1960s excavations were poorly documented. Better evidence of Byzantine period defences can certainly be found lower down the valley at Sassetta di Zignago (Bernabò and De Nevi 1988: 150) and at Filattiera (above 54). Other possible evidence for Byzantine interest in this area can be found in the Ravenna *Cosmographia* which noticed road stations at *Cornelium* (possibly Corniglia or Zignago) and *Cebula* (possibly Montale di Levanto) (Bernabò 1988: 119; Pavoni 1990–1: 50), although the authoritative *Barrington Atlas* does not accept these identifications (Talbert 2000).

The lower Vara valley is for the most part rather better evidenced than the area around Varese. Material remains from several important church sites have survived, including San Venanzio di Ceparana near the confluence of the Vara and the Magra rivers (Vecchi 2004) and nearby San Caprasio di Aulla, a few kilometres to the northeast in the Lunigiana (Arslan et al. 2007; Giannichedda et al. 2003, 2011). The origins of San Venanzio are unclear with some scholars suggesting Byzantine or even earlier Roman origins as Ceparana has been seen by some as the site of the Roman *Boakias* (Bernabò 1988: 117; Vecchi 2004: 121), although again the *Barrington Atlas* prefers nearby Vezzano (Talbert 2000: 598), which became a focus for local power in the early twelfth century for the 'signori di Vezzano' vassals of the Obertenghi whose influence at that time extended to Portovenere southwards and even as far as Sestri Levante westwards (Nobili 1993; Guglielmotti 2005: 45–6). Suggestions that San Venanzio may have been used as an elite burial ground in the sixth century seem equally hard to substantiate and the surviving early medieval sculptured stone fragments seem best interpreted as evidence of later re-use of materials from Luni itself especially given the close relationship later between the Luni bishops and the lords of Vezzano (Vecchi 2004: 130–54).

San Caprasio is better documented, probably being founded in 884 by Adalbert I of Tuscany.[13] It also has more recent archaeology to back up this claim. The current apse was examined in 2000 and radio-carbon dates obtained from charcoal fragments found in the mortar yielded a date of 800–1010 CE (Giannichedda et al. 2003: 99), broadly in line with the documentary story of the monastery's foundation. The excavators estimated that the apse walls to some 2 m in height were of this period. Excavations near the apse resulted in a C14 date of 770–980 CE for a fragment of human bone. This site, therefore, was active at the end of the ninth/early tenth century, demonstrating further that territorial re-organization which included the building of new churches was being successfully undertaken in this part of the Lunigiana by local aristocrats at this time. [1]

The most instructive comparison to San Venanzio and San Caprasio is Brugnato the most significant settlement of the lower Vara and the site of a bishopric since 1133 (Tomaini 1961; Pavoni 1990–1; Ribolla 1988: 106–8; De Nevi 1988: 207–13). Like Varese Ligure it is known today for its planned late medieval *borgo* but in comparison there is much clearer evidence of its earlier medieval history at least as far as its ecclesiastical geography is concerned. The principal site is the current cathedral dedicated to Saints Peter, Lawrence and Columbanus. According to local tradition – and repeated in many scholarly works – a monastery existed here throughout the early medieval period which was connected with the community at Bobbio (Tomaini 1961: 31–3). For some, Brugnato was even a 'Columbanian' foundation perhaps sponsored by the Lombard king Liutprand. In fact there is little authentic written documentation to support any link with Bobbio before the late ninth century by which time Columbanus and his type of monastic practice was of course a distant memory (Pavoni 1990–1: 48–9): when written documentation begins in the 880s with two royal diplomas dated 881 and 882, neither mentions Columbanus.

A charter issued by Charles the Fat in favour of the abbey (2 April 881) records that the community was ruled then by Abbot Erimbert and dedicated to St Peter (Kehr 1937: 57–8). It confirms the earlier actions of Charlemagne, Louis the Pious, Lothar and Louis II, particularly a grant of an estate and wood at *Accola* (most probably Accola near Borghetto Vara) but given that this text has survived only in a very much later copy it would be unwise – as in the example of *Alpe Adra* already examined – to place too much credence on the interesting and detailed boundary description of the *silva* given here (see Pavoni 1990–1: 48–50). Two charters dated 882 (Kehr 1937: 88–90) and 996 (Sickel 1893: 609–11), both claim that the monastery at Brugnato was directly dependent on the papacy, rather than on the nearest bishopric at Luni, but as neither of these texts is entirely reliable in details it is hard to be sure about this. Indeed as they are much later copies there is every chance of interpolation on this important point.

Archaeologically speaking the current cathedral at Brugnato is the best-evidenced early medieval site in the Vara valley as two campaigns of substantial twentieth-century excavations underneath the existing structure have revealed a complex sequence which probably has Roman origins, although exact dating evidence for the earliest phases has proven hard to come by.[14] The current building was begun in the eleventh century and expanded with the twelfth-century foundation of the small adjacent *borgo* and the designation of the place as a bishopric by Innocent II in 1133. Excavations carried out between 1994 and 1998 have revealed some Roman walling, a Byzantine period cemetery and two earlier church buildings (Frondoni et al. 2002: 326–7). It may be that the church began as a small Roman house church (Marcenaro and Frondoni 2006: 33–6; Del Lucchese and Gambaro 2008: 333–5). The double apse arrangement which currently exists can be traced back probably to the eighth or ninth centuries, when a new structure possibly built to house relics came into being. Around the year 1000 this was enlarged again and a circular baptismal font was added. Physical comparisons with early church sites lower down the valley suggest that the Brugnato church was more likely to have been constructed by the bishops of Luni rather than the monks of Bobbio; a similar archaeological sequence has been posited for the cathedral site at Luni and there are parallels with other significant church sites at Migliarina and Vezzano, and on the islands of Tino and Tinetto off La Spezia. Luni, Migliarina and Vezzano all appear to have significant mid-eighth-century phrases of construction (Marcenaro and Frondoni 2006: 23–7). At Vezzano, for example, a church was in use between the seventh and eleventh centuries and tombs have been excavated exterior to the church (Frondoni et al. 2002: 325–6). The graves were fairly simple, dug in bare earth with few frills. Similar style burials of similar date range have been confirmed from Brugnato, Luni and Carpignano (Frondoni et al. 2002: 326–7). The earlier excavations at Tino did not adopt a proper stratigraphic methodology, and so continue to be very difficult to interpret today.

The most interesting recent excavation in the lower Vara valley has been at Corvara (Beverino SP), in the hinterland of La Spezia. When the old village centre – at 320–340 m asl – was being demolished in 2004 a rescue dig yielded very important information about the late tenth/early eleventh-century phases of the site (Cagnana and Gavagnin 2004: 193–5; Cagnana et al. 2008), which demonstrates that occupation can be dated back directly – and continuously – to this period. This fact has potentially important implications for what we think about hillside village settlement in Liguria as a whole because the early eleventh-century date was by radiocarbon and thermo-luminescence and so beyond question. The finds in the eleventh-century phase all pointed to a mixed economy, largely self-sufficient, based on the chestnut. Charcoal evidence revealed the dominance of *Castanea sativa* with only a few other species including the legumes *Vicia sativa* L. and *Lathyrus sativus* L. (Camangi et al. 2009: 182), both used mostly as fodder crops for animals but also edible by humans in hard times. Alongside this were finds of two grinding stones – used to produce chestnut flour – made from sandstone from Monte Gottero some 20 km or so northeast of Corvara. 81.5 per cent of the significant amount of pottery recovered was the remains of *testi*, the typical cooking utensil of this region until the 1950s used to produce bread from chestnut flour (Mannoni 1965). It was possible to trace the clay they were made from to within a radius of 10 km or so, indicating that the pots were of local and probably domestic production, and similar pots have been found near the cathedral at Luni but dated earlier to the seventh and eighth centuries (Cagnana and Gavagnin 2004: 194; Cagnana et al. 2008: 128). There was no imported pottery not even the *vacuolare* type found elsewhere in this valley (Giannichedda and Quiros Castillo 1997). Animal bones from rubbish tips revealed that only domestic (not wild) species were being consumed then: pigs (30% of the samples), sheep (30%) and cattle (40%) (Cagnana et al. 2008: 131). Pigs were likely being slaughtered at less than 18 months old in situ, whereas the cattle were not killed here and probably therefore imported as joints from elsewhere. Sheep cannot survive in woodland as goats can which suggests that – at least in the immediate vicinity of the village – there were sites maintained by and for grazing. How this village site may or may not have interacted with neighbouring sites is not absolutely clear but the excavators made the sensible – and important – point that it was nucleated (Cagnana et al. 2008: 138, 144–6). Aurora Cagnana using *diplomata* of Otto I (19 May 963) and Otto II (18 July 981) in favour of the bishops of Luni argued that Corvara might have been part of a network of nucleated hilltop estate-centres and some fortified sites at Vezzano and Ceparana owned by the bishops of Luni (Cagnana et al. 2008: 138–9, 151).

Conclusion

The Corvara excavation opens up in a really concrete way the possibility that many of the existing hilltop villages of the Vara valley could have their origins at least as far back as the year 1000. We simply need more excavations underneath them to find out. Even so surviving documents suggest as we have seen that in the years either side of the year 1000 both the monks of Bobbio and the bishops of Genoa developed property interests in this region, which helped to form a local aristocracy who rented property from these churches, sometimes for very long periods of time (or even indefinitely). It is likely that other 'outsiders' – such as the bishops of Luni – had earlier been influential here, as the occasional surviving artefact suggests. An interesting case is a re-claimed stone of possibly Byzantine date and style once used as a small door lintel in the village of Porciorasco (Gabrovec 2011: 31).[15] It represents a human and a solar image and is of similar style to objects found at Lucca (Frondoni 1987: 52; Bernabò and De Nevi 1988: 258). It probably came from Tuscany therefore but when is impossible to determine (Figure 6.8). There are other door lintels in Porciorasco with representations of solar phenomena which might possibly be of early medieval production, once again re-cycled as lintels in early modern tenant houses. At nearby Buto – also once part of the diocese of Luni – there are a few fragments of decorated relief re-used in the tower of the parish church which might be of earlier medieval date; but once again precisely where they came from and when is now impossible to say. In this case they most probably came from the demolished church of Cavallanova, recalled by Antonio Cesena in the 1550s as the oldest church in the valley (Lagomarsini 1993: 5, 43).

Such occasional survivals point up just how 'dark' the early medieval period can be in this part of Liguria. In this chapter it has proved impossible to reconstruct any sustained narrative at all until the first surviving written document of 1031. Antonio Cesena was therefore accurate in his assessment that almost all early written documents had perished by his own time. We have to rely on his version of history if we want a narrative history of the early medieval past of his valley, although just enough non-written evidence has survived to show that the Vara valley was not in fact as cut off as Cesena believed and outsiders of many sorts were interested in it pretty much throughout the period. These seemingly

Figure 6.8 Porciorasco, Byzantine carved stone.
Source: Drawing by Ross Balzaretti.

remote hilltop villages may in fact have been created at the end of the first-millennium CE as a result of the competitive behaviour of outsiders including the bishops of Luni and Genoa, the monks of Bobbio and leading local families who interacted with these ecclesiastics, behaviour which demanded more things from more organized, more productive, nucleated sites. This was a moment of fluidity in the history of local territorial organization (Guglielmotti 2005: 29) and perhaps an important turning point in the longer history of the formation of the current landscape. Having surveyed the tantalizingly limited evidence for the early medieval Vara valley we can conclude that more archaeological research – which is badly needed – seems sure to confirm the slowly developing image that this valley while 'dark' in terms of our current knowledge turns out not to have been marginal to history after all.

Notes

1 A parchment fragment of an unidentified theological text written in a practiced late Carolingian minuscule was found in 1982 in the archive of the De Paoli family at Porciorasco, but it has subsequently been mislaid. It may well be part of an early medieval book but when and how it found its way into the possession of the De Paoli is unclear, except to say that there was a medieval church in this village to which it might earlier have belonged.

2 Michael Richter curiously suggested that these boundary phrases must be genuine because 'they are similar to those found in earlier Lombard documents' when those documents survive only as later copies as well (2008: 98). The fact that crosses to mark boundaries are also mentioned by this text – but not in Charlemagne's other Italian *diplomata* – also suggests later interpolation at Bobbio where that custom was normal. See further Balzaretti 2010.

3 The latter road is today signposted on the ground as a path called the 'antica strada del Bracco'.

4 *Cannetum* probably refers to the Giant Cane, *Arundo donax L.* (*cana* in Ligurian dialect) which will tolerate a wide variety of conditions and now grows widely in Liguria (Camangi, Stefani and Sebastiani 2009: 91). As this plant tends to grow at lower altitudes this reference to a reed bed may say something useful about what the Adra estate was like.

5 The principal producer is Azienda Agricola Pino Gino in Missano: they also produce considerable quantities of wine, notably *moscato*. I am very grateful to Maria Antonella Pino for her help on successive field visits.

6 'Up to this point I have, by my own great effort and research, spoken of things very obscure because of their great age . . . because in those old times these places were inhabited in large part by rough shepherds, completely ignorant of letters, who relied solely on their memory of past events; and if there were any feeble [written] memories, these were for the most part consumed by fire and by the bad government which there was during the horrible plague of 1528'. In fact some medieval documents have survived in central archives, especially Genoa, and a few early sixteenth-century property deeds still exist in the parish archive of Varese itself.

7 I have relied on Belgrano's edition here having been unable to see the original on which it is based. This edition has been criticized (e.g. by Calleri 1999) and does not meet modern critical standards. Belgrano's text suggests that the twelfth-century copyist had trouble understanding his model and that numerous spelling errors crept in.

8 This is one of the earliest references to a parish (*plebs*) in this part of Liguria, where the territorial history of parish formation remains obscure: Guglielmotti 2005: 28. The parish of Varese (*de Varia*) is described in similar terms in the mid-twelfth century (Belgrano 1862: 18).

9 Katherine Dunn, Amy Kessler, Philip Leonard and Leonie Watson.

10 Oliver Varney, 'From Romans to Ruminants: the story of five sets of terraces in the Val di Vara' (2004, unpublished undergraduate project, University of Nottingham).

11 I am very grateful to Andreina Giosso (Agriturismo Il Boschetto, Scurtabò) for showing me these exciting finds which she and her husband discovered.

12 Nearby Monte Gottero has also been the subject of speculation about its name, seemingly related to 'Goth' as are Sesta Godano and the River Gotra: Petracco Sicardi and Caprini 1981: 88.

13 The document recording this survives only in a late copy: Giannichedda et al. 2003: 97, 120.

14 Excavations were carried out in the 1950s and 1990s with rather different results. Here I have followed the most recent excavators' opinions, and taken account of a further set of excavations in 2004 (Del Lucchese and Gambaro 2008: 333). As far as I am aware no other early medieval sites have yet been found within the medieval *borgo* of Brugnato, despite recent excavations there (Del Lucchese and Gambaro 2008: 335–6).

15 The stone has now been removed by the owners. It was above the door of a seventeenth-century house, lived in until c. 1990 by the late Sig. Santino Gotelli, the last surviving *mezzadro* of the De Paoli/Gotelli family, who showed me the stone in 1998 shortly before he died.

7

People without History

Dark Age Liguria is, as suggested in Chapter 1, a rather unfashionable way of describing the region's history during the first millennium. It should now be clear that it is intended to reflect the problematic character of the surviving evidence rather than a belief that this region and its people were especially uncivilized or even barbaric. It has proved hard to get much sense of what those who lived in Dark Age Liguria believed about themselves and the world around them because they left so little reflective writing behind them. Even the activities of rulers are little understood most of the time in this context. A history based largely on the surviving written documentation is therefore not really worth writing without the balancing and challenging perspectives offered by archaeology, historical ecology and cognate studies. By adopting a holistic approach to evidence and a healthy dose of imagination, the lives of 'people without history' can be reclaimed from the condescension of those kings and bishops who very occasionally deigned to express an interest in them and in the fruits of their labour if only to fix their obligations and those of future generations in writing. Although most Dark Age Ligurians lived humbly at many of the sites described in this book, they were not barbarians and their lives are as worthy of attention as the next person's.

A belief that everyone should matter to historians, not just those who documented their own existence underpins the decision to begin my Ligurian history with an ecological approach. We can, using complex scientific analyses of pollen remains, fragments of charcoal and excavated animal bones, imagine what 'possible lives' were like and observe that peasant farmers had agency as they managed and worked their landscapes in dynamic ways which complicate the static impressions conjured up by the phrase 'traditional peasant culture' so often employed by anthropologists when observing mountain societies. Importantly, careful site-specific documentation of activation practices such as clearance using fire, high altitude seasonal pasturing and shredding of trees can pinpoint moments of significant historical change as well as explain fairly static cultural habits. One of these turning points occurred in the cold period c. 400–800 CE when open high summer pastures (*alpes*) were deliberately created from existing woodlands using tools specially designed for the purpose. There is no need however to attribute this action to some distant political force such as Charlemagne or the abbot of Bobbio who benefited from his grant of *Alpe Adra* in 774, for local people were entirely capable of adapting plant cover to their needs without outside interference or inspiration: kings and monks themselves were probably responding to an existing situation. Less precisely evidenced but equally vital practices, especially the creation and maintenance, by almost herculean human effort of the terraces so necessary to life in such mountainous terrain must have taken place at some sites around the year 1000 if only because the verb *pastenere* recorded in charters which deal with chestnuts or other fruiting trees implies terracing as part of the 'domestication' of specific productive landscapes. The forms of management implied by written *pastenere* contracts and grants of rights to *alpes* marked a significant change from ancient Roman habits in the region, which were fixated on the sea and the vast inter-connected economy which it represented.

Dark Age people could live quite contentedly, it would seem, in places which now seem hostile to us and in conditions which can seem 'poor'. The history of their settlements can also uncover moments of significant change and in Liguria settlement change ties in closely with the ecological evidence. Lowland nucleation throughout the region was essentially a Roman custom which interrupted a much longer established pattern of more dispersed living on slopes and hilltops for which local production and local or regional exchanges were more important than Mediterranean-wide trade. 'Roman culture' as represented in the very partial surviving evidence was elite culture and wealthy Romans deliberately built their coastal villas where aesthetic pleasures and economic functions could exist together. The physical markers of Roman civilization – roads, villas, military camps, planned towns, apartment blocks, ceremonial buildings, monumental tombs and the like – are relatively few in Liguria because Romans probably had only a superficial impact here. When they eventually left as late as the mid-seventh century, the consequences for local society perhaps were not as great as in other parts of that vast empire. We cannot be certain about this as few archaeologists in Liguria have deliberately set out to find those ordinary Romans who were in the majority. Roman people 'without history' must have lived in places like Porciletto, Gronda, Savignone or Costa Bottuin while the old Empire began to wind down and the fact that their material lives look very like 'early medieval' lives surely renders arguments about Roman cultural 'superiority' largely redundant. Excavation has thoroughly undermined the established view that Roman coastal settlements were simply re-located to nearby hilltops when the Byzantine soldiers departed when the effort of staying seemed no longer worth the cost of it. At Noli, life continued much as before until the eighth century despite the certain collapse of Mediterranean trade because that trade was not necessary for daily existence and arguably had never been for the majority.

Inability to take part in Roman elite culture does not mean that these people can be dismissed as barbarians. If they ate more chestnuts and more animal fat than wheat and olive oil this was not necessarily second best, especially given what we now know about the increasingly cold and wet weather experienced in this period. It was simply practical. Fossilized pollen, pottery 'testi' and the *pastenere* contracts all tell the same story: that a new inland economy had finally replaced the Ancient sea-centred system. This change may have represented, as I have suggested, a reversion to earlier forms of life. Micro-ecological changes (documented by science) may have been easily as important to most people most of the time as political realignments (documented by contemporary written sources). Throughout our period they lived on hills when it was sensible to do so but they did not live on the valley floors until the twelfth century perhaps because then another dry period and the temptations of overseas expansion made living near rivers and coasts both viable and desirable once again.

The people with history – the kings, bishops and monks of our written records – were not of course without importance. Local disengagement from the Byzantine Empire seems to have created a vacuum that went unfilled by Lombards, Carolingians or any of their successors however powerful elsewhere. Instead the Genoese – at least according to the documents they themselves preserved – developed a sense of independence which lasted throughout the medieval period and beyond. This seems to have been a piecemeal process which should not be understood with the benefit of hindsight. Around the year 400 Liguria – even Genoa itself – must have seemed a backwater when viewed from Rome or from Constantinople. Once the reference point of Rome was gone some Genoese constructed a more subtle regional identity which increasingly looked inland and north rather than south and out to sea. Genoa had been within the hinterland of Milan, a very much larger city, from at least the time when it was capital of the Roman Empire (286–402 CE). Genoese churches had Milanese dedications and some elsewhere – most obviously at Albenga – shamelessly borrowed Milanese architecture and ornament. The Gothic wars did little to rupture this relationship, and it was no doubt a sense of deep familiarity which helped to persuade Archbishop Honoratus that Genoa was the best place at which to escape the incoming Lombards in 568. The Lombard 'conquest' of the Byzantine littoral may have helped to create the territorial form taken by Liguria today, even if archaeological evidence now means that we cannot literally believe that Rothari was as successful in this region as Fredegar and others thought at the time. But the fact that seventh-century writers put Genoa rather than Albenga or Savona or Luni at the centre of their narratives surely reflected the real political dominance that this town had already achieved.

The transformation of Genoa from a place which barely registered with well-documented Lombard and Carolingian elites to a town at the centre of a Mediterranean-wide explicitly Christian empire intolerant of other religions was probably a twelfth-century phenomenon. Then the Genoese church collected its old charters and hagiographical narratives into a series of registers and a 'Book of Privileges' which helped to provide the sense of pride in its history which had not apparently been explicit before. These self-representations narrated how successive Genoese bishops had sought to protect their people from Saracen aggression by installing the bones of Saint Romulus in their cathedral of San Lorenzo and arranged hundreds of charters to show how successfully the church's properties had been managed. But at Genoa the bishops' power only extended so far. They did not become counts or acquire comital rights despite having the wherewithal to construct a massive fortress on the ancient hill of Castello which physically must have dominated the town's skyline seen from the sea. Nor did the local aristocracy prevail despite references to a Viscount Ydo in 951 and to a group of citizens who negotiated their privileges from Kings Berengar and Adalbert in 958. Instead local identities firmly rooted in the control of coherent micro-territories began to emerge and some families – such as the tenth-century Counts of Lavagna – started to take political control in ways which would eventually develop into private fiefdoms which challenged Genoese expansionism. If, by the year 1020, Genoa stood on the brink of a new history to be framed with reference to perceived threats of rising Muslim power and the rival economies of Pisa and Venice, local sources remained in the 'dark', largely uninterested in the wider picture for at least another century until the crusader Caffaro wrote his famous annals into the earliest surviving paper book in Europe.

Bibliography

Abbreviations

AM:	*Archeologia medievale*
APM:	*Archeologia postmedievale*
ASLSP:	*Atti della Società Ligure di Storia Patria*
BAR INT:	British Archaeological Reports, International Series
EHR:	*English Historical Review*
EME:	*Early Medieval Europe*
HL:	Paul the Deacon, *History of the Lombards* (see Foulke 1904)
MEFR:	*Mélanges de l'École Française de Rome*
MGH:	*Monumenta Germaniae Historica*
NMS:	*Nottingham Medieval Studies*
PBSR:	*Papers of the British School at Rome*
QS:	*Quaderni storici*
Reg.:	Gregory the Great, *Registrum* (see Martyn 2004)
RMR:	*Reti Medievali Rivista*
RSL:	*Rivista di Studi Liguri*
SM:	*Studi Medievali*
Var.:	Cassiodorus, *Variae* (see Barnish 1992)

References

AA.VV. 1987. *La scultura a Genova e in Liguria dalle origini al Cinquecento* (Genoa: Fratelli Pagano).

Abulafia, David (ed.). 2003. *The Mediterranean in History* (London: Thames and Hudson).

Airaldi, Gabriella. 2010. *Storia della Liguria. Dalle origini al 1492* (Genoa: Marietti).

Alfonso, Isabel (ed.). 2007. *The Rural History of Medieval European Societies. Trends and Perspectives* (Turnhout: Brepols).

Amari, Michele. 1873. 'Nuovi ricordi arabici sulla storia di Genova', *ASLSP*, 5, fasc. 2: 632–3.

Andrews, Alfred C. 1941. 'Alimentary Use of Lovage in the Classical Period', *Isis*, 33: 514–18.

Andrews, David and Pringle, David. 1978. 'Excavations in Medieval Genoa 1971–76. The Palace and Convent of S. Silvestro', in Blake et al. 1978: 334–72.

Agnoletti, Mauro and Anderson, Steven. 2000. *Methods and Approaches in Forest History* (Wallingford: CAB International).

Armiero, Marco and Hall, Marcus (eds). 2010. *Nature and History in Modern Italy* (Athens: Ohio University Press).

Arobba, Daniele, Caramiello, Rossana and Del Lucchese, Angiolo. 2003. 'Archaeobotanical Investigations in Liguria: Preliminary Data on the Early Iron Age at Monte Trabocchetto (Pietra Ligure, Italy)', *Vegetation History and Archaeobotany*, 12: 253–62.

Arobba, Daniele, Caramiello, Rossana and Martino, Gian Piero P. 2007. 'Indagine paleobotanica su sedimenti di età altomedievale da livelli profondi dell'arenile di Pietra Ligure (Savona)', *Ligures*, 5: 88–95.

Arslan, Ermanno A. 2005. *Repertorio dei ritrovamenti di moneta Altomedievale in Italia (489–1002)* (Spoleto), at: www.ermannoarslan.eu/index.php

—. 2007. 'Il gruzzolo di monete d'oro', in Frondoni 2007: 52–6.

Arslan, Ermanno A., Tiziano Mannoni, Enrico Giannichedda, Rita Lanza, Fulvio Bartoli, Riccardo Boggi. et al. (eds). 2007. *Gli scavi di San Caprasio ad Aulla* (Florence: All'Insegna del Giglio).

Arthur, Paul. 2004. 'From Vicus to Village: Italian Landscapes, AD 400–1000', in Christie 2004: 103–34.

Assereto, Giovanni and Doria, Marco. 2007. *Storia della Liguria* (Bari: Laterza).

Ausenda, Giorgio, Delogu, Paolo and Wickham, Chris (eds). 2009. *The Langobards before the Frankish Conquest* (Woodbridge: Boydell and Brewer).

Azzara, Claudio and Gasparri, Stefano (ed. and tr.). 1992. *Le leggi dei Longobardi. Storia, memoria e diritto di un popolo germanico* (Milan: Ed. La Storia).

Azzara, Claudio and Moro, Pierandrea (ed. and tr.). 1998. *I capitolari italici. Storia e diritto della dominazione carolingia in Italia* (Rome: Viella).

Baker, Polydora. 1994. 'A Preliminary Assessment of the Role of Hunting in Early Medieval Subsistence in the Alpine, Preapline and Lowland Areas of Northern Italy on the Basis of Zoo-archaeological Data', in Biagi and Nandris 1994: 307–16.

Baker, Polydora and Clarke, Gillian. 1993. 'Archaeozoological Evidence for Medieval Italy: A Critical Review of the Present State of Research', *AM*, 20: 45–77.

Bakirtzis, Nikolas. 2010. 'The Practice, Perception and Experience of Byzantine Fortification', in Stephenson 2010: 352–71.

Balbis, Giovanni. 1979. 'La Liguria bizantina: una presenza del passato', *Nuova Rivista Storica*, 63: 149–86.

Balletto, Laura (ed.). 1997. *Oriente e Occidente tra Medioevo ed Età Moderna. Studi in onore di Geo Pistarino* (Genoa: G. Brigati).

Balzaretti, Ross. 2004. 'The History of the Countryside in sixteenth-century Varese Ligure', in Balzaretti, Pearce and Watkins 2004: 123–38.

—. 2009. 'Review of Roberta Cevasco, Memoria Verde', *Environment and History*, 15.2: 257–9.

—. 2010. 'Review of Michael Richter, Bobbio in the Early Middle Ages', *Catholic Historical Review*, 96: 98–100.

—. 2011. 'Victorian Travellers, Apennine Landscapes and the Development of Cultural Heritage in Eastern Liguria, c. 1875–1914', *History*, 96: 1–23.

Balzaretti, Ross, Pearce, Mark J. and Watkins, Charles (eds). 2004. *Ligurian Landscapes* (London: Accordia Research Institute).

Banti, Ottavio. 2009. 'L'epitafio di "Leodegar" di Filattiera (a. 752)', *SM*, 50.2: 815–32.

Barker, Graham and Lloyd, John (eds). 1991. *Roman Landscapes: Archaeological Survey in the Mediterranean Region* (London: British School at Rome).

Barnish, Samuel (tr.). 1992. *The Variae of Magnus Aurelius Cassiodorus* (Liverpool: Liverpool University Press).

Basili, Aurelia and Pozza, Luciana (eds). (1974). *Le carte del Monastero di San Siro di Genova dal 952 al 1224* (Genoa: Società Ligure di Storia Patria).

Behringer, Wolfgang. 2010. *A Cultural History of Climate* (Cambridge: Polity Press).

Belgrano, Tommaso (ed.). 1862. 'Il registro della curia arcivescovile di Genova', *ASLSP*, 2, part 2.

—. 1887. 'Il secondo registro della curia arcivescovile di Genova', *ASLSP*, 18.

Bellatella, Emiliano, Bertino, Antonio and Gardini, Alexandre. 1989. 'Lo scavo dell'area suburbana di via S. Vincenzo a Genova', *AM*, 16: 357–410.

Bellini Cristina, Cevasco Roberta, Moreno Diego, Guido Maria A. and Montanari Carlo. 2009. 'The Mogge di Ertola Site, High Aveto Valley, Ligurian Apennines (N Italy): Bronze Age, Medieval and Present Cultural Landscapes', in Krzywinski et al. 2009: 108–9.

Bellini, Cristina, Mariotti-Lippi, Marta and Montanari, Carlo. 2009. 'The Holocene Landscape History of the NW Italian Coasts', *The Holocene*, 19: 1161–72.

Benente, Fabrizio. 2000. 'Incastellamento e poteri locali in Liguria. Il Genovesato e l'area del Tigullio', in Benente and Garbarino 2000: 61–83.

Benente, Fabizio and Garbarino, Gian Battista. (eds). 2000. *Incastellamento, popolamento e signoria rurale tra Piemonte meridionale e Liguria* (Bordighera: Istituto Internazionale di Studi Liguri).

Benente, Fabrizio, Andreazzoli, Federico, Baldassarri, Monica, Codovilla, Roberto, Dentonie, Marzia, Garbarino, Gian Battista, Lasssa, Sara, Parise, Alexander, Pastorino, Fabrizio, Piombo, Nadia. 2004. 'San Nicolao II. Lo scavo dell'ospedale di San Nicolao di Pietra Colice (Castiglione Chiavarese). Relazione preliminare avanzata delle campagne di scavo 2001, 2003, 2004', in Vecchi 2004: 23–114.

Benvenuti, M., Mariotti-Lippi, Marta, Pallecchi, P. and Sagri, M. 2006. 'Late-Holocene Catastrophic Floods in the Terminal Arno River (Pisa, Central Italy) from the Story of a Roman Riverine Habour', *The Holocene*, 16: 863–76.

Bernabò, Barbara. 1988. 'Viabilità romana nella valle', in De Nevi 1988: 116–22.

—. 1999. 'I Fieschi e la Val di Vara', in Calcagno 1999: 1–28.

Bernabò, Barbara and De Nevi, Paolo. 1988. 'Le pievi e i castelli', in De Nevi 1988: 128–55.

Bernabò Brea, Luigi. 1946. *Gli scavi della Caverna delle Arene Candide. Pt I. Gli strati con ceramiche* (Bordighera: Istituto Internazionale di Studi Liguri).

Bertelli, Carlo and Brogiolo, Gian Pietro (eds). 2000. *Il futuro dei Longobardi. L'Italia e la costruzione dell'Europa di Carlo Magno* (Milan: Electa).

Bertinelli, Maria Gabriella A. 2007. 'Da Liguria a Romani', in Assereto and Doria 2007: 5–23.

Bertolotto, Sabrina and Cevasco, Roberta. 2000. 'The "Alnoculture" System in the Ligurian Eastern Apennines: Archive Evidence', in Agnoletti and Anderson 2000: 189–202.

Biagi, Paolo and Nandris, John (eds). 1994. *Highland Zone Exploitation in Southern Europe* (Brescia: Museo Civico di Scienze Naturali di Brescia).

Biagini, M., Melli, Piera and Torre, Eleonora. 1998. 'La ceramica comune in Liguria nel VI e VII secolo', in Saguì 1998: 577–84.

Bianchi, Ettore. 1996. 'La Tavola di Polcevera e l'occupazione del Genovesato in epoca tardorepubblicana', *Archeologia uomo territorio*, 15: 63–80.

—. 2006-7. 'Il castello bizantino di Perti. Revisione critica', *Archeologia uomo territorio*, 25–6: 11–25.

Biasotti, Mirella and Giovinazzo, Rossana. 1982. 'I reperti faunistici di Filattiera', *AM*, 9: 358–62.

Bintliff, John and Pearce, Mark (eds). 2011. *The Death of Archaeological Theory?* (Oxford and Oakville: Oxbow).

Blake, Hugo, Potter, Tim and Whitehouse, David (eds). 1978. *Papers in Italian Archaeology*, II (Oxford: British Archaeological Reports).

Boccardo, Piero and Di Fabio, Clario (eds). 2005. *Genova e l'Europa. Opere, artisti, committenti, collezionisti* (Cinisello Balsamo: Silvana).

Bonora, Ferdinando. 1986. 'L'indagine archeologica sul complesso architettonico di San Fruttuoso di Capodimonte – Camogli (GE). Notizia preliminare sulla campagna 1985', *AM*, 13: 191–208.

Bonora, Ferdinando, Murialdo, Giovanni, Mannoni, Tiziano. 1988. 'Il "castrum" tardo-antico di S. Antonino di Perti, Finale Ligure (Savona): fasi stratigrafiche e reperti dell'area D. Seconde notizie preliminari sulle campagne di scavo 1982–1987', *AM*, 15: 335–93.

Bordone, Renato and Jarnut, Jörg (eds). 1988. *L'evoluzione delle città italiane nell'XI secolo* (Bologna: Il Mulino).

Bordone, Renato, Guglielmotti, Paola, Lombardini, S. and Torre, Alessandro (eds). 2007. *Lo spazio politico locale in età medievale, moderna e contemporanea* (Alessandria: Edizioni dell'Orso).

Borzani, Luca, Pistarino, Geo and Ragazzi, Franco (eds). 1993. *Storia Illustrata di Genova*. vol. 1, *Genova Antica e Medievale* (Milan: Sellino).

— (eds). 1993. *Storia Illustrata di Genova*. vol. 5, *Genova nell'età contemporanea: economia, culture e società tra '800 e '900* (Milan: Sellino).

Bradley, Guy, Isayev, Elena and Riva, Corinna (eds). 2007. *Ancient Italy. Regions without Boundaries* (Exeter: University of Exeter Press).

Branch, Nick. 2004. 'Late Würm Lateglacial and Holocene Environmental History of the Ligurian Apennines, Italy', in Balzaretti, Pearce and Watkins 2004: 7–70.

Branch, Nick, Guido, Maria Angela, Menozzi, Bruna I., Montanari, Carlo and Placereani, Sandra. 2002. 'Prime analisi polliniche per il sito "Moggia di Pian Brogione" (Casanova di Rovegno – GE)', *APM*, 6: 125–31.

Brogiolo, Gian Pietro. 2005. 'Risultati e prospettiva della ricera archeologica sulle campagne altomedievali italiani', in Brogiolo, Chavarria and Valenti 2005: 7–16.

—. 2006. 'Le campagne italiane tra tardo antico e altomedioevo nella ricera archeologica', in Galetti 2006: 11–32.

Brogiolo, Gian Pietro (ed.). 1994. *Edilizia residenziale tra V e VIII secolo* (Mantua: Parini).

—. 1996a. *La fine delle ville romane: trasformazioni nelle campagne tra tarda antichità e alto medioevo* (Mantua: Parini).

—. 1996b. *Early Medieval Towns in the Western Mediterranean* (Mantua: SAP).

—. 2001. *Le chiese tra VII e VIII secolo in Italia settentrionale* (Florence: All'Insegna del Giglio).

Brogiolo, Gian Pietro and Cantino Wataghin, Gisella (eds). 1998. *Sepolture tra IV e VIII secolo* (Mantua: Parini).

Brogiolo, Gian Pietro and Castelletti, Lanfredo (eds). 1992. *Il territorio tra tardo antico e alto medioevo* (Florence: All'Insegna del Giglio).

Brogiolo, Gian Pietro and Chavarría Arnau, A. 2008. 'El final de las villas y las transformaciones del territorio rural en Occidente (siglos v–viii)', in Ochoa, García-Entero and Gil Sendino 2008: 193–213.

Brogiolo, Gian Pietro and Gelichi, Sauro. 1998. La città nell'altomedioevo italiano. *Archeologia e storia* (Bari: Laterza).

Brogiolo, Gian Pietro and Gelichi, Sauro (eds). 1996a. *Le ceramiche altomedievali (fi ne vi–x secolo) in Italia settentrionale: produzione e commerci* (Mantua: Parini).

—. 1996b. *Nuove ricerche sui castelli altomedievali in Italia settentrionale* (Florence: All'Insegna del Giglio).

Brogiolo, Gian Pietro, Chavarria Arnau, A. and Valenti, Marco (eds). 2005. *Dopo la fine delle ville. Evoluzione nelle campagne tra VI e IX secolo* (Mantua: SAP).

Brogiolo, Gian Pietro, Gauthier, Nathalie and Christie, Neil (eds). 2000. *Towns and their Territories between Late Antiquity and the Early Middle Ages* (Leiden: Brill).

Brown, Thomas S. 1984. *Gentlemen and Officers: Imperial Administration and Aristocratic Power in Byzantine Italy A.D. 554–800* (London: British School at Rome).

Brown, Thomas S. and Christie, Neil. 1989. 'Was there a Byzantine Model of Settlement in Italy?' *MEFR, Moyen Age*, 101: 377–99.

Brubaker, Leslie. 2004. 'The Elephant and the Ark: Cultural and Material Interchange across the Mediterranean in the Eighth and Ninth Centuries', *Dumbarton Oaks Papers*, 58: 175–95.

Bullough, Donald A. 1956. 'A Byzantine (?) Castle in the Val di Magra: Surianum-Filattiera', *PBSR*, 24: 14–21.

Burns, Thomas S. 1984. *A History of the Ostrogoths* (Bloomington: Indiana University Press).

Cabona, Danilo, Mannoni, Tiziano and Pizzolo, Onofrio. 1982. 'Gli scavi nel complesso medievale di Filattiera in Lunigiana. 1. La collina di San Giorgio', *AM*, 9: 331–57.

—. 1984. 'Gli scavi nel complesso medievale di Filattiera in Lunigiana. 2. La collina di Castelvecchio', *AM*, 11: 243–7.

Cabona, Danilo, Giannichedda, Enrico and Gambaro, Luigi. 1990. 'Scavo dell'area est del villaggio abbandonato di Monte Zignago: Zignago 4', *AM*, 17: 355–408.

Cagnana, Aurora. 1994. 'Considerazioni sulle strutture abitative liguri fra VI e XIII secolo', in Brogiolo 1994: 169–77.

—. 1998. 'Il sottosuolo della Cattedrale: gli scavi del 1966 e le ricerche successive', in Di Fabio 1998: 38–43.

Cagnana, Aurora and Gavagnin, S. 2004. 'Indagini archeologiche nel borgo arroccato di Corvara (Beverino, La Spezia)', *AM*, 31: 187–99.

Cagnana, Aurora, Cabella, Roberto, Capelli, Claudio, Castiglioni, Elizabetta, Marrazzo, Daniela, Piazza, Michele and Spinetti, Alessandra. 2008. 'L'abitato d'altura di X–XI secolo a Corvara di Beverino (SP). Contributo all'archeologia del paesaggio altomedievale in Lunigiana', in Del Lucchese and Gambaro 2008: 123–51.

Calandra, Elena. 2002. 'Val d'Aveto e Val Trebbia fra età del Ferro ed età romana. Una traccia dei problemi', *APM*, 6: 17–23.

Calcagno, Daniele. 2004. "Ianuenses facient iurare Lavaninis et Paxaninis et illis de Lagneto": alle origini del potere dei Conti di Lavagna', in Vecchi 2004: 161–76.

Calcagno, Daniele (ed.). 1999. *I Fieschi tra Medioevo ed Età Moderna* (Genoa: Associazione "A Compagna").

Calleri, Marta. 1999. 'Gli usi cronologici Genovese secoli X–XII', *ASLSP*, 39/1: 25–100.

Calleri, Marta (ed.). 1997. *Le carte del monastero di San Siro di Genova (951/952–1224)* (Genova: Società Ligure di Storia Patria).

—. 2009. *Codice diplomatico del monastero di Santo Stefano di Genova*, vol. 1 (965–1200) (Genoa: Società Ligure di Storia Patria).

Camangi, Fabiano, Stefani, Agostino and Sebastiani Luca. 2009. *Etnobotanica in Val di Vara. L'uso delle piante nella tradizione popolare* (La Spezia: Provincia della Spezia).

Campana, Nadia and Cevasco, Roberta. 2001. 'Un'area di interesse archeologico ambientale: studi di ecologia storica a "Pian delle Gròppere" (Casanova di Rovengo – GE)', in Stringa and Moreno 2001: 225–32.

Campoltrini, Giulio. 1989. 'Due orecchini bizantini da Luni', *AM*, 16: 737–40.

Caneva, Giulia. (ed.). 2005. *La biologia vegetale per i beni culturali*, vol. 2 (Florence: Nardini).

Cantino Wataghin, Gisella. 2000. 'Christianisation et organisation ecclésiastique des campagnes: l'Italie du nord aux ive–viiie siècles', in Brogiolo, Gauthier and Christie 2000: 209–34.

Capo, Lidia (ed. and tr.). 1992. *Paolo Diacono, Storia dei Longobardi* (Vicenza: Mondadori).

Carobene, Luigi, Firpo, Marco and Melli, Piera. 2006. 'Aspetti geoarcheologici nel Porto Antico di Genova', in Cucuzza and Medri 2006: 295–9.

Carobene, Luigi, Firpo, Marco and Rovere, Alessandra. 2009. 'Le variazioni ambientali nell'area di Vado Ligure dal Neolitico ad oggi', *Il Quaternario*, 21: 433–56.

Carpaneto, Angelo. 1975. *Langasco dall'epoca romana ad oggi* (Genoa: Comune di Langasco).

Castagnetti, Andrea, Luzzati, Michele, Pasquali, Gianfranco and Vasina, Augusto (ed.). 1979. *Inventari altomedievali di terre, coloni e redditti* (Rome: Istituto Storico per il Medioevo).

Castelletti, Lanfredo. 1976. 'Resti vegetali macroscopici da Refondou presso Savignone', *AM*, 3: 326–8.

Cavaciocchi, Simonetta (ed.). 1996. *L'uomo e la foresta secc. XIII–XVIII* (Florence: Le Monnier).

Cavallaro, L. 1993. 'Da Genua a Ianua', in Borzani, Pistarino and Ragazzi 1993 (vol. 1): 33–48.

Cera, Giovanna (ed.). 2000. *La Via Postumia da Genova a Cremona* (Rome: Bretschneider).

Cesana, D., Giovinazzo, R., Marrazzo, D., Melli, Piera and Spinetti, A. 2007. 'The medieval diet in Genoa (NW Italy) through the analysis of faunal remains from archaeological sites', at: http://medieval-europe-paris-2007.univ-paris1.fr/

Cevasco, Roberta. 2004. 'Multiple Use of Tree-land in the Northern Apennines in the Post-medieval Period', in Balzaretti, Pearce and Watkins 2004: 155–77.

—. 2007. *Memoria verde. Nuovi spazi per la geografia* (Reggio Emilia: Diabasis).

—. 2010. 'Environmental Heritage of a Past Cultural Landscape. Alder Woods in the Upper Aveto Valley of the Northwestern Apennines', in Armiero and Hall 2000: 126–40.

Cevasco, Roberta, Menozzi, Bruna I., Molinari, Chiara, Moreno, Diego, Vaccarezza, Claudia, Guido, Maria Angela and Montanari, Carlo. 2010. 'The Historical Ecology of Ligurian Chestnut Groves: Archival Documentation and Field Evidence', *Acta Horticulturae (ISHS)* 866: 43–50, at: www.actahort.org/books/866/866_2.htm

Cevasco, Roberta and Moreno, Diego. 2009. 'Wood-pasture and Wood-meadow in the Ligurian-Tuscan-Aemilian Apennines, Italy', in Krzywinski et al. 2009: 104–5.

Cevasco, Roberta, Moreno, Diego, Poggi, Giuseppina and Rackham, Oliver. 1997–9. 'Archeologia e storia della copertura vegetale: esempi dall'Alta Val di Vara', *Memorie della Accademia Lunigianese di Scienze 'Giovanni Capellini'*, 62–63–64: 241–61.

Chazelle, Celia and Cubitt, Catherine (eds). 2007. *The Crisis of the Oikoumene: The Three Chapters and the Failed Quest for Unity in the Sixth-century Mediterranean* (Turnhout: Brepols).

Chazelle, Celia and Lifshitz, Felice (eds). 2007. *Paradigms and Methods in Early Medieval Studies* (New York: Palgrave).

Cheyette, Fredric L. 2008. 'The Disappearance of the Ancient Landscape and the Climatic Anomaly of the Early Middle Ages: A Question to be Pursued', *EME*, 16: 127–65.

Chiaramonte Trevé, C. (ed.). 2003. *Antici liguri sulle vie appenniniche tra Tireno e Po. Nuovi contribute* (Cisalpino: Milan).

Christie, Neil. 1990. 'Byzantine Liguria: An Imperial Province against the Lombards, AD 568–643', *PBSR*, 58: 229–71.

—. 1995. 'Late Antique Cavemen in Northern and Central Italy', in Christie 1995: 311–16.

—. 2006. *From Constantine to Charlemagne. An Archaeology of Italy AD 300–800* (Aldershot: Ashgate).

Christie, Neil (ed.). 1995. *Settlement and Economy in Italy 1500 BC to AD 1500. Papers of the Fifth Conference of Italian Archaeology* (Oxford: Oxbow).

—. 2004. *Landscapes of Change. Rural Evolutions in Late Antiquity and the Early Middle Ages* (Aldershot: Ashgate).

Cipolla, Carlo (ed.). 1918. *Codice Diplomatico del monastero di San Colombano di Bobbio*, 3 vols (Rome: Tipografia del Senato).

Clark, Gillian. 1987. 'Stock Economies in Medieval Italy: A Critical Review of the Archaezoological Evidence', *AM*, 14: 7–17.

Cleary, Mark and Delano-Smith, Catherine. 1990. 'Transhumance Reviewed: Past and Present Practices in France and Italy', *RSL A*, 56, 1–4: 21–38.

Colardelle, Michel (ed.). 1996. *L'homme et la nature au Moyen Age* (Paris: Editions Errance).

Collins, Roger. 1998. *Charlemagne* (London: Palgrave).

—. 2007. *Die Fredegar-Chroniken* (Hannover: Monumenta Germaniae Historica).

—. 2009. 'Review-Article. Making Sense of the Early Middle Ages', *EHR*, 124: 641–65.

Cruise, Gillian M. 1990. 'Pollen Stratigraphy of Two Holocene Peat Sites in the Ligurian Apennines, Northern Italy', *Review of Palaeobotany and Palynology*, 63: 299–313.

—. 1992. 'Environmental Change and Human Impact in the Upper Mountain Zone of the Ligurian Apennines: The Last 5000 Years', *RSL*, 56: 169–88.

Cruise, Gillian M., Macphail, R. I., Linderholme, J., Maggi, Roberto and Marshall, P. D. 2009. 'Lago di Bargone, Liguria, N Italy: A Reconstruction of Holocene Environmental and Land-use History', *The Holocene*, 19.7: 987–1003.

Cucuzza, Nicola and Medri, Maura (eds). 2006. *Archeologie. Studi in onore di Tiziano Mannoni* (Bari: Edipuglia).

Davite, Chiara. 1988. 'Scavi e riconizioni nel sito rurale tardo-antico di Gronda (Luscignano, MC)', *AM*, 15: 397–406.

Davite, Chiara and Moreno, Diego. 1996. 'Des "saltus" aux "alpes" dans les Apenninsdu nord (Italie): une hypothese sur la phase du haut Moyen Age (560–680 ap. J. C) dans la diagramme pollinique du site de Prato spilla', in Colardelle 1996: 138–42.

Davite, Chiara, Gardini, Alexandre, Ridella, R. and Torre, Eleanora. 1986. 'Lo scavo nell'Abbazia di San Fruttuoso di Capodimonte-Camogli (GE). Notizia preliminare sulla campagna 1985', *AM*, 16: 209–24.

Decker, Michael. 2009. *Tilling the Hateful Earth. Agricultural Production and Trade in the Late Antique East* (Oxford: Oxford University Press).

Delano Smith, Catherine. 1979. *Western Mediterranean Europe. An Historical Geography of Italy, Spain and Southern France since the Neolithic* (London: Academic Press).

—. 2004. 'A Perspective on Mediterranean Landscape History', in Balzaretti, Pearce and Watkins 2004: vii–ix.

Delano Smith, Catherine, Gadd, D., Mills, N. and Ward-Perkins, Bryan. 1986. 'Luni and the "Ager Lunensis". The Rise and Fall of a Roman Town and its Territory', *PBSR*, 59: 81–146.

Delogu, Paolo. 1994. 'La fine del mondo antico e l'inizio del medioevo: nuovi dati per un vecchio problema', in Francovich and Noyé 1994: 7–29.

—. 2009. 'Kingship and the Shaping of the Lombard Body Politic', in Ausenda, Delogu and Wickham 2009: 251–74.

Del Lucchese, Angiolo and Gambaro, Luigi (eds). 2008. *Archeologia in Liguria. Nuova serie*, vol. 1, 2004–5 (Genoa: De Ferrari).

De Maestri, S. and Moreno, Diego. 1980. 'Contribuito alla storia della costruzione a secco nella Liguria rurale', *AM*, 7: 319–41.

De Marchi, Paola M. 2003. 'La ceramica longobarda: osservazioni', in Fiorillo and Peduto 2003: 14–20.

De Maria, Lorenza and Turchetti, Rita (eds). 2004. *Rotte e porti del Mediterraneo dopo la caduta dell'Impero romano d'Occidente* (Soveria Manelli: Rubbettino).

De Negri, Teofilo O. and Mazzino, E. 1964. 'Il castello di Varese e il suo restauro', *Bollettino Ligustico*, 16: 143–89.

De Nevi, Paolo. 1988. *Val di Vara. Un grido, un canto* (Sarzana: Centro Studi Val di Vara).

De Pascale, Andrea, Maggi, Roberto, Montanari, Carlo and Moreno, Diego. 2006. 'Pollen, Herds, Jasper and Copper Mines: Economic and Environmental Changes during the 4th and 3rd Millennia BC in Liguria (NW Italy)', *Environmental Archaeology*, 11: 115–24.

Destefanis, Eleanora. 2002a. *Il monastero di Bobbio in età altomedievale* (Florence: All'Insegna del Giglio).

—. 2002b. 'La Valle dell'Aveto in età altomedievale: alcuni spunti di riflessione', *APM*, 6: 25–34.

Devroey, Jean-Pierre, Feller, Laurent and Le Jan, Regine (eds). 2010. *Les élites et la richesse au haut Moyen Âge entre vi^e et xie siècles* (Turnhout: Brepols).

De Vingo, Paolo. 2010a. 'Archaeology of Power in the Rural Cemeteries of Western Liguria Maritima between Late Antiquity and the Beginning of the Early Middle Ages', in Ebanista and Rotili 2010: 79–96.

—. 2010b. 'Le village de Noli en Ligurie occidentale entre l'Antiquité tardive et le haut Moyen Âge', *Archéologie Médiévale*, 40: 89–114.

—. 2011. 'Food Preparation and Preservation in North-west Italy: A Comparative Assessment in the Study of Early Medieval Eating and Cooking Utensils in the Settlement of Sant'Antonino in Western Liguria and the Village of Trino Vercellese in the Po valley', in Klápŝte and Sommer 2011: 7–89.

De Vingo, Paolo and Frondoni, Alessandra. 2003. 'Fonti scritte e cultura materiale del territorio fra tardoantico e altomedioevo in val Polcevera (GE): problemi aperti e prospettive di ricerca', in Fiorillo and Peduto 2003: 32–6.

Dewing, H. B. (ed. and tr.). 1919. *Procopius, History of the Wars*, 7 vols. (Cambridge, MA: Harvard University Press).

Di Dio, M. 2006. 'Le vicende storiche della chiesa di San Paragorio di Noli alla luce degli esiti del recente restauro', in Cucuzza and Medri 2006: 57–61.

Di Fabio, Clario. 1990. 'San Tommaso', in Dufour Bozzo and Marcenaro 1990: 21–142.

—. 2003. 'Alle origini della Cattedrale di Genova. Temi di Christiana Signa', in Frondoni 2003a: 33–8.

Di Fabio, Clario (ed.). 1998. *La cattedrale di Genova nel medioevo, secoli vi–xiv* (Cinisello Balsamo: Silvana).

Dreslerová, Dagmar and Mikuláš, Radek. 2010. 'An Early Medieval Symbol Carved on a Tree Trunk: Pathfinder or Territorial Marker?' *Antiquity*, 84: 1067–75.

Dueck, Daniela. 2000. *Strabo of Amasia: A Greek Man of Letters in Augustan Rome* (London and New York: Routledge).

Dufour Bozzo, Colette. 1987. 'Dal Mediobizantino al Protoromanico: dalla "città vescovile" alla "città communale". X–XI secolo', in AA. VV. 1987: 63–81.

Dufour Bozzo, Colette and Marcenaro, Mario (eds). 1990. *Medioevo demolito. Genova 1860–1940* (Genoa: Pirella).

Dutton, Paul E. 2004. *Charlemagne's Mustache and Other Cultural Clusters of a Dark Age* (New York: Palgrave).

Dyson, Steven L. 2003. *The Roman Countryside* (London: Duckworth).

Ebanista, Carlo and Rotili, Marcello (eds). 2010. *Ipsam Nolam barbari vastaverunt. L'Italia ed il Mediterraneo occidentale tra il V secolo e la metà del VI* (Cimitile: Tavolario Ediz.).

Epstein, Steven A. 1996. *Genoa and the Genoese, 958-1528* (Chapel Hill: University of North Carolina Press).

Everett, Nicholas. 2002. 'The Earliest Rcension of the Life of Sirus of Pavia (Vat. Lat. 5771)', *SM*, 43: 857-957.

—. 2003. *Literacy in Lombard Italy, c. 568-774* (Cambridge: Cambridge University Press).

Fazzini, Paolo and Maffei, Marina. 2000. 'The Disappearance of the City of Luni', *Journal of Cultural Heritage*, 1: 247-60.

Ferrando Cabona, I., Gardini, Andrea and Mannoni, Tiziano. 1978. 'Zignano 1: gli insediamenti e il territorio', *AM*, 5: 272-374.

Ferrari, I., Scipioni, Sara, Menozzi, Bruna I. and Montanari, Carlo. 2006. 'Studi antracologici in siti archeologici medievali dell'Italia Nord-occidentale', *Informatore Botanico Italiano*, 38: 55-60.

Figone, Fausto. 1995. *La Podesteria di Castiglione. Lineamenti storici* (Chiavari).

Filangieri, Luca. 2006. 'La canonica di San Lorenzo a Genova. Dinamiche istituzionali e rapporti sociali (secoli X–XII)', *RMR*, VII: 1-37.

Fiorillo, Rosa and Peduto, Paolo (eds). 2003. *III Congresso Nazionale di Archeologia Medievale* (Florence: All'Insegna del Giglio).

Fischer Drew, Katherine (tr.). 1973. *The Lombard Laws* (Philadelphia: University of Pennsylvania Press).

Fossati, Severino, Bazzurro, Sergio and Pizzolo, Onofrio. 1976. 'Campagna di scavo nel villaggio tardoantico di Savignone (Genova)', *AM*, 3: 309-25.

Foulke, William Dudley (tr.). 1907. *Paul the Deacon, History of the Lombards* (Pennsylvania: University of Pennsylvania Press).

Francovich, Riccardo and Hodges, Richard. 2003. *From Villa to Village: The Transformation of the Roman Countryside in Italy* (London: Duckworth).

Francovich, Riccardo and Noyé, Ghislaine (eds). 1994. *La Storia dell'alto medioevo Italiano (vi–x secolo) alla luce dell'archeologia* (Florence: All'Insegna del Giglio).

Francovich, Riccardo and Valenti, Marco (eds). 2006. *IV Congresso Nazionale di Archeologia Medievale* (Florence: All'Insegna del Giglio).

Frondoni, Alessandra. 1987. 'L'altomedioevo: età longobarda e carolingia. VII-IX secolo', in AA.VV. 1987: 35-59.

—. 1998. *Archeologia cristiana in Liguria. Aree ed edifici di culto tra IV e XI secolo* (Genoa: B. N. Marconi).

—. 2003. 'Christiana signa: perché e come', in Frondoni 2003: 23-32.

—. 2005. 'Tra bisanzio e l'Occidente. Scultura e plastica a San Siro, San Tommaso e San Fruttuoso di Capodimonte', in Boccardo and Di Fabio 2005: 14–39.

—. 2008. 'Archeologia in Liguria tra tardoantico e altomedioevo: recenti scoperte, problem e prospettive di ricerca', *Bulletin du Musée d'anthropologie préhistorique de Monaco*, Supplement no. 1: 167–84.

Frondoni, Alessandra (ed.). 2003. *Romana pictura e Christiana signa. Due mostre in confronto. Arte figurativa in Liguria fra età imperiale e altomedioevo* (Genoa: De Ferrari).

—. 2007. *Il Tesoro svelato. Storie dimenticate e rinvenimenti straordinari riscrivono la storia di Noli antica* (Genoa: De Ferrari).

Frondoni, Alessandra, Geltrudini, F. and De Vingo, Paolo. 2002. 'Cemetery Contextsin Mid Eastern Liguria in the Medieval Centuries', in Helmig, Scholkmann and Untermann 2002: 324–35.

Frondoni, Alessandra, Benente, Fabrizio, Murialdo, Giovanni, Palazzi, P. and Pellegrineschi, L. 1997. 'Indagini archeologiche a Varigotti (Savona). Il castrum e la chiesa di San Lorenzo', in Gelichi 1997: 102–8.

Frondoni, Alessandra, Geltrudini, F., Pampaloni, A., De Vingo, Paolo and Cirnigliaro, E. 2006. 'Noli (Savona), via XXV Aprile. Analisi della sequenza insediativa di un contesto pluristratificato tra tardoantico e bassomedioevo', in Francovich and Valenti 2006: 95–103.

Frondoni, Alessandra, Parodi, Valentina and Torre, Eleanora. 2006. 'Archeologia urbana a Noli (SV): nuove acquisizioni sul villaggio altomedievale dagli scavi del vecchio piazzale ferroviario', in Francovich and Valenti 2006: 104–8.

Frova, Antonio. 1977. *Scavi di Luni*, 3 vols (Rome: Bretschneider).

Gabrovec, Sergio. 2009. *Teviggio* (Chiavari: Grafiche Rotomec).

—. 2011. *Porciorasco* (Varese: Comunità parrocchiale di Varese Ligure).

Galetti, Paola. 1997. *Abitare nel Medioevo: forme e vicende dell'insediamento rurale nell'Italia altomedievale* (Florence: Le lettere).

Galetti, Paola (ed.). 2006. *Forme del popolamento rurale nell'Europa Medievale: l'apporto dell'archeologica* (Bologna: Università di Bologna).

Gambaro, Luigi. 1999. *La Liguria costiera tra III a I secolo A. C. Una lettura archeologica della romanizzazione* (Mantua: Societá Archeologica Padana).

—. 2003. 'Insediamenti e commerci in Lunigiana in età imperiale e tardo-antica', in Giannichedda and Lanzi 2003: 62–6.

Gambaro, Luigi and Lambert, Chiara. 1987. 'Lo scavo della cattedrale di San Lorenzo di Genova e i centri episcopali della Liguria', *AM*, 14: 199–254.

Gambogi, Pamela and Firmati, M. (1998). 'Frequentazione tardoantica e altomedievale nell'isola di Gorgona', in Saquì 1998: 635–8.

Gandolfi, Daniela. 1998. 'Ceramiche fini di importazione di VI–VII secolo in Liguria. L'esempio di Ventimiglia, Albenga e Luni', in Saquì 1998: 253–74.

Ganz, David. 2004. 'Dúngal (fl. c.800–827)', ODNB, at: www.oxforddnb.com/view/article/8263

Gardini, Alexandre. 1993. 'La ceramica bizantina in Liguria', in Gelichi 1993: 47–78.

Gardini, Alexandre and Melli, Piera. 1988. 'Necropoli e sepolture urbane ed extraurbane a Genova tratardo-antico ed alto-medioevo', *RSL*, A. 14, 1–4: 159–78.

Gardini, Alexandre and Milanese, Marco. 1979. 'L'archeologia urbana a Genova negli anni 1964–1978', *AM*, 6: 129–70.

Gardini, Alexandre and Murialdo, Giovanni. 1994. 'La Liguria', in Francovich and Noyé 1994: 159–82.

Gelichi, Sauro (ed.). 1993. *La ceramica nel mondo bizantino tra XI e XV secolo e i suoi rapporti con l'Italia* (Florence: All'Insegna del Giglio).

—. 1997. *I Congresso nazionale di archeologia medievale* (Florence: All'Insegna del Giglio).

Gelichi, Sauro. 2002. 'The Cities', in La Rocca 2002: 168–88.

Gelzer, Henricus (ed.). 1890. *Georgii Cyprii [George of Cyprus], Descriptio orbis Romani* (Leipzig: Teubner).

Gentili, R., Gentili, E. and Sgorbato, S. 2009. 'Crop Changes from the XVI Century to the Present in a Hill/Mountain Area of Eastern Liguria (Italy)', *Journal of Ethnobiology and Ethnomedicine*, 5, at: www.ncbi.nlm.nih.gov/pmc/articles/PMC2679714/ (unpaginated).

Ghizzoni, F. (ed.). 1990. *Storia di Piacenza I. Dalle origini all'anno Mille* (Piacenza: Cassa di Risparmio di Piacenza e Vigevano).

Giannattasio, Bianca Maria. 2007. *I Liguri a la Liguria. Storia e archeologia di un territorio prima della conquista romana* (Milan: Longanesi).

Giannichedda, Enrico. 1993. 'Una padella altomedievale da Rossiglione (Genova)', *AM*, 20: 579–90.

—. 1995. 'Monte Castello: L'altomedioevo fra protostoria ed età Moderna. In risposta ad interpretazioni conclusive di ricerche in corso', *AM*, 22: 531–5.

—. 2003. 'Insediamenti e culti in Lunigiana', in Giannichedda and Lanza 2003: 76–86.

—. 2006. *Uomini e cose. Appunti di archeologia* (Bari: Edipuglia).

Giannichedda, Enrico (ed.). 1998. *Filattiera-Sorano: l'insediamento dell' età romana e tardoantica. Scavi 1986–1995* (Florence: All'Insegna del Giglio).

Giannichedda, Enrico and Lanza, Rita. 2003. *Le ricerche archeologiche in provincia di Massa-Carrara* (Florence: All'Insegna del Giglio).

Giannichedda, Enrico and Mannoni, Tiziano. 1990. 'Alcuni dati archeologici sullapastorizia nell'Appennino settentrionale tra protostoria e medioevo', *RSL*, 16: 279–313.

Giannichedda, Enrico, Lanza, Rita and Ratti, Olivia. 2003. 'Lo scavo archeologico di San Caprasio ad Aulla', in Giannichedda and Lanza 2003: 97–104.

—. 2011. 'Indagini nella canonica e nel chiostro dell'abbazia di San Caprasio ad Aulla (MS)', *AM*, 38: 287–318.

Giannichedda, Enrico and Quiros Castillo, Juan Antonio. 1997. 'La ceramica vacuolare nell'Appennino Ligure e Toscano', in Gelichi 1997: 379–83.

Graham-Campbell, James and Valor, M. 2007. *The Archaeology of Medieval Europe.* vol. 1, *Eighth to Twelfth Centuries AD* (Aarhus: Aarhus University Press).

Grendi, Edoardo. 1996. *Storia di una storia locale. L'esperienza ligure 1792–1992* (Venice: Marsilio).

—. 2006. 'Ripensare la microstoria?' in Revel 2006: 227–37 (orig. pub. 1977).

Greppi, Paola. 2008. *Provincia maritima Italorum: fortificazioni altomedievali in Liguria*, BAR INT 1839 (Oxford: John and Erica Hedges Ltd).

Grey, Cam. 2011. *Constructing Commmunities in the Late Roman Countryside* (Cambridge: Cambridge University Press).

Grove, Alfred Thomas and Rackham, Oliver. 2001. *The Nature of Mediterranean Europe – An Ecological History* (Yale: Yale University Press).

Guglielmotti, Paola. 2005. *Ricerche sull'organizzazione del territorio nella Liguria medievale* (Florence: Firenze University Press).

—. 2007a. 'Definizione e organizzazione del territorio nella Liguria orientale del secolo XII', *ASLSP*, n. s. 47, 1: 185–213.

—. 2007b. 'Linguaggi del territorio, ligueggi sul territorio: la val Polcevera genovese (secoli X–XII)', in Petti Balbi and Vitolo 2007: 241–68.

Guido, Maria Angela, Menozzi, Bruna I., Montanari, Carlo and Scipioni, Sara. 2002a. 'Il sito "Mogge di Ertola" come potenziale fonte per la storia ambientale del crinale Trebbia/Aveto', *APM*, 6: 111–16.

Guido, Maria Angela, Scipioni, Sara and Montanari, Carlo. 2002b. 'Il paesaggio colturale nei dintorni di Casanova di Rovengo (GE) dal VII–VIII d.c: dati archeobotanici per l'area di Pian delle Groppere', *APM*, 6: 117–24.

Hallenbeck, Joel T. 2000. *The Transferal of the Relics of St. Augustine of Hippo from Sardinia to Pavia in the Early Middle Ages* (Lewiston, NY: Edward Mellen Press).

Hansen, Inge L. and Wickham, Chris (eds). 2000. *The Long Eighth Century* (Leiden: Brill).

Häussler, Ralph. 2007. 'At the Margins of Italy: Celts and Ligurians in the North-West Italy', in Bradley, Isayev and Riva 2007: 45–78.

Helmig, Guido, Scholkmann, Barbara and Untermann, Mattias (eds). 2003. *Medieval Europe, Basel 2002* (Basel: ABBS).

Herring, Edward, Whitehouse, Ruth and Wilkins, John (eds). 1991. *Papers of the Fourth Conference of Italian Archaeology, 2. The Archaeology of Power, Part 2* (London: Accordia Research Centre).

Hodges, Richard. 1982. *Dark Age Economics: The Origins of Towns and Trade* (London: Duckworth).

—. 1989. 'Charlemagne's Elephant and the Beginnings of Commodisation in Europe', *Acta Archaeologica*, 59: 155–68,

Hodges, Richard and Bowden, William (eds). 1998. *The Sixth Century: Production, Distribution and Demand* (Leiden: Brill).

Horden, Peregrine and Purcell, Nicholas. 2000. *The Corrupting Sea. A Study in Mediterranean History* (Oxford: Blackwell).

Howard, R., Lavers, Chris and Watkins, Charles. 2002. 'Dendrochronology and Ancient Oak Trees: Preliminary Results for Sherwood Forest, UK and the Val di Vara, Italy', *APM*, 6: 35–48.

Imperiale di Sant'Angelo, Cesare (ed.). 1936. *Codice diplomatico della repubblica di Genova*, vol. 1 (Rome: Tipografia del Senato).

Jarnut, Jörg. 1995. *Storia dei Longobardi* (Turin: Einaudi).

Kedar, Benedict Z. 1997. 'Una nuova fonte per l'incursione musulmana del 934–935 e le sue implicazione per la storia genovese', in Balletto 1997: 605–16.

Kehr, Paul Fridolin. 1937. *Die Urkunden Karls III* (Berlin: Weidmann).

King, Paul D. (tr.). 1987. *Charlemagne: Translated Sources* (Kendal, Cumbria).

Klápšte, Jan and Sommer, Petr (eds). 2011. *Processing, Storage, Distribution of Food* (Turnhout: Brepols).

Krusch, Bruno (ed.). 1888. *Fredegarii et aliorum chronica, MGH, Scriptorum Rerum Merovingicarum, II* (Hannover: Monumenta Germaniae Historica).

Krzywinski, Knut, O'Connell, Michael and Küster, Hansjörg (eds). 2009. *Cultural Landscapes of Europe* (Bremen: Aschenbeck Media).

Kulikowski, Michael. 2007. 'Drawing a Line under Antiquity: Archaeological and Historical Categories of Evidence in the Transition from the Ancient World to the Middle Ages', in Chazelle and Lifshitz 1997: 171–84.

Lagomarsini, Sandro (ed.). 1993. *Relatione dell'origine et successi della terra di Varese descritta dal rev. prete Antonio Cesena l'anno 1558* (La Spezia: Accademia Luniganese di Scienze "Giovanni Capellini").

Lagomarsini, Sandro. 2004. 'Urban Exploitation of Common Rights: Two Models of Land Use in the Val di Vara', in Balzaretti, Pearce and Watkins 2004: 179–88.

La Guardia, Rina. 1987. *Scritti in ricordo di Graziella Massari Gaballo e Umberto Tocchetti Pollini* (Milan: Ediz. ET).

Lamboglia, Nino and Pallarès, Francisca. 1985. *Ventimiglia romana*, 3rd edn (Bordighera: Istituto internazionale di studi liguri).

La Rocca, Cristina (ed.). 2002. *Italy in the Early Middle Ages* (Oxford: Oxford University Press.

Laurent, Marie-Aline. 2010. 'Organisation de l'espace et mobilisation des resources autour de Bobbio', in Devroey, Feller and Le Jan 2010: 479–94.

Lavagna, Rita. 1998. 'Savona. Complesso monumentale del Priamàr. La ceramica comune', in Sagui 1998: 585–90.

Lavagna, Rita and Varaldo, Carlo. 1997. 'Osservazioni sui corredi funerari nella necropoli tardoantica e altomedievale del Priamàr a Savona', in Gelichi 1997: 296–301.

Lees, Frederic. 1912. *Wanderings on the Italian Riviera. Recollections of a Leisurely Tour* (London: Pitman and Sons).

Liebeschuetz, J. H. W. G. 2001. 'Late Antiquity and the Concept of Decline', *NMS*, 45: 1–11.

Lowe, J. John, Branch, Nick and Watson, Clare. 1994. 'The Chronology of Human Disturbance of the Vegetation of the Northern Apennines during the Holocene', in Biagi and Nandris 1994: 169–88.

Lowe, J. John and Watson, Clare. 1993. 'Lateglacial and Early Holocene Pollen Stratigraphyof the Northern Apennines, Italy', *Quaternary Science Review*, 12: 727–38.

Lowe, J. John, Davite, Chiara, Moreno, Diego and Maggi, Roberto. 1994. 'Holocene Pollen Stratigraphy and Human Interference in the Woodlands of the Northern Apennines, Italy', *The Holocene*, 4.2: 133–46.

Lusuardi Siena, Silvia. 1985. 'Lo scavo nella cattedrale di Luni (SP). Notizie preliminare sulle campagne 1976–1984', *AM*, 12: 303–11.

—. 2006. 'Una furnace per campane carolingia nella cattedrale di Luni (La Spezia) nel quadro di recenti rinvenimenti lunigianesi', in Cucuzza and Medri 2006: 235–43.

Lusuardi Siena, Silvia and Murialdo, Giovanni. 1991. 'Le ceramiche mediterranee in Liguria durante il periodo bizantino (VI–VII secolo)', in *A cerâmica medieval no mediterrâneo ocidental* (Campo arqueológico de Mértola: Lisbon): 123–46.

McCormick, Michael. 2001. *Origins of the European Economy. Communications and Commerce AD 300–900* (Cambridge: Cambridge University Press).

McCormick, Michael, Dutton, Paul, E. and Mayewski, Paul A. 2007. 'Volcanoes and the Climate Forcing of Carolingian Europe, A.D. 750–950', *Speculum*, 82: 865–95.

McCullagh, Michael J. and Pearce, Mark. 2004. 'Surveying the Prehistoric Copper Mine at Libiola (Sestri Levante – GE), Italy', in Balzaretti, Pearce and Watkins 2004: 83–95.

Macchi Jánica, Giancarlo (ed.). 2009. *Geografie del popolamento. Casi di studio, metodi e teorie* (Siena: Università degli studi di Siena).

Macchiavello, Sandra. 1997. 'Per la storia della cattedrale di Genova. Percorsi archeologici e documentari', *ASLSP*, n.s. 37/2: 21–36.

Maffeis, L. and Negro Ponzi Mancini, M. M. 1995. 'La ceramica commune nei siti dell'Italia settentrionale dall'età tardo antica al medioevo: variazioni tipologiche e funzionali del corredo domestico', in Christie 1995a: 591–602.

Maggi, Roberto. 1988. 'Archeologia della preistoria', in De Nevi 1988: 85–92.

—. 1999. 'Coasts and Uplands in Liguria and Northern Tuscany from the Mesolithic to the Bronze Age', in Tykot, Morter and Robb 1999: 47–65.

—. 2003. 'Suoli sepolti e paesaggio sull'Appennino ligure', in Chiaramonte Trevé 2003: 161–74.

—. 2004. 'I monti sun eggi', in Balzaretti, Pearce and Watkins 2004: 71–82.

Maggi, Roberto (ed.). 1992. *Archeologia preventiva a lungo il percorso di un metanodotto, Quaderni della Suprintendenza della Liguria* 4 (Genoa: Soprintendenza Archeologica della Liguria).

Maggi, Roberto and Campana, Nadia. 2002. 'Frammenti di paletnologia fra Trebbia e Aveto', *APM*, 6: 185–94.

Maggi, Roberto and Nisbet, Roberto. 1990. 'Prehistoric Pastoralism in Liguria', *RSL*, 56: 265–96.

Maggi, Roberto and Pearce, Mark. 2005. 'Mid Fourth-millennium Copper Mining in Liguria, North-west Italy: The Earliest Known Copper Mines in Western Europe', *Antiquity*, 79: 66–77.

Maggi, Roberto, Nisbet, Roberto and Barker, Graham (eds). 1990 'Archeologia della pastorizia nell'Europa meridionale', *RSL*, 56, 1–4.

Maggi, Roberto, Nadia Campana, Negrino, Fabio and Ottomano, Carlo. (1995). 'The Quarrying and Workshop Site of Valle Lagorara (Liguria-Italy)', *ARP*, 4: 73–96.

Mannoni, Tiziano. 1965. 'Il "testo" e la sua diffusione nella Liguria di Levante', *Bollettino Ligustico*, 17: 49–64.

—. 1974. 'Il Castello di Molassana e l'archeologia medievale in Liguria', *AM*, 1: 11–17.

—. 1983a. 'Vie a mezzi di communicazione', *AM*, 10: 214–19.

—. 1983b. 'Insediamenti poveri nella Liguria di età romana e bizantina', *RSL*, 49: 254–65.

—. 1987. 'Archeologia della produzione', *AM*, 14: 559–64.

—. 2000. 'L'archeologia dei castelli condotta in Liguria negli anni '60 e '70', in Benente and Garbarino 2000: 71–9.

—. 2004a. 'Aspetti di topografia antica e di archeologia Cristiana dei territori della Lunigiana occidentale', in Vecchi 2004: 17–22.

—. 2004b. 'Rapporti tra i porti e la rete stradale in Liguria tra età romana e medievale', in De Maria and Turchetti 2004: 275–90.

—. 2004c. 'Case di città e case di campagna', in Puncuh 2004: 227–60.

Mannoni, Tiziano and Murialdo, Giovanni. 1990. 'Insediamenti fortificati tardoromani e altomedievali nell'arco alpino. L'esperienza ligure', *AM*, 17: 9–15.

Mannoni, Tiziano and Murialdo, Giovanni (eds). 2001. S. *Antonino: un insediamento fortificato nella Liguria bizantina* (Bordighera: Istituto Internazionale di Studi Liguri).

Mannoni, Tiziano and Poleggi, Ennio. 1974. 'Fonti scritte e strutture medievali del "Castello" di Genova', *AM*, 1: 171–94.

—. 1976. *Archaeology and the City of Genoa* (Lancaster: Lancaster University Press).

Marazzi, Federico. 1998. 'The Destinies of the Late Antique Italies: Politico-economic Developments of the Sixth Century', in Hodges and Bowden 1998: 119–60.

Marcenaro, Mario. 2006. *Il Battistero monumentale di Albenga* (Albenga: Istituto Internazionale di Studi Liguri).

Marcenaro, Mario and Frondoni, Alessandra. 2006. *Tra Milano e la Provenza. Guida agli edifici cristiani della Liguria Marittima tra IV e X secolo* (Albenga: Istituto Internazionale di Studi Liguri).

Mariotti Lippi, Marta, Guido, Maria Angela, Menozzi, Bruna I., Bellini, Cristina and Montanari, Carlo. 2007. 'The Massaciuccoli Holocene Pollen Sequence and the Vegetation History of the Coastal Plains by the Mar Ligure (Tuscany and Liguria, Italy)', *Vegetation History and Archaeobotany*, 16: 267–77.

Markus, Robert. 1997. *Gregory the Great and his World* (Cambridge: Cambridge University Press).

Mårtensson, Linda, Nosch, Marie-Louise and Strand, Eva Andersson. 2009. 'Shape of Things: Understanding a Loom Weight', *Oxford Journal of Archaeology*, 28: 373–98.

Martyn, John R. C (tr.). 2004. *The Letters of Gregory the Great*, 3 vols (Toronto: Pontifical Institute).

Massabò, Bruno (ed.). 1999. *Dalla villa al villaggio. Corti: scavo di un sito archeologico di età romana e altomedievale lungo il metanodoto del Ponente Ligure* (Genoa: Erga).

Massabo, Bruno. 2004. *Albingaunum. Itinerari archeologici di Albenga* (Genoa: Fratelli Frilli).

Medri, Maura (ed.). 2006. *Villa romana della Foce, San Remo* (Imperia) (San Remo: Istituto Internazionale di Studi Liguri).

Meiggs, Russell. 1982. *Trees and Timber in the Ancient Mediterranean World* (Oxford: Clarendon Press).

Melli, Piera (ed.). 1996. *La città ritrovata. Archeologia urbana a Genova 1984–1996* (Genoa: Tormena).

Melli, Piera. 1998. 'Il sito fi no all'eta tardoantica. I dati archeologici', in Di Fabio 1998: 28–37.

Melli, Piera, Bulgarelli, Francesca, Ferraris, Maria Rosa, Parodi, Gianluca and Torre, Eleonora. 2006. 'Per la ricostruzione del popolamento dell'appennino ligure: ricerche a Mezzanego (GE), località Porciletto', in Cucuzza and Medri 2006: 87–90.

Mennella, Giovanni and Coccoluto, Giovanni (eds). 1995. *Liguria reliqua trans et cis Appenninum*, Inscriptiones Christianae Italiae 9 (Bari: Edipuglia).

Menozzi, Bruna I., Bellini, Cristina, Cevasco, Andrea, Cevasco, Roberta, de Pascale, Andrea, Guido, Maria, Maggi, Roberta, Moe, Dagfinn, Montanari, Carlo and Moreno, Diego. 2007. 'The Archaeology of a Peat Bog in Context: Contribution to the Study of Biodiversification Processes in Historical Time (Ligurian Appennines, NW Italy)', at: http://medieval-europe-paris-2007.univ-paris1.fr/ (2007 conference paper).

Menozzi, Bruna I., Zotti, M. and Montanari, Carlo. 2010. 'A Non-pollen Palynomorphs Contribution to the Local Environmental History in the Ligurian Apennines: A Preliminary Study', *Vegetation History and Archaeobotany*, 19: 503–12.

Milanese, Marco. 1978. 'Un castello militare della Liguria orientale: Castronovo di Salino (La Spezia)', *AM*, 5: 452–60.

—. 1987. *Scavi nell'oppidum preromano d Genova* (Genova –S. Silvestro I) (Rome: Bretschneider).

—. 1993. *Genova romana. Mercato e città dalla tarda età repubblicana a Diocleziano dagli scavi del colle di Castello* (Rome: Bretschneider).

—. 1995. 'La ceramica romana a Genova: nuovi dati archeologici e archaeometrici su produzione e commercio', in Olcese 1995: 189–96.

Milanese, Marco and Giardi, Marisa. 1987. 'L'insediamento preromano di Monte Dragnone (La Spezia). Relazione preliminare', in La Guardia 1987: 71–8.

Milburn, Robert. 1988. *Early Christian Art and Architecture* (Berkeley and Los Angeles: University of California Press).

Milella, Marisa. 1989. 'Ceramica e vie di communicazione nell'Italia bizantina', *MEFR*, 101: 533–57.

Miller, Maureen C. 2000. *The Bishop's Palace. Architecture and Authority in Medieval Italy* (Ithaca and London: Cornell University Press).

Mommsen, Theodore (ed.). 1877. *Corpus Inscriptionum Latinarum*, vol. V, Inscriptiones Galliae Cisalpinae Latinae (Georgium Reimerus: Berlin).

Montanari, Carlo and Guido, Maria Angela. 2006. 'Esperienze di storia ed archeologia ambientale in Liguria', in Cucuzza and Medri 2006: 95–8.

Montanari, Massimo. 1979. *L'alimentazione contadina nell'altomedioevo* (Naples: Liguori).

—. 1994. *The Culture of Food* (Oxford: Blackwell).

Moreland, John. 1991. 'Method and Theory in Medieval Archaeology in the 1990's', *AM*, 38: 7–42.

—. 2001. *Archaeology and Text* (London: Duckworth).

—. 2010. *Archaeology, Theory and the Middle Ages* (London: Duckworth).

Moreno, Diego. 1990. *Dal documento al terreno. Storia e archeologia dei sistemi agro-silvo-pastorali* (Bologna: Il Mulino).

—. 1997a. 'Pastori e serpi nelle alpi liguri (1890–1990)', in Mornet and Morenzoni 1997: 313–30.

—. 1997b. 'Storia, archeologia e ambiente. Contribuito alla definizione ed agli scopi dell'archeologia postmedievale in Italia', *APM*, 1: 89–94.

—. 2004a. 'Escaping from "Landscape": The Historical and Environmental Identification of Local Land-management Practices in the Post-medieval Ligurian Mountains', in Balzaretti, Pearce and Watkins 2004: 129–40.

—. 2004b. 'Activation Practices, History of Environmental Resources and Conservation', in Sanga and Ortalli 2004: 386–90.

Moreno, Diego and Cevasco, Roberta. 2007. 'Appunti dal terreno: storia locale, storia territoriale ed ecologia storica', in Bordone, Guglielmotti, Lombardini and Torre 2007: 313–28.

Moreno, Diego and Montanari, Carlo. 2008. 'Más alla de la percepción: hacia una ecología histórica del paisaje rural en Italia', *Cuadernos Geográficos*, 43: 29–49 [in English].

Moreno, Diego and Poggi, Giuseppina. 1996. 'Storia delle risorse boschive nelle montagne mediterranee: modelli di interpretazione per la produzione foraggere in regime consuetudinario', in Cavaciocchi 1996: 635–45.

Moreno, Diego and Raggio, Osvaldo. 1990. 'The Making and Fall of an Intensive Pastoral Land-use System. Eastern Liguria, 16–19th centuries', *RSL*, A. 56, 1–4: 193–217.

Moreno Diego, Cevasco, Roberta, Guido, Maria Angela and Montanari, Carlo. 2005. 'L'approccio storico-archeologico alla copertura vegetale: il contributo dell'archeologia ambientale e dell'ecologia storica', in Caneva 2005: 463–98.

Mornet, Élisabeth and Franco Morenzoni, Franco (eds). 1997. *Mileux naturels, espaces sociaux: études offertes à Robert Delort* (Paris: Publications de la Sorbonne).

Mosca, A. 2004. 'Il viaggio di Rutilio Namaziano: una ricostruzione degli approdi tirrenici', in De Maria and Turchetti 2004: 311–31.

Murialdo, Giovanni. 1985. 'Alcune considerazioni sulle anfore africane di VII secolo dal "castrum" di S. Antonino nel Finale', *AM*, 22: 433–53.

—. 1988. 'Necropoli e sepolture tardo-antico del Finale', *RSL*, 54: 230–42.

—. 1998. 'Il "castrum" tardo-antico di S. Antonino di Perti', *AM*, 25: 354–70.

Murialdo, Giovanni, Olcese, Gloria, Palazzi, P. and Parodi, Lidia. 1998. 'La ceramica commune in Liguria nel VI e VII secolo', in Saguì 1998: 227–51.

Mussi, Margherita, Bahn, Paul and Maggi, Roberto. 2008. 'Parietal Art Discovered at Arene Candide Cave (Liguria, Italy)', *Antiquity*, 82: 265–70.

Navoni, Marco. 1990. 'Dai longobardi ai Carolingi', in Caprioli, Rimoldi and Vaccaro 1990: 83–122.

Nobili, Mario 1993. 'Formarsi e definarsi dei nomi di famiglia nelle stirpi marchionali dell'Italia centro-settentrionale: il caso degli Obertenghi', in Violante 1993: 77–96.

Ochoa, Carmen F., García-Entero, Virginia and Gil Sendino, Fernando (eds). 2008. *Las villas tardorromanas en el occidente del Imperio: arquitectura y función* (Gijón: Ediciones Trea).

Olcese, Gloria (ed.). 1995. *Ceramica romana e archeometria: lo stato degli studi* (All'Insegna del Giglio: Florence).

Origone, Sandra. 1974. 'Mulini ad acqua in Liguria nei secoli X–XV', *Clio*, 10: 89–120.

—. 2000. 'Liguria bizantina: 538–643', in Scholz and Makris 2000: 272–89.

Ortenberg, Veronica. 1990. 'Archbishop Sigeric's journey to Rome in 990', *Anglo-Saxon England*, 19: 197–246.

Palazzi, Paolo, Parodi, Loredana, Falcetti, C., Frondoni, Alessandra and Murialdo, Giovanni. 2003. 'Archeologia urbana a Finalborgo (1997–2001)', *AM*, 30: 183–243.

Paltineri, Silvia. 2002. 'Territorio come manufatto e manufatti nel territorio: i cumuli di spietramento a Pian delle Gròppere (Casanova di Rovengo – GE)', *APM*, 6: 83–7.

Paroli, Lidia (ed.). 1992. *La ceramica invetriata tardoantica e altomedievale in Italia* (Florence: All'Insegna del Giglio).

Pasini, Cesare. 1991. 'Chiesa di Milano e Sicilia: punti di contatto dal iv all'viii secolo', in Pricoco 1991: 365–98.

Patterson, John. 1991. 'Villae or vici?' in Barker and Lloyd 1991: 117–79.

Pavoni, Romeo. 1988. 'L'evoluzione cittadina in Liguria nel secolo XI', in Bordone and Jarnut 1988: 241–53.

—. 1990–1. 'Brugnato e i confini fra Genova e Luni', *Memorie della Accademia Lunigianese di Scienze 'Giovanni Capellini'*, 60–1: 47–71.

—. 1992. *Liguria medievale. Da provincia romana a stato regionale* (Genoa: ECIG).

—. 2003. 'Società e cultura della Liguria fra tardoantico e altomedioevo', in Frondoni 2003: 79–88.

Pearce, Mark. 2002. 'Reconstructing Past Transapennine Routes: The Trebbia Valley', *APM*, 6: 181–3.

—. 2011. 'Have Rumours of the "Death of Theory" been Exaggerated?' in Bintliff and Pearce 2011: 80–9.

Penco, Giorgio. 1955. 'Le origini del monachesimo in Liguria', *Benedictina*, 9: 15–30.

—. 1956. 'Centri e movimenti monastici nella Liguria altomedievale', *Benedictina*, 10: 1–21.

—. 1961. 'La vita monastica in Italia all'epoca di S. Martino di Tours', *Studia Anselmiana*, 46: 67–83.

Pergola, Paolo 1999. 'La Corsica dell'Alto Medioevo: un crocevia politico, economico e militare tra l'Africa e la costa tirrenica', *Medioevo. Saggi e Rassenge*, 24: 11–26.

Petracco Sicardi, Giulia. 1962. *Toponomastica di Pigna* (Bordighera: Instituto Internazionale di Studi Liguri).

—. 2003. 'Riflessi linguistici dei mutamenti storici fra tardoantico e altomedioevo', in Frondoni 2003: 89–90.

Petracco Sicardi, Giulia and Carpini, Rina. 1981. *Toponomastica storica della Liguria* (Genoa: Sagep).

Petti Balbi, Giovanna. 2007. *Governare la città: prattiche sociali e linguaggi politici a Genova in età medievale* (Florence: Firenze University Press).

Petti Balbi, Giovanna and Vitolo, Giovanni (eds). 2007. *Linguaggi e pratiche del potere. Genova e il Regno di Napoli tra medioevo ed età moderna* (Salerno: Laveglia).

Picard, Jean-Charles. 1988. *Le Souvenir des Évêques. Sépultures, listes episcopales et culte des évêques en Italie du Nord des origines au Xe siècles* (Rome: École Française de Rome).

Pighi, Giovanni Battista (ed.). 1960. *Versum de Mediolano Civitate/Versus de Verona* (Bologna: Zanichelli).

Pistarino, Giovanni. 1979. *Liguria monastica* (Cesena: Badia di Santa Maria del Monte).

Pluskowski, Aleks (ed.). 1996. *Breaking and Shaping Beastly Bodies: Animals as Material Culture in the Middle Ages* (Oxford: Oxbow).

Poleggi, Ennio. 1973. *Santa Maria di Castello e il romanico a Genova* (Genoa: Sagep).

Poleggi, Ennio and Cevini, Paola. 2003. *Genova*, 5th edn (Rome-Bari: Electa).

Polonio, Valeria. 1997. 'Il monachesimo femminile in Liguria dalle origini al XII secolo', in Zarri 1997: 87–119.

—. 1999. 'Tra universalismo e localismo: costruzione di un sistema (569–1321)', in Puncuh 1999: 77–120.

—. 2002. *Istituzioni ecclesiastiche della Liguria medievale* (Rome: Herder).

—. 2007. 'Dalla marginalità alla potenza sul mare: un lento itinerario tra v e xiii secolo', in Assereto and Doria 2007: 24–42.

Pricoco, Salvatore (ed.). 1991. *Sicilia e Italia suburbicaria tra IV e VIII* (Soveria Manelli: Rubbettino).

Provero, Luigi. 2007. 'Forty Years of Rural History for the Italian Middle Ages', in Alfonso 2007: 141–72.

Pryor, John. 2003. 'The Mediterranean Breaks Up: 500–1000', in Abulafia 2003: 155–77.

Puncuh, Dino (ed.). 1962. *Liber privilegiorum Ecclesiae Ianuensis* (Genoa).

—. 1999. *Il cammino della chiesa genovese dalle origini ai nostri giorni* (Genoa: Società ligure di storia patria).

—. 2004. *Storia della cultura ligure*, 2 vols (Genoa: Società ligure di storia patria).

Quaini, Massimo. 1973. *Per la storia del paesaggio agrario in Liguria* (Savona: Camera di commercio, industria, artigianato e agricoltura).

Raggio, Osvaldo. 1991. 'Social Relations and Control of Resources in an Area of Transit: Eastern Liguria, Sixteenth to Seventeenth Centuries', in Woolf 1991: 20–42.

—. 2004. 'Microhistorical Approaches to the History of Liguria: From Microanalysis to Local History. Edoardo Grendi's Achievements', in Balzaretti, Pearce and Watkins 2004: 97–103.

Raggio, Osvaldo and Torre, Angelo (eds). 2004. *Edoardo Grendi. In altri termini: etnografia e storia di una società di antico regime* (Milan: Feltrinelli).

Revel, Jacques (ed.). 2006. *Giochi di scala. La microstoria alla prova dell'esperienza* (Rome: Viella).

Reynolds, Paul. 1995. *Trade in the Western Mediterranean, AD 400–700: The Ceramic Evidence*, BAR INT 604 (Oxford: Tempus Reparatum).

Ribolla, Paolo. 1988. 'Archeologia d'età protostorica, romana e medievale in Val di Vara', in De Nevi 1988: 105–12.

Ricci, Roberto. 2002. *Poteri e territorio in Lunigiana storica (VII–XI secolo). Uomini, terra e poteri in una territorio di confine* (Spoleto: Fondazione Centro italiano di studi sull'alto Medioevo).

—. 2007. *La marca della Liguria orientale e gli Obertenghi (945–1056)* (Spoleto: Fondazione Centro italiano di studi sull'alto Medioevo).

Richter, Michael. 2008. *Bobbio in the Early Middle Ages. The Abiding Legacy of Columbanus* (Dublin: Four Courts Press).

Ripoll, Gisella and Arce, Javier. 2000. 'The Transformation and End of Roman Villae in the West', in Brogiolo, Gauthier and Christie 2000: 63–114.

Rotoli, Mauro and Negri, Stefania. 2003. 'I resti vegetali carbonizzati', in Giannichedda and Lanza 2003: 198–212.

Rovere, Alessandra. 1990. 'La tradizione del diploma di Berengario II a Adalberto del 958 in favore dei Genovesi', *Rassegna degli Archivi di Stato*, 50: 371–7.

Rovere, Alessandra (ed.). 1992. *I libri iurium della Repubblica di Genova*, vol. 1 (Rome: Ministero per i beni culturali e ambientali).

Russo, Eugenio. 2003. 'La scultura in Liguria dal VI all'VIII secolo. Stimoli per un'approfondimento', in Frondoni 2003: 73–7.

Saguì, Lucia (ed.). 1998. *Ceramica in Italia: VI–VII secolo*, 2 vols (Florence: All'Insegna del Giglio).

Salvadori, Frank. 2003. 'Archeozoologia e medioevo: lo stato degli studi', in Rosa and Peduto 2003: 176–81.

Sanga, Glauco and Ortalli, Gherardo (eds). 2004. *Nature Knowledge. Ethnoscience, Cognition, and Utility* (New York and Oxford: Berghahn).

Sarris, Peter. 2009. 'Introduction: Aristocrats, Peasants and the Transformation of Rural Society, c. 400–800', *Journal of Agricultural Change*, 9: 3–22.

Scholz, Cordula and Makris, Georgios (eds). 2000. *Polypleuros nous: Miscellanea für Peter Schreiner zu seinem 60. Geburtstag* (Munich: Saur).

Schreiner, Peter. 1997. 'Bisanzio e la Liguria', in Balletto 1997: 1097–108.

Schwarcz, Andreas. 1997. 'Die Liguria zwischen Goten, Byzantinern, Langobarden und Franken im 6. Jahrhundert', in Balletto 1997: 1109–31.

Scipioni, Sara. 2002. 'Dati antracologici da due pratiche attuali: la produzione del carbone vegetale nelle alte valli Scrivia e Trebbia (Appennino Ligure)', *APM*, 6: 49–66.

Sherratt, Andrew. 1993. 'The Relativity of Theory', in Yoffee and Sherratt 1993: 119–30.

Sickel, Theodor von. 1893. *Die Urkunden Otto des III, MGH Diplomata regum et imperatorum Germaniae*, Bd. 2 Tl. 2 (Hannover: MGH).

Skinner, Patricia. 1995. *Family Power in Southern Italy: The Duchy of Gaeta and its Neighbours, 850–1139* (Cambridge: Cambridge University Press).

Spadea, Giovanni and Martino, Gian Piero. 2004. 'La Liguria marittima dopo la caduta dell'Impero, il quadro delle ricerche archeologiche', in De Maria and Turchetti 2004: 253–73.

Squatriti, Paolo. 2002. 'Digging Ditches in Early Medieval Europe', *P&P*, 176: 11–65.

— 2010. 'The Floods of 589 and Climate Change at the Beginning of the Middle Ages: An Italian Microhistory', *Speculum*, 85: 799–826.

Squatriti, Paolo (tr.). 2007. *The Complete Works of Liudprand of Cremona* (Washington, DC: Catholic University of America Press).

Stagno, Anna Maria. 2009. 'Geografia degli insediamenti e risorse ambientali: un percorso tra fonti archeologiche e documentarie', in Macchi Jánica 2009: 301–10.

Stephenson, Paul (ed.). 2010. *The Byzantine World* (London and New York: Routledge).

Stringa, Paolo and Moreno, Diego (eds). 2001. *Patrimonio storico-ambientale. Esperienze, progetti, e prospettive per la valorizzazione delle aree rurali* (Officine Grafiche Canessa: Rapallo).

Talbert, Richard J. A. (ed.). 2000. *The Barrington Atlas of the Greek and Roman World* (Princeton: Princeton University Press).

Tinner, Willy, Lotter, André F., Ammann, Brigitta, Conedera, Marco, Hubschmid, Priska van Leeuwen, Jacqueline F. N. and Wehrli, Michael. 2003. 'Climatic Change and Contemporaneous Land-use Phases North and South of the Alps 2300 BC to 800 AD', *Quaternary Science Reviews*, 22: 1447–60.

Tomaini, Placido. 1961. *Brugnato città abbaziale e vescovile*, 2nd edn (Città di Castello: Ed. Arti Grafiche).

—. 1978. *Varese Ligure. Insigne borgo ed antica pieve* (Città di Castello: Ed. Arti Grafiche).

Torre, Angelo. 2002. 'La produzione storica dei luoghi', *QS*, 37: 443–75.

—. 2008. 'Un "tournant spatial" en histoire? Paysages, regards, ressources', *Annales. Histoire, Sciences Sociales*, 63 n. 5: 1127–44.

Tosi, Michele. 1990. 'Bobbio e la Valle del Trebbia', in Ghizzoni 1990: 395–499.

—. 1992–3. 'I monaci colombiniani del sec. VII portano un rinnovmento agricolo-religioso nella fascia littorale Ligure', *Archivium Bobiense*, 14/15: 5–246.

Tykot, Robert H., Morter, Johnathan and Robb, John E. (eds). 1999. *Social Dynamics of the prehistoric Central Mediterranean* (London: Accordia Research Institute).

Tyler, Elizabeth and Balzaretti, Ross (ed.). 2006. *Narrative and History in the Early Medieval West* (Turnhout: Brepols).

Uhlirz, Mathilde. 1957. 'Die rechtliche Stellung der Kaiserinwitwe Adelheid im Deutschen und im Italischen Reich', *Zeitschrift der Savigny-Stiftung für Rechtsgeschichte: Germanistiche Abteilung*, 74: 85–97.

Urbani, Rossana and Zazzu, Guido Nathan. 1999. *The Jews in Genoa*, vol. 1, 570–1681 (Leiden: Brill).

Valabrega, Guido. 1986. 'Le Présence des Sarrasins à Varigotti', *Cahiers de Tunisie*, 34: 139–47.

Valenti, Marco. 2000. 'Il villaggio altomedievale di Poggio Imperiale a Poggibonsi. Dall'età longobarda all'età carolingia', in Bertelli and Brogiolo 2000: 194–9.

Valenti, Marco and Salvadori, Frank. 2006. 'Animal Bones: Synchronous and Diachronic Distribution as Patterns of Socially Determined Meat Consumption in the Early and High Middle Ages in Central and Northern Italy', in Pluskowski 2006: 171–88.

Varaldo, Carlo. 1996. 'Lo scavo della Contrada di S. Domenico al Priamàr (Savona). Relazioni preliminari sulle campagne di scavo 1989–1995', *AM*, 23: 309–20.

Varaldo, Carlo, Lavagna, Rita, Benente, Fabrizio, Ramagli, Paolo and Ventura, Donatella. 2003. 'Il castello di Andora (SV): dalle tracce di frequentazione romana al castello signorile', in Atti III Convengo di Archeologia Medievale (Salerno): 191–200.

Vecchi, Elizabetta M. 2004. 'Contributo all'archeologia cristiana nella diocese di Luni. Frammenti marmorei di reimpiego a San Venanzio di Ceparana', in Vecchi 2004a: 115–60.

Vecchi, Elizabetta M. (ed.). 2004. *Poteri signorili ed enti ecclesiastici dalla Riviera di Levante alla Lunigiana. Aggiornamenti storici ed archeologici* (La Spezia: Istituto Internazionale di Studi Liguri).

Violante, Cinzio (ed.). 1993. *Nobiltà e chiese nel medioevo e altri saggi. Scritti in onore di Gerd G. Tellenbach* (Rome: Jouvence).

Wallis, Faith (tr.). 1999. *Bede, The Reckoning of Time* (Liverpool: Liverpool University Press).

Wanner, Kurt (ed.). 1994. *Ludovici II diplomata* (Rome: Istituto Storico Italiano per il Medio Evo).

Ward-Perkins, Bryan. 1981. 'Two Byzantine Houses at Luni', *PBSR*, 49: 91–8.

—. 1984. *From Classical Antiquity to the Middle Ages. Urban Public Building in Northern and Central Italy AD 300–850* (Oxford: Clarendon Press).

—. 1997. 'Continuitists, Catastrophists and the Towns of Post-Roman Northern Italy', *PBSR*, 65: 157–76.

—. 2005. *The Fall of Rome: And the End of Civilization* (Oxford: Oxford University Press).

Watkins, Charles (ed.). 1993. *Ecological Effects of Afforestation: Studies in the History and Ecology of Afforestation in Western Europe* (Wallingford: CAB International).

Watkins, Charles. 2004. 'The Management History and Conservation of Terraces in the Val di Vara, Liguria', in Balzaretti, Pearce and Watkins 2004: 141–54.

Watson, Clare S. 1996. 'The Vegetational History of the Northern Apennines, Italy: Information from Three New Sequences and a Review of Regional Vegetation Change', *Journal of Biogeography*, 23: 805–41.

Watson, Clare, Branch, Nick and Lowe, John J. 1994. 'The Vegetation History of the Northern Apennines during the Holocene', in Biagi and Nandris 1994: 153–68.

White, Jeffrey A. (ed. and tr.). 2005. *Biondo Flavio, Italy Illuminated*, vol. 1, Books I–IV (Cambridge, MA: Harvard University Press).

Whittow, Mark. 2009. 'Early Medieval Byzantium and the End of the Ancient World', *Journal of Agrarian Change*, 9: 134–53.

Wickham, Chris. 1988. *The Mountains and the City. The Tuscan Appennines in the Early Middle Ages* (Oxford: Oxford University Press).

—. 1994. *Land and Power. Studies in Italian and European Social History, 400–1200* (London: British School at Rome).

—. 1998. 'Overview: Production, Distribution, Demand', in Hodges and Bowden 1998: 272–92.

—. 1999. 'Early Medieval Archaeology in Italy: The Last Twenty Years', *AM*, 26: 7–20.

—. 2000. 'Overview: Production, Distribution and Demand, II', in Hansen and Wickham: 345–78.

—. 2002. 'Edoardo Grendi e la cultura materiale', *QS*, 110: 323–32.

—. 2005. *Framing the Early Middle Ages. Europe and the Mediterranean, 400–800* (Oxford: Oxford University Press).

—. 2009. *The Inheritance of Rome from 400 to 1000* (London: Penguin).

Wood, Ian N. 1997. 'Report: The European Science Foundation's Programme on the Transformation of the Roman World and Emergence of Early Medieval Europe', *EME*, 6: 217–27.

—. 2001. *The Missionary Life. Saints and the Evangelisation of Europe 400–1050* (London: Longman).

Wood, Susan. 2006. *The Proprietary Church in the Medieval West* (Oxford: Oxford University Press).

Woolf, Stuart (ed.). 1991. *Domestic Strategies: Work and Family in France and Italy 1600–1800* (Cambridge: Cambridge University Press).

Yoffee, Norman and Sherratt, Andrew (eds). 1993. *Archaeological Theory: Who Sets the Agenda?* (Cambridge: Cambridge University Press).

Zanini, Enrico 2010. 'Le città dell'Italia bizantina: qualche appunto per un'agenda della ricerca', *RMR*, XI.

Zarri, Gabriella (ed.). 1997. *Il monachesimo femminile in Italia dall'alto Medioevo al secolo XVII a confronto con l'oggi* (Verona: Il Segno).

Zironi, Alessandro 2004. *Il monastero longobardo di Bobbio. Crocevia di uomini, manoscritti e culture* (Spoleto: Fondazione Centro italiano di studi sull'alto Medioevo).

'Zone umide 2009'. Proceedings of the International Workshop 'Le Zone Umide. Archivi del paesaggio culturale tra ricerca e gestione', *Archivio di Stato di Genova*, 29–30 January 2009, at: www.dismec.unige.it/zum/atti.html

Index

Page numbers in *italics* refer to figures.